THE HAZARAS AND THE AFGHAN STATE

NIAMATULLAH IBRAHIMI

The Hazaras and the Afghan State

Rebellion, Exclusion and the Struggle for Recognition

HURST & COMPANY, LONDON

First published in the United Kingdom in hardback in 2017 by
C. Hurst & Co. (Publishers) Ltd.
This paperback edition first published in 2022 by
C. Hurst & Co. (Publishers) Ltd.
New Wing, Somerset House, Strand, London, WC2R 1LA
© Niamatullah Ibrahimi, 2022
All rights reserved.
Printed in the United Kingdom

Distributed in the United States, Canada and Latin America by
Oxford University Press, 198 Madison Avenue, New York, NY
10016, United States of America.

A Cataloguing-in-Publication data record for this book
is available from the British Library.

ISBN: 9781787387744

This book is printed using paper from registered sustainable
and managed sources.

www.hurstpublishers.com

To my parents for their unconditional love

CONTENTS

CONTENTS

CONTENTS

ACKNOWLEDGEMENTS

This book is the outcome of several years of research at a number of institutions, and friendship and intellectual exchange with many individuals. As a result, I owe enormous intellectual and personal debts to many more people than I can mention here.

Prior to developing a long-term research interest in the politics and history of Hazaras in Afghanistan, I worked for the International Crisis Group from 2003 to 2005. It was my first opportunity to visit most of Afghanistan and meet and talk to people from all social, political and ethnic groups of the country. I wish to thank Dr Samina Ahmed, Mr Nick Grono, Mr Bob Templer, Mr Vikram Parekh, Ms Joanna Nathan, Ms Candace Rondeaux, Mr Michael Shaikh and Mr Faiz Ali for all their support and assistance in enabling me to witness and research the first few years after the toppling of the Taliban regime by the US-led international intervention in 2001.

The idea for this book was born with my work for the Crisis States Research Centre of the London School of Economics from 2005 to 2010 in Afghanistan. Two of the research papers that I published by the centre have now been revised and appear as Chapters IV and V of this book. My work with the Crisis States Research Centre kindled my research interest in the politics of Hazaras and of Afghanistan more generally. I am extremely grateful to Professor James Putzel, Dr Antonio Giustozzi and Ms Wendy Foulds for their support and cooperation in those years.

In 2012, I spent six months as a Visiting Fellow at the Centre for Development Studies of the Free University of Berlin. I wish to thank

ACKNOWLEDGEMENTS

Professor Hermann Kreutzmann and Dr Stefan Schütte from the Centre for Development Studies for hosting me and making me feel at home in Berlin, and Professor Ingeborg Baldauf and Mr Ahmad Azizi from Humboldt University, and Professor Conrad Schetter from the University of Bonn, with whom I conversed at several workshops and seminars of the Crossroads Asia Network.

In Kabul, I have greatly benefited from the help of the Afghanistan Centre at Kabul University (ACKU), founded by the legendary American scholar of Afghanistan, Nancy Dupree. Mr Waheed Wafa, Haji Daoud, Mr Ali Basharyar and other staff at the centre always made me feel welcome and helped me find, access and photocopy materials that were otherwise unavailable in Kabul.

I also owe a debt to my colleagues at the Asia-Pacific College of Diplomacy at The Australian National University where the book took its final shape. I am particularly indebted to Professor William Maley for his invaluable support, friendship and generosity with his time, extensive personal collection of books on Afghanistan and most importantly his insights and knowledge of Afghanistan. I would also like to thank Dr Jochen Prantl, the Director of the APCD, Mrs Andreas Haese and Mr Craig Hanks for all their support for my research, and Dr Srinjoy Bose for his friendship and intellectual conversations on Afghanistan's politics and history.

My work on the Hazaras has benefited immensely from existing historical, ethnographic and anthropological literature on the Hazaras and other ethnic groups in Afghanistan. I am delighted especially to acknowledge my immensely useful conversations over many years with Dr Sayed Askar Mousavi, Professor Alessandro Monsutti, Dr Kristian Berg Harpviken and Haji Kazim Yazdani. I have also greatly benefited from both the works of, and my own personal conversations with, Professor Nazif Shahrani.

Over the years, I have profited greatly from my friendship with a number of other scholars and practitioners both in and out of Afghanistan. Mr Daoud Yosufi was particularly helpful in connecting me with so many valuable people in Kabul, Mazar-e Sharif, Ghazni and Hazarajat. In the summer of 2009, Mr Mir Khadim Baig Karbalaye invited me, together with Mr Kazim Yazdani, to make a trip from Kabul to his home district, Laal wa Sarjangal, where he hosted us with

ACKNOWLEDGEMENTS

immense hospitality and generosity. I would also like specially to thank Mr Abbas Agah, Mr Abbas Farasso, Mr Ali Amiri, Mr Akram Gizabi, Mr Amir Foladi, Mr Ali Reza Younespour, Mr Asadullah Walwalji, Ms Fatema Karbalaye, Mr Hadi Marefat, Mr Hafiz Mansour, Mr Ishaq Muhammadi, Mr Jalal Awhidi, Mr Khudadad Bisharat, Dr Liza Schuster, Mr Matin Alizadah, Dr Muhammad Qasim Wafayezada, Mr Nader Nadery, Mr Najeeb Asadi, Ms Najla Ayubi, Dr Nasir Andisha, Professor Nazif Shahrani, Dr Nemat Bizhan, Dr Nishank Motwani, Mr Rahmuddin Haji Agha, Mr Sakhi Darwish, Mr Shahmahmood Miakhel, Ms Seema Ghani, Dr Susanne Schmeidl, Mr Qurban Ali Erfani, Dr Saifuddin Saihun, Dr Sima Samar, Dr Timor Sharan and Mr Zia Muhammadi for having helped me in my research on Hazaras or my broader research interests on Afghanistan's politics and history in various ways.

Over the course of my research, I interviewed many people, some of whom I have chosen not to mention by name as the topics of our conversations involved sensitive issues with continuing social, security and political significance. They were extremely generous with their time and I particularly thank them for the faith and trust they placed in me by sharing their personal histories.

I could not have completed this long journey without the love and support I received from my family. I cannot thank my parents enough for their unwavering determination to support my education under extremely difficult circumstances. Gul Begum, my wife, has been a source of love and inspiration and has been extremely patient with my long hours at the office and work at home. I acknowledge that she often reminded me of my approaching deadlines. Along the journey that led to the publication of this book, we have also been blessed by our two wonderful sons, Hazhir and Shahir, who are our incredible sources of strength and inspiration.

Lastly, I would like to express my sincere gratitude to Michael Dwyer of Hurst Publishers for his support and patience as I worked on the manuscript over a few years. I am also delighted to acknowledge Alasdair Craig who coordinated the review of the manuscript by two excellent peer reviewers, Rebecca Wise who took care of its final copy editing, Jon de Peyer who was responsible for the coordination and final production and to Sebastian Ballard for his redrawing of the maps.

GLOSSARY

Arbaab	landlord, chief of the village, master
Amir al-Momenin	commander of the faithful, ruler
Asl	original, founded, authentic, root
Askar	soldier
Badraqa	accompaniment, escort
Baig	lord, chieftain (title of honour)
Bida't	invented, unfounded and unauthentic
Daneshgah	university
Dodi	bread (Pashto)
Fiqh	jurisprudence, Islamic law
Gelim	rug, traditional woolen carpet in Afghanistan
Gerawi	mortgaged, pledged, given as security in a traditional mortgage system that is similar to a pawn agreement
Haakim	governor, ruler, district or province administrator
Halqa	circle, ring
Harakat	movement, motion, departure
Hawzah	centre, area, electoral district
Hezb	party, organisation. group
Inqilaab	revolution
Irshad	guidance, giving direction
Ittehadiah	association, union, alliance
Jabhah	front line
Jagir / Jahgir	areas or land granted to military or administrative officials by the ruler in lieu of regular salary (the

	recipients, Jagirdar, were expected to provide support and personnel to the military)
Jambast	as a whole, in total, a land tax system in which the amount of tax was fixed according to the size of land
Jawanan	young people
Jehad	struggle, fight, holy war
Jirga	assembly, meeting
Junbesh	movement, shaking, motion
Kaafir	infidel, unbeliever, non-Muslim
Kaali	bread (Pashto)
Kata	big, large
Khaalisa	pure, unmixed, crown land
Khalq	people, masses, creation
Khan	landlord, influential person (title of honour)
Kharwaar	a unit of weight equal to 573.4 kilograms, a large amount of something
Khoms	one-fifth, according to Shi'a law one-fifth of the annual surplus of a household to be designated for charity and religious affairs
Kot	a historical tax system whereby a share of the yearly produce was collected based on an annual assessment of the amount of the harvest
Kour	home, accommodation (Pashto)
Kufr	infidelity, blasphemy
Lashkar	army, many people
Kuchi	nomad (usually used to refer to Pashtun nomadic tribes)
Madrasah	Islamic boarding school
Malik	chieftain, head of a clan or a village
Mostaza'fin	dispossessed, poor, oppressed
Motaraqqi	advanced, progressive
Mulk	land, property, country
Munazzam	regular, organised
Mir	head, leader, chief of a region or tribe
Mujahed	fighter, warrior
Mujtahid	highest religious scholar among the Shi'as who is entitled to interpret Islamic laws

Naaqilin	transferees, people who were resettled by the government
Nezamnamah	code of laws, regulations, legislation
Nahzat	rise, awakening
Paaygah	station, military base
Paaw	unit of weight equal to 448 rams, one-quarter
Pairaw	follower
Pishkhedmat	personal attendant, servant
Pohantun	university (Pashto)
Qarargaah	headquarters, military base
Qand	lump sugar, unrefined sugar
Qolba	plough, a unit in traditional land measurement based on the size of land that could be ploughed by a pair of oxen in a day
Qomandaan	commander, military leader
Rahbar	leader, guide
Ra'iyat	subjects, followers, people
Rawshanfikr	intellectual, open-minded, a graduate of modern schools and universities
Roghan	ghee, cooking oil
Sardaar	a person of high rank, military commander, title of high ranking tribal leaders and members of the ruling dynasties in Afghanistan
Saazman	organisation
Shaakh puli	a kind of tax on livestock
Sho'al	flame
Shura	council, assembly
Sir	a traditional unit of weight in Afghanistan equal to 7.168 kilograms
Talib	seeker, student of an Islamic school, a member of the Taliban fundamentalist movement (Taliban is the plural form of Talib in Dari)
Tanzim	arrangement, organisation, one of the several anti-Soviet mujahedin groups formed in the 1980s
Taqiyyah	caution, prudence, a Shi'a Islamic principle which permits its followers to dissimulate their religious practices in the face of persecution and high risk

GLOSSARY

Tazkera	biography, national identity card in Afghanistan
Tiyul	a system in which the right to use land or collect revenues of an area was granted in exchange for military services, particularly during wars
Ulema	Islamic scholars, religious clerics
Wakil	delegate, representative, attorney
Waqf	dedication, religious endowment
Welayat e Faqih	Guardianship of the Jurist, founding theory of the Islamic Republic of Iran
Welaayat	province, guardianship
Wuluswali	district, district administration centre
Yaaghi	rebel, insurgent, mutinous
Yaaghistan	land of rebels, areas outside central government control

INTRODUCTION

THE MODERN STATE, WARS AND ETHNIC POLITICS
IN AFGHANISTAN

What happens to the Hazaras is not just the story of this people. It's the story of the whole country. It's everybody's story!

Dan Terry (an aid worker, interview with Zabriskie, 2008)

This book is about the Hazara people and the Afghan state. It traces the historical trajectory of the Afghan state from the advent of the Durrani Empire in 1747 until the present to explain how it interacted with and shaped the destiny of the Hazaras in modern Afghanistan.

By examining the debate about the rise and crisis of the modern state and ethnic politics in Afghanistan, I focus on the intersection of two separate but highly interdependent levels of politics in the country: first, the impact of the modern Afghan state since its formation towards the end of the nineteenth century on the Hazara people, and, second, intense and at times highly violent competition among Hazara elites for internal political leadership as well as strategies towards the state's demand for control, submission to its authority and extraction of revenues. By focusing on the intersection of national state politics and internal dynamics of the Hazara people, I aim to explore patterns of continuity and change in the relations of the Afghan state with one of the principal ethnic groups of the country over the *longue durée*.

This book is the product of several years of intermittent research and inquiry that were driven by a combination of my own personal curiosity and scholarly research interests. It began with investigation of dynamics of wars and politics in the 1980s in Hazarajat, the Central Highlands of Afghanistan, which is home to most of the Shi'a Hazaras of Afghanistan. At this stage, my research was motivated by my own personal experience of growing up and witnessing violent conflicts in the region during the 1980s. I was personally motivated to understand the social and political groups, the historical events and the domestic and foreign factors that affected me at the personal level and made Afghanistan the country it is: a land torn by wars of foreign invasions, domestic conflicts and endless suffering for its people.

In focusing on the Hazaras and modern state in Afghanistan, I also highlight the tensions and contradictions that drive Afghanistan's political instability and discuss the role of foreign powers and the Afghan rulers and political elites, past and present, in the suffering of their own people. While I will highlight mass killings, displacement and dispossession of Hazaras and their persecution and marginalisation by the Afghan state and rulers, I acknowledge the sufferings of other peoples of the country, and seek to contribute to a broader understanding of Afghanistan and its people by discussing patterns of continuities and changes in the national politics of the country. Similarly, although I focus on the domestic politics, throughout the book I acknowledge and mention the role of external influences and players in shaping Afghan politics and contributing to the rise and fall of political elites in Kabul.

Broadly speaking, my discussion of the relations between Hazaras and the modern state in Afghanistan unfolds over three separate periods: a period of state-building and rebellion by Hazaras that culminated in the Hazara War of 1891–1893; a period of state consolidation and exclusion of Hazaras from political participation and distribution of the benefits of the modern state that roughly extended from 1901 to 1978; and a period of state crisis and fragmentation that overlaps with what I call the Hazaras struggle for recognition, beginning with the fall of the central state institutions in the Hazarajat region in 1979.

To set the scene for the subsequent chapters, in the following two sections, I will introduce the main ethnic groups in Afghanistan and offer some explanations for how ethnicity and the Afghan state may be conceptualised to help understand the story of Hazaras and the Afghan state.

INTRODUCTION

The ethnic landscape of afghanistan

Afghanistan is often described as a crossroads and heart of Asia. Historically, as a land bridge that connected empires and centres of civilization in Central and South Asia, the Middle East and China, and thus as a meeting point of cultures, civilizations, armies and trade caravans, the country is endowed with a rich cultural heritage and ethnocultural diversity. According to one estimate, the country is home to fifty-five major and smaller ethno-linguistic groups, making it one of the most diverse countries in the world (Orywal, 1986). Dupree (1980, pp. 58–64) lists twenty-one identifiable groups. The 2004 constitution of the country names fourteen ethnic groups as comprising the 'nation of Afghanistan'. These are Pashtun, Tajik, Hazara, Uzbek, Turkman, Baluch, Pashayi, Nuristani, Aymaq, Arab, Qirghiz, Qizilbash, Gujur and Brahwui. Pashto and Dari were recognised as official languages of the state.

For the first time in the country's history, the 2004 constitution also recognised Shi'a jurisprudence as applicable for the private matters of its followers, and minority languages like Uzbeki as the third official languages in areas where they are spoken by the majority of the population (Articles 4, 16 and 131).

Pashtuns, Tajiks, Hazaras and Uzbeks are usually recognised as the largest ethnic groups. As Map 1.1 shows, Pashtuns predominantly live in the south and east, Tajiks in the west and the areas between Kabul and Badakhshan, the Shi'a Hazaras in the central highlands and Uzbeks and Turkmen in the northwest of the country. Having said that, it is important to remember that maps can be very poor indicators of the diversity and real complexity of geographical distribution of social groups. For example, there are significant Pashtun communities in the north and northeast of Afghanistan who are locally known as *Naaqilin* (transferees), because they were transferred at various times from the south and east to these historically non-Pashtun areas (see Chapter 4 of this book). In the same manner, there are substantial communities that can potentially be described as Tajiks, Hazaras or people of various Turkic backgrounds who live in the largely Pashtun provinces of the south and east.

The Pashtuns, Tajiks and Uzbeks are predominantly followers of Sunni Islam and Hazaras are mainly Shi'a Muslims. Most followers of

3

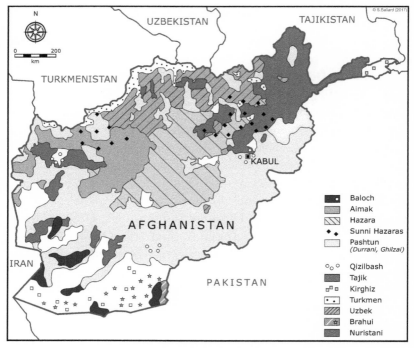

Map 1.1: Ethnolinguistic Groups in Afghanistan
[Source: University of Texas 1997].

Sunni Islam adhere to the Hannafi school of thought, founded by the great Islamic legal scholar, Numan Ibn Thabit known as the Imam Abu Hanifah, which is known for its moderation and respect towards Shi'a Islam. While there are smaller followers of Shi'a Islam among the Pashtuns and Tajiks, there are substantial Sunni Hazara communities in the northeastern provinces of Panjshir, Baghlan, Parwan, Takhar and Qunduz, as well as the western province of Badghis. Similarly, there are substantial communities of Ismaili Shi'a among the Hazaras of Eastern Hazarajat as well as among the Tajiks and other ethno-linguistic groups of Badakhshan.

Each of the major ethnic groups has its own views of a common origin. Some of these views are myths conceived by Western orientalists during the nineteenth century or nationalist historians, and then adopted by members of an ethnic group, while others were views traditionally held within each group before the rise of modern state. For example, as will be discussed in Chapter 5, traditionally many Pashtuns conceived of themselves as descendants of the lost tribe of Israel but during the 1930s Afghan nationalist historians and politicians who were influenced by the rise of nationalist ideologies in Europe began to redefine Pashtun identity as part of the Aryan race, and then turn it into official policy of the country. Similarly, the idea of Hazaras as descendants of a division of the army of Genghis Khan in the thirteenth century, promoted by Western orientalists, is being challenged by Hazara and other scholars of Afghanistan who trace a much longer history for the group that became Hazaras (Mousavi, 1998; Yazdani, 2008).

Dari and Pashtu are the most spoken and official languages of Afghanistan. Dari is the official name of the Farsi or Persian spoken in Afghanistan. Tajiks and Hazaras speak various dialects of the language, including substantial communities that may not easily fit into either group known as Parsiwans. Dari is the lingua franca of the country and has historically been the main language of arts, culture and administration. Pashtuns speak various dialects of Pashtu, although there are significant Pashtun communities in the cities who speak Dari as their first language. The Uzbeks and Turkmen speak Uzbeki and Turkmeni respectively. There are a number of other languages spoken by small minority groups including Baluchi, Pashayi, and Nuristani languages.

The description of Afghanistan's ethno-linguistic groups becomes most sensitive when it comes to the size of each group as a proportion of the overall population of the country. The first attempt to conduct a national census was interrupted by the outbreak of armed conflict in 1979. Although the holding of a national census was part of the 2001 Bonn Agreement, it has repeatedly been delayed for technical, security and political reasons as a national census that can show clear ethnic breakdown of the population may also challenge powerful historical perceptions and deeply held myths about the power and size of the dominant groups. Consequently, the issue of the size of each group is highly political because ethnic elites tend to frame their claim for a share of political power based on the alleged size of groups they claim to represent.

In the absence of reliable national figures, western estimates of the total population of the country and various ethnic groups have become the most widely cited sources. Ironically, one of the most popular of these is the World Factbook of the US Central Intelligence Agency (CIA), which provided such estimates until 2015. In 2016, the agency stopped providing such figures citing unavailability of such data 'on the sensitive subject of ethnicity in Afghanistan'. However, a comparison of the figures of the Factbook over the previous years provides interesting insights into these estimates and the nature of ethnicity in Afghanistan. First, the estimated figure of each ethnic group as a percentage of the total population of the country has significantly changed over time. For example, the percentage of Pashtuns increased from 38 per cent in 1996 and 2001 to 42 per cent in subsequent years. By contrast, the estimates of Hazaras has decreased from 19 per cent in 1996 and 2001, to less than half, 9 per cent from 2004 to 2014. During the same period, the estimates of Tajiks and Uzbeks increased from 25 to 27 and from 6 to 9 per cent respectively. These numbers are used as a basis for distribution of political power and national resources and underpin an ethnic hierarchy that is reinforced by inadvertent or consciousness approval, or outright manipulation of such figures by foreign actors.

Table 1.1: Estimated Size of the Major Ethnic Groups in Afghanistan

Major Ethnic Groups	1996 estimates %	2001 estimates %	2004 and 2014 estimates %
Pashtuns	38	38	42
Tajiks	25	25	27
Hazaras	19	19	9
Uzbek	6	6	9
Chahar Aimaks, Turkmen, Baloch and others	12		
Aimaks, Turkmen, Baloch and others		12	
Aimaq			4
Turkmen			3
Baloch			2
Others			4
Total	100	100	100

Source: CIA World Factbook, 1996, 2001 and 2004–2014.

Another important pattern in the CIA World Factbook concerns identification of some communities as separate ethnic groups. For example, Aimaqs appeared as a separate ethnic group in the CIA figures beginning from 2004. The community presents a curious case of ethnic identity in Afghanistan. They are Sunni and Farsi speaking people that predominantly live in Ghur and western Afghanistan but are also found in substantial numbers in northeast and urban centres of the country. If Sunni Islam and language are the main markers of ethnic identity, they are closer to most Tajiks. By contrast, if a shared belief in a common origin is the central marker of ethnic identity they might have closer affinity to most Hazaras as descendants of the Turkic tribes of the region. Nonetheless, as the CIA estimates show, over time they are increasingly recognised as a distinct ethnic group.

The modern state and ethnic politics in Afghanistan

As has become apparent, the description of ethnic groups in Afghanistan presents a puzzle: ethnicity is often blamed for political fragmentation and social division of the country but ethnic groups as solid social entities are harder to define. Ethnic identity as a phenomenon that is socially, culturally or politically salient and yet difficult to define is not unique to Afghanistan. Ethnicity is often believed to be at the heart of many complex challenges facing fragile states. Politicised ethnic identities are believed to be a major source or facilitating factor in many intractable conflicts around the world (Eck, 2009; Cederman, Wimmer & Min, 2010). Horrific atrocities that are described as ethnic cleansing and genocide are only the worst of what have been perpetrated in the name of some groups against others that are believed to belong to rival ethnic groups. Ethnic political mobilisation is believed to threaten young democracies by turning elections into an ethnic referendum in which people are mobilised to express primordial grievances rather than vote on political and socioeconomic policies of governments. Hence, it transforms voters from rational actors who vote for socioeconomic policies of governments to impulsive followers of ethnic entrepreneurs and populist demagogues (Horowitz, 1985). Ethnicity is also believed to hamper socioeconomic development by making inter-group cooperation difficult and diverting resources away from developmental objectives to destructive rivalries and competition (Montalvo & Reynal-Querol, 2005). In short, ethnicity is blamed for causing wars, undermining democracies, distorting socioeconomic development and preventing the emergence of effective states.

However, defining what constitutes ethnicity and when it assumes political significance is a precarious task (Chandra, 2006). Some scholars have attempted to define ethnic groups by delineating the core elements of an ethnic group. For example, Smith (2009) defined an ethnic group as a 'named and self-defined human community whose members possess a myth of common ancestry, shared memories, one or more elements of common culture, including a link with a territory, and a measure of solidarity, at least among the upper strata' (p. 27). While these elements are obviously important markers of group identities, the practical significance of each element or a combination of them may have different meanings and consequences in different contexts. A more helpful approach was advanced by Barth (1969), when he defined an ethnic group as a population which:

1. Is largely biologically self-perpetuating;
2. Shares fundamental cultural values, realized in overt unity in cultural forms;
3. Makes up a field of communication and interaction;
4. And has a membership which identifies itself, and is identified by others, as constituting a category distinguishable from other categories of the same order (pp. 10–11).

Barth's approach is useful because he shifted the focus of the debate from identifying shared cultural features of ethnic identities to exploring how those symbolic and cultural features constituted social boundaries. He emphasised that ethnic identities are not mere products of geographical or social isolation, or lack of contacts, between groups. On the contrary, ethnic identities persist with remarkable strength even in situations where members of different groups have close and frequent interaction. Barth's definition of ethnic groups as separate 'fields of communication and interaction' pointed to the resilience and endurance of shared group characteristics, in spite of frequent interaction and contact across the boundaries between groups.

In a similar manner, Glatzer (1998) also emphasises the role of ethnic identities in the making and maintaining of social boundaries. He proposed the following definition with a specific view to aiding understanding of ethnic identities in Afghanistan:

...a principle of social order and of social boundary based on the identification of oneself and of others with social units or categories which combine the following properties: (a) they comprise both genders, all age groups and transcend generations; (b) they are believed to have distinctive cultural qualities by which the members of that unit would differ from comparable neighbouring units; (c) members identify themselves and their families with the past and future of that unit; (d) members and neighbours give them a name (ethnonym); and they are not sub-units of other ethnic groups (p. 168).

However, ethnic identities are not the only principles of social orders and social boundaries. Social boundaries can form and evolve along a range of other ascriptive and acquired markers of identities such as kinship ties, place of residence, socio-economic status, political views, religion and occupational positions. Furthermore, even if ethnic identities are one of the major principles of social divisions they need not have political significance and implications. As experiences of many multi-ethnic countries around the world show, the significance of ethno-cultural differences may be limited to their social and cultural functions with few if any political consequences. The main task ahead of us is then to identify the circumstances and conditions under which ethnic identities assume political relevance by becoming the main base, or one of the main bases, of social and political mobilisation, by fashioning a framework according to which groups evaluate their socioeconomic status and political power, and by creating conditions in which individuals' security and life chances are closely intertwined with those of their groups.

State Disruption and Ethnic Politics

If ethnic identities are one of several competing fields of 'communication and interaction' or principles of 'social boundary-making' then we need to identify the mechanisms and conditions that elevate it above other completing principles and fields. In this book I contend that the state in Afghanistan is the chief source of elevation of ethnic identities over other principles of social divisions and boundaries.

To begin with, the history of modern Afghanistan is a history of constant 'struggle and survival' (Saikal, 2006) and recurrent disruptions to becoming a modern nation state. Ethnic identities gain significance in the process of the recurrent disruptions and contestation for control and meaning of the would-be state as both the centralising elites and challenging groups compete for political power and align themselves with foreign powers to shape ideas and consequences of statehood and nationhood in Afghanistan.

The historical contestation over the nature and institutions of political, administrative and financial control of the state demonstrates two major dynamics of national politics of the country. First, the historical trajectory of the Afghan state is periodically disrupted by its deep tensions and contradictions that surface in intense and violent competition for political power between centralising elites, on the one hand, and excluded challenging social groups, on the other. I contend that a key reason why the Afghan state faced regular upheavals and interruptions is the particular nineteenth century model it aspires to emulate: the centralised state left behind by Amir Abdur Rahman Khan in 1901. The model, achieved through a combination of British support, brutal violence and extensive manipulation of sociocultural differences, excluded many groups and demonstrated the capacity of the modern state to threaten profoundly the security and survival of groups. Hence, the significance of control of the state institutions became abundantly clear. This founding period in the history of the country set in motion complex dynamics of exclusion and inclusion and tensions between centripetal and centrifugal tendencies that continue to shape periodic disruptions, setbacks and even reversals of politics in the country. The pattern of disruption and instability in the state-building process is most clearly demonstrated by violent ends to the reigns of Afghan rulers. Of sixteen rulers between 1901 and 2016, Hamid Karzai is the only Afghan ruler to have peacefully transferred power to his successor. The only three other rulers who came close to transferring power without causing a major conflict are Babrak Karmal (1979–1986) Sebghatullah Mojaddedi (April–June 1992), and (in a formal sense) Burhanuddin Rabbani (1992–2001). But even in these three examples the transfer of power should be interpreted more as a sign of weakness of the capacity of the rulers to hold power against more powerful forces such as Soviet influence in the 1980s and the dynamics of civil war in the 1990s. All others were either assassinated or violently overthrown and forced into exile by coups, armed uprisings and foreign invasions. This has meant that the state capacity to exercise effective control across the country and time is limited and weak. Consequently, if assessed against standards of Western statehood such as the level of its monopoly over means of violence, extraction of revenue and administrative control and penetration of the society, the Afghan state has been weak for most of its history.

Second, since its emergence as a modern state Afghanistan has lacked sufficient domestic revenues to fund the state apparatus and its developmental programmes. The inability to develop a domestic revenue base, which I argue is partly a product of its internal contradictions and periodic disruptions, has made Afghanistan dependent on the patronage of foreign powers. Thus, it should come as no surprise that the Afghan state is often described as weak and fragile, a rentier state with limited stable sources of revenues and uncertain control over its territory (Suhrke, 2008; Rubin, 2002; Verkoren & Kamphuis, 2013).

The periodic crises and disruption of the Afghan state and its dependence on foreign patronage should not be interpreted as necessarily signs of a weak capacity to affect the fate of its society and to inflict massive violence on its people. On the contrary, I argue that the volatility of the Afghan state and its dependence on the patronage of foreign powers has increased its tendency to inflict massive violence, collect exorbitant taxes and impose highly centralised control over its people. Furthermore, the dependence on foreign patronage played an important role in the domestic contestation for control of the state institutions: it shaped the outcomes of internal contestation in favour of some groups over their rivals by giving them an edge over their rivals through provision of financial, military or political support.

In this book, I am primarily interested in ethnicity identities as 'fields of communication and interaction' and their roles in creation and maintenance of 'social boundaries'. Consequently, aiming to capture the simultaneous fluidity and significance of ethnic identities, I will not be concerned much with specific elements of an ethnic identity such as the idea of ethnic and racial origins except when they play a role in formation of social boundaries.

War-centric and state-centric explanations

To elaborate my argument, I make a distinction between two ideal-type explanations in the literature on Afghanistan: state-centric and war-centric. Although at the extremes such distinctions between the two accounts can amount to crude simplification of both the scholarship and the practical realities of Afghanistan, I argue that it is important to make such an analytical distinction for two reasons: first, it helps in understanding not only the nature and types of problems identified by students of Afghanistan but also the strategic options and policy solutions they propose for addressing them. Second, the distinction illuminates unchallenged normative assumptions that pervade the thinking of Afghanistan's political elites and much of the scholarship and historiography of the country. Two aspects of these assumptions are worth highlighting here: first, the centralised state is often equated with order, progress and some forms of general public good and then contrasted to rebellious and unruly peoples, peripheries and tribes that stand in the way of order and progress. Second, Afghanistan's political instability and the suffering of its people are blamed on machinations and meddling of foreign powers and the domestic causes and drivers of the war and violence are treated as subsidiary issues, if acknowledged at all.

To begin with, for most war-centric accounts ethnicity as a political phenomenon did not precede but rather resulted from the vicious cycles of war that have raged in the country since 1978. These explanations focus on the war and upheaval of the last four decades as the primary cause of politicisation of ethnic identities. A solution that might result from this prognosis is that the crisis of Afghanistan can be addressed by reconstituting the historical, centralised state. In other words, if ethnic politics is a product of the crisis and disintegration of institutions of the Afghan state after 1978, then the task is to identify ways of reversing and restoring or at least firmly reconnecting the country to its historical past.

By contrast, the state-centric accounts contend that ethnicity as a political phenomenon preceded the outbreak of war in 1978. As a result the country should take a closer look at longer periods of its political history to identify the conditions that led to the outbreak of the war in the first place. It is worth emphasising that both accounts put the centralised state at the centre of analysis but the underlying assumption of most war-centric accounts is that prior to 1978, Afghanistan was a cohesive and united country, and that ethnic politics are the result of foreign meddling, and machinations and instrumentalisation of ethnic identities by warlords and ethnic entrepreneurs. Consequently, this account carries the risk of equating popular mobilisation and legitimate aspirations for political participation and equality among ethnic groups with warlords and ethnic fiefdoms, and as such has a tendency to gloss over even legitimate ethnic grievances and aspirations.

Various forms of these two accounts can also be found in popular perceptions. In many of my own interviews and conversations, I came across a strong sense of nostalgia for the past: the pre-1978 Afghanistan that is believed to have been known for its peace, political stability and social harmony. Such narratives that usually blame everything on the war in Afghanistan were most passionately told by those who have roots in enclaves of modernisation in pre-war cities such as Kabul. By contrast, I also heard numerous stories that stressed persecution, political and socioeconomic exclusion, excesses at the hands of state authorities, and grinding poverty among the people. These accounts that tend mostly to come from the rural countryside closely overlap with what I call state-centric accounts.

While certainly far from nostalgic accounts of Kabuli elites displaced by war, many scholars also argue that ethnic politics is the product of war in Afghanistan. For example, Rais (2008) notes that 'primordial ethnic identity and Islam emerged as powerful tools of social and political mobiliation at the end of the long years of war' (p. 5). He argues that wars have narrowed the space for 'social contract and political consensus' by polarising the society along ethnic lines. Similarly, Glatzer (1998) sees ethnicity as an 'epiphenomenon in the Afghan war', that is to say it is a secondary factor that is largely a by-product of the war. However, he noted that once the war began, 'ethnically-motivated aggression' led to particular 'aggressiveness' because ethnic identities carry high levels of 'emotional content'. Schetter (2005) also points to a process of 'ethnicization of the conflict' that occurred during the war but argues that 'ethnicization of the masses failed' (2005, p. 2). The main point to note is that in these accounts ethnic divisions, like many other problems in the country, are the corollary of absence or weakness of the Afghan state.

By contrast, a state-centric explanation shifts the focus of the debate to the broader historical trajectory and evolution of Afghanistan as a modern state. The centralised Afghan state that extended its control over the territory that became Afghanistan at the end of the nineteenth century becomes a major object of analysis and scrutiny. Consequently, the policies and approaches of the centralising elites are held as responsible for ethnicisation of politics. Shahrani (1986; 2008) argues that the process of construction of the first centralised state towards the end of the nineteenth century caused a simultaneous process of social fragmentation along ethnic, linguistic and sectarian lines. He argues that ethnicity, kinship and Islam have historically been available to both the state elites and social groups as sources of collective identities. However, the failure of the Afghan state to become more than a corrupt bureaucracy and offer its citizens just treatment fragmented the country. In Shahrani's account, the legacy of the first state-building continues to shape the more recent crisis of the Afghan state. Consequently, the genesis of the Taliban and Talibanism as a political and ideological movement can be traced to 'Afghanistan's creation a century before the Soviet invasion of 1979', and the civil war of the 1990s is 'in fact the virulent manifestation of Pashtun-dominated state-building policies' of the past Afghan state (Shahrani, 2008, pp. 155–6).

In a similar manner, Mousavi (1998) shifts the focus of debate to the basic tenets of 'Afghan nationalism', which he uses to describe 'the whole arrays of attitudes and beliefs which lie at the basis of the notion, held by the Afghans, of their racial supremacy over and above all the ethnic groups in Afghanistan' (pp. 5–6). A combination of nationalist historiography and policies by the Pashtun elites since the early twentieth century, and a romanticised image of Afghanistan as developed around myths about the Pashtun tribes by the colonial and western officials and historians, is responsible for a false national identity and history which excludes other ethnic groups and inhabitants of Afghanistan. Mousavi argues that a new approach to scholarship in Afghanistan requires challenging the nationalist narrative that was formulated by Pashtun elites. He argues that:

> It was an ideology created and sustained by the Afghan or Pashtun people with the aim of establishing political control over the area known today as Afghanistan. In order to exercise this control, it needed to deny the exis-

INTRODUCTION

tence of the area's other ethnic groups, cultures and languages. To do this it had to rewrite history and redefine the area's cultural heritage. (p. 2)

More recently, Wafayezadah's *Ethnic Politics and Peacebuilding in Afghanistan* (2013, p. 279) also argued that the over the past century the Afghan state's exclusive identity construction and discriminatory policies created 'dominant and dominated groups' and contributed to the rise of 'out-group and in-group divisions' along ethnic lines.

If both war and fragmentation of state authority lead to ethnicisation of politics, the question that poses itself is, what are the mechanisms and pathways through which state-building and state fragmentation lead to ethnic politics? It is obvious that war and collapse of central authority can profoundly affect the character and consequences of ethnic identities. Thus, war-centric accounts have important points to make when they indicate increased salience of ethnic identities during armed conflicts. With the collapse of state institutions, ethnic communities might also become security communities as political, security and social and cultural dynamics interact and reinforce one another. Maley (2006) provides an elaborate explanation of the mechanisms that are responsible for particular salience of ethnicity at times of war and the collapse of state institutions. He argues that war and foreign interferences severely disrupted the Afghan state. As a result, the state suffered the dual problems of capacity and legitimacy, which are respectively reduced ability to exercise authority and claim popular normative support. The effects of disruption of the state are most acutely felt in the security sphere as the police and the military lose their capacity and legitimacy to provide protection for ordinary people. Societies disrupted by war and state failure also experience severe erosion of trust in state institutions, which creates a situation in which it becomes rational for people to resort to clientelism, nepotism and identity politics. Consequently, tribal or ethnic groups take the role of 'mutual-support association, bound together by strong norms of reciprocity based on shared lineage' (p. 19).

The link between the rise of modern states and ethno-nationalist conflicts is not unique to Afghanistan. There is an extensive literature that links politicisation of ethnic identities to the rise of modern states. I will briefly provide an overview of two such accounts before discussing how they might help explain the situation of Afghanistan. First,

Smith (1986; 1991; 2009) has consistently stressed the role of pre-modern ethnic ties and identities in shaping the character and content of modern states and nationalist projects. The ethno-symbolic approach he has developed focuses on 'networks of ethnic ties (and the activities subsumed under them) as the single most important factor in the rise and persistence of nations and nationalisms' (2009, p. 27). In explaining the transition from ethnic pasts to national present, Smith (2009) focuses on what he describes as dynamics of 'selection' or 'proposal' by the nation-building elites and the 'responses' by the majority of the masses. Put simply, national identities are formed or challenged as a result of processes whereby nation-building elites select some language, cultural symbol or religion as building blocks of the nation, which are then accepted, rejected or renegotiated by the ordinary people (2009, p. 31). Thus, the process of construction of national identities begins with a choice by the elites to select from among the pre-existing cultural forms, languages, religions and cultural symbols of the populations of a country. And ethnic identities are activated as political factors when they are included or excluded in the selection process. The selection by the elites does not always succeed, but when it does, it is likely to involve some kind of compromise and mutual negotiation between the elite projects and the responses by the majority of the population.

The second account, which helps my discussion of ethnic politics in Afghanistan, is formulated by Wimmer (2002; 2008; 2013). For Wimmer, the process of selection and resonance, which is a key moment of nation-building in Smith's account, is also a key driver of many conflicts and wars around the world. Wimmer advances a more recent modernist account by focusing on the role of nation-state formation in the politicisation of ethnic identities. He departs from the earlier modernist account (Gellner, 1983; Anderson, 1991), which emphasised on large-scale socioeconomic transformations such as industrialisation and mass education as the driving forces behind nationalism, by emphasising the significance of a shift in political legitimation in the transition from pre-modern polities to modern nation-states. His basic starting point is that in contrast to pre-modern states, where political power was legitimated through dynastic and religious principles, modern states base their claim to legitimate authority on national principles and as a result presuppose and require a nation. The transition from the traditional to the national principles of legitimacy is a major cause of wars of the last five centuries. In an analysis of extensive global datasets, he finds that the likelihood of armed conflicts doubled across the world as traditional empires gave way to modern nation-states. In the process, ethnic groups challenged the hierarchies of power that were the foundation of the traditional empires and the new states began to compete for the loyalty of people and the control of territories.

The profound shift in the nature of power and legitimacy also determines whether countries develop overarching frameworks of national identity or politicise sub-national identities. This depends on the outcome of particular political alliances and distribution of resources during the process of political modernisation. As Wimmer (2013) puts it,

> …depending on how the distribution of resources and power between rulers and ruled change, political alliances form along ethnic lines, or the population at large shifts its loyalty to the state elite and identifies with the overarching national category. Ethnic groups and nations thus both represent equilibrium outcomes of [the] modernization process. (p. 5)

The essential point to remember from these two accounts is that state-building is, by definition, a highly exclusionary and selective process. States exclude not only externally, the peoples who are outside their borders, but also internally through selection of cultural symbols and distribution of resources and political power. As a result, modern states can potentially exclude some, perhaps the majority, of their own social and cultural groups, particularly in situations where nationhood and national principles are weak or non-existent at the time of the rise of states. In such situations, the state-building elites may need to make more consequential decisions in choosing from among traditional cultural, linguistic and religious reservoirs, the building blocks of a national identity.

The argument and approach of this book

In the previous two sections, I discussed some of the pertinent ways in which the Afghan state and the ethnic groups constituting the nation in Afghanistan can interact and shape one another. To recap briefly, I use the term 'the Afghan state' to refer to the institutions of political, coercive and administrative control as well as the ideas and strategic approaches of the Afghan rulers that underpinned those institutions. I conceive ethnicity as a 'field of communication and interaction' and as a 'principle of social boundary making' that consists of both ascriptive elements such as language, religion and place of residence as well as acquired and imposed elements such as socioeconomic and political status. I also assume ethnicity to be one of several competing such fields and principles and I use the word ethnicisation to describe situations where ethnicity becomes the overriding or predominant principles of boundary-making. I argue that the Afghan state is the main source of the added and imposed significance of ethnic difference and thus the main driver of ethnicisation of politics in Afghanistan. State fragmentation and war in recent decades further contributed to the process. To put it simply, the modern state politicised ethnic identities, before war and violence securitised them. Three aspects of my argument are worth highlighting here.

First, the first modern state in Afghanistan was built towards the end of the nineteenth century through a series of wars of internal conquest that were led by a coalition of Pashtun political elites and sponsored by foreign financial, military and political support. This centralised state dominated the political imagination of subsequent generations of Afghan centralisers and created lasting relations of domination and subordination that shaped the subsequent contestation for the control and nature of the Afghan state. The process of centralisation of power began with the selective distribution of rewards, and at times extremely violent exclusion, among the Pashtun tribes. However, at the national level the control of the state by coalitions of Pashtun monarchies and tribal elites brought sufficient levels of power and resources to a larger proportion of the Pashtun elites that placed them in a comparatively advantaged position in relation to other ethnic groups. Hence, the state became a vehicle of Pashtun political domination.

Second, in their rise to power and in extending their control over the country the centralising elites engaged in a selective distribution of the benefits of control of the state. Two aspects of the selection process are worth highlighting: first, members and supporters of the winning coalitions were rewarded with tangible and material rewards. In addition to a privileged access to institutions of the state, these selective incentives and rewards included the property, land and even the persons of those who were defeated in the contestation for control of the state and were as a result excluded from power. Second, the centralising elites mostly engaged in selective representation of the history, culture and tradition as symbols of cultural and political authority in the country. The process of selection and exclusion made the contestation for control of the state a zero-sum game, in which the losing parties' socioeconomic status, security and even survival were put at risk. Hence, the more the state was worth controlling, the fiercer became the contestation for its control.

Third, as a principle of social boundary-making and mobilisation, ethnicity has been available to both the state elites that sought to centralise power and impose their own vision of statehood and nationhood and the social groups that challenged and resisted the expansion of state authority in their own areas. It was most powerful when it overlapped and fused with Islam, another principle of boundary-making, as the overarching framework in struggles for political competition and survival. In the first few decades of the twentieth century, Afghan nationalism manifested as Pashtun nationalism, a state-sponsored ideology that sought to select, invent and elevate Pashtun cultural traditions as symbols of national political authority. Over time, the process of the selective distribution of the benefits of the state and selective cultural and political representation increased the salience of ethnicity by adding economic, political and security dimensions to its ascriptive significance. In the face of the dynamics of selection and exclusion, the Hazaras became more aware of themselves as political group and turned to their ethnic identity as a source of solidarity and a basis for resisting and challenging their exclusion from the state. The salience and politicisation of ethnic identities result from cumulative effects of successive rounds of centralisation and unravelling of political power in Afghanistan.

These three aspects of my argument explain three periods of the relationship of Hazaras and the Afghan state. The first period of the relationship was characterised by traditional and mostly spontaneous rebellions during the nineteenth century. These predominantly local and tribal rebellions reached their peak with the intensification of centralising efforts by Amir Abdur Rahman Khan (1880–1901). I argue that the main driving force behind the coincidence of state-formation and frequent rebellions is a broad historical shift that I describe as 'internalisation' of economy of conquest and plunder. In the course of the nineteenth century, the Afghan state, which succeeded the Durrani Empire built in 1747, lost the revenues of the empire, which mostly came from tributes and plunders of wars of conquests from the Indian subcontinent. To compensate for the loss, the centralising elites embarked on a series of wars of internal conquest and reconquest of the peoples and territories that became Afghanistan.

The wars of conquests of the Durrani Empire in the Indian Sub-continent, and the internal wars of conquests, shared a similar socio-economic dynamic: a pact between state elites and Pashtun tribal aristocracy over the distribution of the revenues of the conquests and plunder. Hence, the state which emerged as a result of the wars of conquests rested on a pact between some Pashtun elites who dominated the state and others who represented the tribes. Hence, the selective distribution of the rewards and benefits of state formation.

I argue that long-term the success of the state- and nation-building processes in Afghanistan required the broadening of relations of exchange between Pashtun centralisers and Pashtun tribal elites to include other ethnic groups in the country. This would require a shift away from the policy of selective distribution and representation to creating a system of exchange in which political loyalty, taxation and military service were exchanged for political participation and equitable distribution of public goods. I argue that, despite some haphazard efforts, the Afghan state failed to create such a broad-based system of exchange, which brings me to the second phase of the relationship between the Hazaras and the Afghan state: exclusion and marginalization, 1901–1978. The Hazara integration into the Afghan state during the 1890s was followed by a period of prolonged systematic exclusion of the Hazaras from the material and symbolic benefits of modern Afghanistan. The system of exclusion that existed into the 1970s imposed costs of the modern state on Hazaras such as taxation, direct political control from Kabul and military service without offering a commensurate level of political participation or public goods in the form of socioeconomic development or rule of law and security.

The history and legacy of several decades of exclusion and persecution underscore the third phase of the relationship between the Hazaras and the Afghan state: struggle for recognition. From the 1970s, the Hazaras gained greater collective awareness as a group, transformed their identity from being a source of humiliation and marginalisation to a resource for political mobilisation, and attempted to revive and reclaim their culture and identity. These major shifts spawned violent internal conflicts among the Hazaras and posed a major challenge to the dynamics and processes of selective distribution and representation of the Afghan. I argue that during this period, struggles over the terms of the contract between the state and the peoples of Afghanistan have continued in parallel with wars of foreign invasion and external meddling in Afghanistan affairs. In short, the contestation over the Afghan state is also a contestation about whether state-building is a process of historical reconstruction.

The structure of this book

The following three chapters provide a historical background to the events that unfolded after 1979. Chapter 1 provides a broad historical background to the emergence of modern Afghanistan. It focuses on the Durrani Empire that was established in 1747 in Qandahar and discusses the main features of the tribal kingdom, and its impact on the nature and future of ethnic relations in the country. Chapter 2 discusses the advent of the centralised state during the reign of Amir Abdur Rahman Khan (1880–1901). It contends that the centralised state in Afghanistan emerged as the culmination of three interrelated historical shifts: internalisation of the wars of conquests; increased significance of Islam as a source of legitimation and popular mobilisation; and transformation of Afghanistan from an independent tribal kingdom to a fiscal colony of the British. The chapter looks closely at the Hazara War from 1891 to 1893, one of the four major civil wars of Abdur Rahman's reign, to discuss the role of selective promise and distribution of rewards of expansion of state control over the Hazarajat in the most known extensive ethnic and tribal mobilisation against the Hazaras. It contends that war resulted in the most significant instance of genocide in the modern history of Afghanistan.

Chapter 3 covers the long period between 1901, when Amir Abdur Rahman Khan died, and 1978, when Afghanistan descended into its most recent period of turmoil and bloodshed. It maintains that in the twentieth century the centralised state that was formed at the end of the wars of internal conquests needed to transition from being an instrument of domination to institutions of governance and the development of political representation. The chapter argues that while short periods of democratic and liberal reforms provided windows of opportunity, a genuine transformation of the state was undermined by a combination of traditionalist reaction and exclusionary Afghan nationalism, which was formulated as essentially Pashtun nationalism.

The bulk of this study is dedicated to the period after the April 1978 coup of the pro-Soviet People's Democratic of Afghanistan. This is a period broadly characterised by a Hazara 'struggle for recognition'. If there is one central theme to the role of the Hazaras in Afghanistan's politics, society and culture in the last few decades, it is an earnest desire for recognition as equal citizens, and as participants and beneficiaries of political and socioeconomic development of Afghanistan. Besides the more tangible demands such as political representation, the process also involves Hazara writers, historians, poets, singers and artists who are united by a desire to overcome the humiliation and invisibility to which they were subjected after incorporation into the Afghan state.

In contrast to the previous chapters that are mainly based on secondary sources, the last four chapters are based on my own primary research interviews and informal conversations with Hazara political leaders, former military figures, intellectuals and businessmen in Kabul, Mazar-e Sharif, Herat, districts of Hazarajat and the Hazara diaspora in Quetta Pakistan and elsewhere.

Chapter 4 provides an in-depth account of the rise and fall of the Shuray-e Enqelab-i Ittefaq-e Islami Afghanistan, the first region-wide organisation formed after the collapse of central government control in Hazarajat in 1979. The chapter assesses the organisation against the ambition of its leaders to create a proto-state, and the ambivalent position of its founders in relation to the idea and institutions of the Afghan state. Chapter 5 looks at the consequences of the disintegration of the Shura: bloody and protracted armed conflicts among several Hazara mujahedin organisations through much of the 1980s. It discusses the role of the clergy, the traditional Hazara landed elites and the intelligentsia in the armed conflict to account for the victory of the Islamist clergy as the dominant political force in the region.

Chapter 6 is dedicated to a renewed effort by Hazara elites who emerged victorious from the local civil wars of the 1980s to assert their role in the rapidly changing national politics after the 1989 withdrawal of Soviet troops from the country. It focuses on Hezb-e Wahdat Islami Afghanistan, which was formed in 1989, and discusses its strategies and political alignments at the national level, from the civil wars in Kabul from 1992 to 1996 to the fight against the Taliban movement from 1996 to 2001.

The intra-Hazara conflict demonstrated the intensity and ferociousness of the internal struggle for construction and meaning of ethnic identity, and how it interacted with external dynamics, which at this stage included a plethora of domestic and foreign actors, including the Afghan government in Kabul, the Soviet military forces, other Sunni mujahedin organisations and the institutions and factions within Pakistan and the Islamic Republic of Iran. The chapter discusses the role of the clergy, the traditional elites and the intelligentsia in a series of bloody civil wars that engulfed the Hazarajat region during the decade. It demonstrates that a combination of external support provided by the revolutionary Islamic Republic of Iran, and greater organisational skills, contributed to the victory of the Islamist clergy over the intelligentsia, the khans and the traditional clergy. The chapter shows how Hezb-e Wahdat progressively moved away from its Islamist ideological rhetoric to become a vehicle for expression of Hazara concerns and interests. It argues that a profound fear of reconstitution of the Afghan state as an 'instrument of domination' was a major cause of the ferociousness of the competition for control of Kabul and the central state it embodied throughout the 1990s.

Chapter 7 is dedicated to the dynamics of state-building and ethnic politics after international intervention in 2001. It highlights tension between the stated goals of the state-building process to establish a 'broad-based and representative' political order and powerful forces that sought to reconceive the process as a historical reconstruction. It shows that the result was a *de facto* distribution of power along ethnic lines in a highly centralised presidential system. The arrangement is based on an ethnic hierarchy, in which the Hazaras occupy the third layer, and in which ethnic representation, including in the position of vice-presidents, become highly symbolic and ceremonial. It argues that the influence of historical narratives of Afghan nationalism has combined with the domestic and international actors' desire for convenient and quick fix solutions to make the war-centric account the dominant framework for understanding, articulating and addressing the problem in Afghanistan. The war-centric account has achieved the victory by side lining the state-centric account, foreclosing the possibilities of alternative imaginations and solutions for governance and development of the country. In short, the victory has been achieved as a result of a collective denial, which refuses to admit the problems of the state or the causes and history of the war itself.

The conclusion revisits the main theme of the book by assessing the practical implications of the war-centric and state-centric accounts for resolution of the crisis in Afghanistan.

1

ETHNIC AND TRIBAL POLITICS IN TRANSITION FROM EMPIRE TO STATEHOOD

The entire community [Hazaras] faces a perilous future; they have ugly and detestable faces. Their men and women are related and mixed up with one another like insects on the earth. The creator of human kind planted this cursed community as fruitless trees that do not bear the essence of humanity and reason. The farmer of destiny has never sown the seeds of beauty and humanity in the soil of nature of these beast-like creatures. In designing their faces, it appears the painter of the universe has not meant to portray a human face.

Jami (2007, p. 516)

Introduction

The dominant narrative of the history of Afghanistan usually traces its genesis as a modern country to the foundation of the Durrani Empire by Ahmad Shah Durrani in 1747. In this narrative, the foundation of the empire is also the moment of the founding of Afghanistan. It is surrounded by myths and mysteries and Ahmad Shah is widely eulogised as *Baba* or father of the nation. Mir Ghulam Muhammad Ghubar, one of the most prominent historians of the country, reflected this narrative in claiming that 'Ahmad Shah is recognised and respected as a great Afghani king as much for his military conquests as, and even more, for his invaluable services for national and political unification of Afghanistan'

(Ghubar, 2008, p. 2). Ghubar also contends that Ahmad Shah 'made consolidation of political unification the foundation [of his rule]. To achieve this goal, he respected the legal equality among the inhabitants of Afghanistan and did not recognise much distinction on the basis of religion, language, region and tribe' (Ghubar, 1997, p. 359).

Ahmad Shah is also generally believed to have been elected as king of Afghanistan after a nine-day intensive deliberation by a *jirga* or council of tribal leaders in Qandahar. According to this account, Sufi Saber, a mendicant and spiritual figure from Kabul, who had foretold that Ahmad Shah would become the king after Nadir Shah Afshar, placed a bunch of wheat on his cap and declared him sovereign. In their efforts to construct a long history of a nation in Afghanistan governed by consensual and deliberative norms, some authors have gone as far as to describe the meeting as a 'national jirga' which was 'seeking a candidate for the kingship that could fit the free Afghani character and their principles of jirga and national democracy' (Habibi, 1967, p. 334).

In this chapter, I critically engage with this period of the history of Afghanistan to provide a historical background to the emergence of Afghanistan as a state with centralised authority and well-defined borders at the end of the nineteenth century. Understanding this period is important for appreciating modern Afghanistan because it presented Afghanistan's rulers with challenges of transition from traditional empires as models of political order to a modern state. The transition induced by European colonialism involved major shifts, which I argue profoundly shaped Afghanistan as a country. In this chapter, I focus on the reigns of Ahmad Shah (1747–1772), and Amir Dost Muhammad Khan (1826–1838 and 1842–1863), who founded the Durrani Empire and the Muhammadzai dynasty respectively. Ahmad Shah belonged to the Sadozai branch of the Popalzai Durrani tribe and Dost Muhammad Khan came from the Barakzai tribe of the same federation.

I argue that central to rise and fall of the Sadozai and Muhammadzai dynasties was a particular pact between the Sadozai and Muhamamdzai rulers and the Pashtun tribes. I look at patterns of distribution of land and revenues to account for this relationship. At the time of Ahmad Shah and his immediate successors the Indian sub-continent was the source of three-quarters of the empire's revenues. With the advent of the Sikh Empire and later the British, the Durrani Empire permanently lost its control over areas to the south of the Khyber Pass. This spawned a process of 'internalisation of conquest and plunder', in the form of efforts for extraction of greater resources and occupation of lands within the territories that became Afghanistan. The process, which began with Amir Dost Muhammad Khan and reached its zenith at the time of Abdur Rahman Khan, also overlapped with greater colonial influence and increased influence of Islam as a source of legitimation of political power and wars.

The first section of this chapter provides a broad overview of the rise and disintegration of the Durrani Empire with a focus on its relations with the tribes and ethnic groups. The second section takes a closer look at patterns of collection and distribution of revenues and land to account for material and political inequalities between various Pashtun tribes and between Pashtuns and other groups. The third section will assess the impact of the Durrani Empire on the Hazara population of the country. It will look at instances of conflict and cooperation of three Hazara leaders with the Durrani ruler to explore the role of ethnic identity in political alignments at that time. The conclusion argues that despite much bloodshed and violence used by the Durrani rulers against Pashtun tribes, the Durrani Empire marked Pashtun hegemony and institutionalised their political, social and economic dominance over other ethno-linguistic groups.

Transition from the Durrani empire to the kingdom of Kabul

The Durrani Empire was the last of a series of traditional 'conquest empires' that historically dominated much of the Islamic world. With the gradual encapsulation of the South and Central Asia by Western colonialism, these vast and powerful empires disintegrated, giving way to the modern system of nation states during the nineteenth century. Similar to the Mughal Empire in the Indian sub-continent, the Safavid in Iran and the Ottomans in Turkey, the Durrani Empire expanded and contracted through the ability of its rulers to lead campaigns of military conquests. Ahmad Shah who founded the empire, ran a series of relentless military campaigns to expand the empire towards the north, east and south. During his reign, he led ten major military campaigns to expand his influence to the north, the west and to the Indian sub-continent in the south. When he died in 1772, in addition to Afghanistan with its present boundaries, the Durrani Empire also included Panjab, Kashmir, Sindh and Baluchistan in the Indian subcontinent, and Mashhad and Nishabur, now in Iran. To the north, its influence ended at the Amu River.

In comparison to the Mughal, Savaid and Ottoman dynasties that ruled for centuries, the life span of the Durrani Empire was relatively short. Timur Shah, Ahmad Shah's son and first successor died in 1793 without naming a successor from among his numerous sons. The number of Timur Shah's wives and concubines is not known but he left behind some seventy daughters and sons. At the time of his death, thirty-two of his sons were alive and potentially each a contender of the throne (Farhang, 1988, p. 176). By the early nineteenth century, Ahmad Shah's vast empire was rapidly disintegrating as a result of bloody internal wars of succession among numerous Durrani princes. The effects of this polygamous rivalry within the royal families was so detrimental that some regard it as one of the major factors that prevented the country from 'developing solid domestic structures of statehood and stability' (Saikal, 2004, p. 3).

These internal wars were partly a product of the tribal organisation of the Pashtun society. Ahmad Shah, the founder of the empire, belonged to the Sadozai branch of Popalzai, one of the seven major Durrani tribes. The closest rival of the Popalzai were the Barakzais who played important roles as ministers at the Durrani courts. During the first two decades of the century, as the plots and wars of succession among the Sadozai princes unravelled the empire, the Barakzais gradually rose to power. By 1818, the contenders for the Durrani throne had effectively lost control of its territories and the empire was reduced to a number of competing principalities. In 1826, Dost Muhammad Khan, a member of the Muhammadzai clan of the Barakza tribe, took control of Kabul from where he expanded his control over the territories that became modern Afghanistan by the time he died in 1863. Except for short-term disruptions to their rule, members of the Muhammadzai dynasty ruled Afghanistan until the outbreak of war in Afghanistan in 1978.

The transition from the Sadozai to the Muhammadzai dynasty marked important changes. These changes shaped the relationship that the Durrani Empire and Afghanistan's successive rulers developed with the diverse people who lived in its territories. Among the Pashtuns, it marked the transfer of power from the Popalzai to the Barakzai tribe of the same confederation. The transition occurred in a broader context of the decline of the Durrani Empire as a system of governance. Whereas Ahmad Shah rose in a world where empires would rise and fall as individual conqueror warriors organised armies of conquests to challenge existing dynasties or create new ones, Amir Dost Muhammad Khan founded the Muhamamdzai dynasty in a world that was profoundly being shaped by Western colonialism.

In 1834, Amir Dost Muhammad Khan assumed the title of Amir-ul-Momenin or commander of the faithful in a jehad or holy war against the growing power of the Sikh Empire founded by Ranjit Singh in Punjab that had also extended its control over Peshawar. He failed to regain control of these territories but jehad remained a significant instrument for his successors in their foreign as well as internal wars. Henceforth, in the face of the overwhelming power of the non-Muslim Sikhs and later the British, the nature of the Afghan state shifted towards greater application of religious symbolism. Whereas the Sadozai rulers claimed the secular title of Shah (king), their Muhammadzai successors claimed more divinely-sanctioned authority as Amirs. Although the title was assumed in a holy war against the non-Muslims Sikhs, it signified a fundamental shift in the nature of the Afghan state with important implications for the predominantly Shi'a Hazaras in a Sunni majority country. (The most recent attempt to establish a similar system was the 'Islamic Emirate of Afghanistan' of the Taliban (1996–2001) in which Mullah Omer, the Taliban leader, also claimed the title of Amir-ul-Momenin.)

Despite its chronic instability and regular crisis, the Durrani Empire created the lasting foundation of a tribally and ethnically stratified system in which the Durranis were privileged over other Pashtuns and the entire Pashtuns over the other ethnic communities of the country. In the words of Singh (1977), at the centre of the system, Ahmad Shah 'exalted the Saddozeis—the members of his own clan—and added to the lustre of the halo that already surrounded the descendants of Saddo and Khwaja Khizar' (p. 34). Ahmad Shah appointed his sons as governors of key provinces. Next in the hierarchy were the chiefs of the major Durrani tribes who formed a council of nine tribal chiefs 'without whose consultation and advice he [Ahmad Shah] would adopt no measure of importance' (Singh, 1977, p. 34; Elphinstone, 1842, pp. 534–5).

Although there are few written records of the history of the Durrani Empire, there is evidence that shows that the Durrani kings and Amirs presided over massive changes in the social landscapes of the region. It was founded on a system of economic and political inequalities among tribes and ethnic groups and its life span coincided with extensive displacements of mostly non-Pashtun ethno-linguistic groups between Herat in the West and Kabul in the centre of Afghanistan. The dominant position of the Durrani tribes was most significantly symbolised in renaming of the tribal confederation from its previous name, Abdali, to Durrani, which meant pearl and in in which Ahmad Shah himself was cast as *durri-dauran* (pearl of the age) or *durri durran* (pearl of the pearls) (Singh, 1977, p. 27). On the other hand, perhaps for the first time references are made to Hazaras as a distinct group. As the quotation at the beginning of the chapter from Jami, the official Durrani historian shows, the Hazaras began to be the subject of references such as 'insects on the earth' with 'ugly and detestable faces' facing a 'perilous future'. These statements indicate that the Durrani Empire's political hierarchy was producing social stereotypes based on ethnic groups.

Land and power

The symbolic status of the Durrani tribes, as pearls of the hierarchy, was reinforced by significant material advantages, ranging from monopoly over key political and military positions to highly favourable land redistribution and taxation practices. This is most evident in patterns of distribution of land, which in eighteenth-century Afghanistan, in the words of Gankovsky (1981), constituted, 'the economic foundation of the Durrani Empire' (p. 77). Generally speaking, during this period, land ownership was of three distinctive kinds: crown lands (*khaalisa*) which were mainly located in the immediate environs of major cities like Qandahar, Kabul, Herat and Peshawar; private land (*mulk*) which included most land; and religious endowments (*waqf*) (Gankovsky, 1981, pp. 76–7; Noelle, 1997, p. 269). After the plunders of foreign conquests, land, produce of crown lands and levies and customs collected from the towns were the principal internal source of revenues for the Sadozai rulers. As will become evident later, land and customs became the primary sources of revenues for subsequent Afghan rulers after the Indian subcontinent was lost to the British and the Sikh Empire in Punjab during the first half of the nineteenth century.

The advantage granted to the Durrani tribes in the distribution of land gradually spawned patterns of settlements of different tribal and ethnolinguistic groups. Historically, as centres of trade and commercial exchange that connected the historical Silk routes, Afghanistan's major regions such as Herat, Qandahar, Kabul, Balkh and Ghazni attracted diverse linguistic, religious and cultural groups. In addition to the ethnocultural groups that today make up the main ethnic groups of Pashtuns, Tajiks, Hazaras, Uzbeks and Baluchs, these centres of trade were home to significant communities of Jews, Hindus and Sikhs. In the sixteenth century, Babur, the founder of the Mughal Empire, noted that in Kabul alone eleven or twelve separate languages were spoken. He was so impressed with the diversity of the population of the city that he remarked that 'if there be another country with so many different tribes and such a diversity of tongues, it is not known' (Babur, 1922, p. 207).

Southern Afghanistan offers a particularly illustrative case of the transformation of a multi-ethnic region. As one of the agriculturally fertile and politically and commercially important centres of the region, situated on the route between Iran and India, it was inhabited by diverse ethnic groups. In addition to the Pashtuns who predominate today, there were Hazaras, Baluch and another group of people known as *Farsiwan* or Farsi speakers. As late as the early nineteenth century, Afghans constituted only one quarter of approximately 5,000 houses in the city of Qandahar, the remainder including a substantial community of Hindu traders (Hopkins, 2008, p. 155). British colonial sources suggest that even by the early eighteenth century, the expansion of the Pashtun settlement and power had not changed the heterogeneous mix of the population in the region and that Durrani Pashtuns were only beginning to make their presence felt:

> The Durrani tribes were first located in the neighborhood of Qandahar by Nadir Shah...Before that period the land had been cultivated by a mixed peasantry, composed of Parsiwans, Hazaras, Baluchis etc., with a small proportion of Afghan colonists. (Rawlinson, 1841, p. 509)

Over the past few centuries, the social composition of southern Afghanistan changed from being multi-ethnic and multi-religious to being a predominantly Pashtun region. The roots of such large-scale transformation lay in the system of political and military alliance that developed between the rulers and their subjects. In a longstanding tradition of war and conquests by conquerors of the region, a conqueror looked at the territories and population he controlled as imperial assets that could 'be transferred from one polity to another through inheritance, gift, marriage alliances, and peace agreements' (Barfield, 2010, pp. 71–2). As such, by virtue of his conquest of Qandahar, Ahmad Shah claimed the right to transfer ownership of the assets from one group to another to reward and promote his military dependents or punish and exile others. In practice, this meant changing patterns of settlements and land ownership to fit the new hierarchy of power in his empire.

After ascending the throne of the empire he founded, Ahmad Shah launched a major land assessment and redistribution scheme in the Qandahar region that entrenched the position of the Durranis. The land in Qandahar was divided into *qolba*, a unit in traditional measurement of land which 'which could be laid under cultivation by one *burzgar* (or busbanman), one yoke of oxen and one plough' (Rawlinson, 1841, p. 510). Durrani tribes received 5,206 *qolbas* for which they were required to provide 5,710 horsemen, while non-Durrani Pashtuns would provide 1,890 horsemen for only 110 *qolbahs* of land (Ghani, 1982, p. 355).

Ahmad Shah's land redistribution scheme occurred about a decade after a similar land redistribution in 1738 by Nadir Shah, the Turkic conqueror from the north of Iran, in whose army Ahmad Shah grew to prominence. Nadir Shah had ordered the irrigated land in Qandahar to be divided into three categories. Some 500 *qolba* were reserved as *khaalisa* (state land) which was given to the Farsiwans who cultivated it in return for half of its produce and the other half was assigned to the state. Some 6,000 *qolbas* were given to the Durrani tribes as *tiyul*, a system in which they were obliged to provide one horseman for the army in return for every *qolba*. In addition to their largest share of the irrigated land in the centre of Qandahar, the Durrani tribes were also given considerable land in the valleys of the Kadanai, Dori, Arghastan, and Tarnak rivers which because of water scarcity were called Khoshkaba (dry or waterless). In a broader distribution of the important valleys in and around Qandahar, Arghandab was given to Alkozais, Zamindawar to Alizais and other fertile valleys went to the Barakzais (Singh, 1977, pp. 17–18; Farhang, 1988, pp. 96–7; Ghani, 1982, pp. 336–7).

Two rounds of systematic land redistribution which entailed mass displacement and dispossession of native cultivators such as the Hazaras, Baluch, Tajiks or smaller Pashtun tribes like Kakars, gave rise to another social class in Qandahar that became known as *ra'iyat* or subjects. These landless tribes were required to contribute 2,959 soldiers to Ahmad Shah. In the words of Ghani (1982, p. 348), 'it was through the agency of the state that class positions were seen to be derived and coincide with ethnic identities'.

The Hazaras were most affected in the extensive territories between Kabul and Qandahar. Besides the Hazara population in the centre of Qandahar, extensive areas of Southern Afghanistan were entirely populated by Hazara communities. Before the Durrani Empire, the Hazara homeland extended from Kabul in the east, Ghazni, Qalat and vicinity of Qandahar to the southeast and south, Ghur to the west and Balkh to the north of present day Afghanistan (Babur, 1922, pp. 200, 207, 218; Mousavi, 1998, pp. 65–73). In the areas between Kabul and Qandahar, the Hazaras were pushed towards the Central Highlands from the plains of Qalat, Ghazni and Wardak. Qalat, which became known as Qalat Ghilzai after it was taken over by Ghilzai Pashtuns, was a Hazara territory known as Qalat Barluk at the time of Babur. During the same time, the areas south and east of Ghazni were populated by Hazara communities. The present-day Wardak region west of Kabul was also taken over by Pashtuns in the course of the seventeenth century (Kakar, 2006, p. 127). Masson (Masson, 1842), who travelled through the region in 1830s, remarks:

> We were now in the district of Wardak, which extends to Shekhabad and yields a revenue of ninety thousand rupees. It was anciently possessed by the Hazaras, who, about one hundred years since, were expelled by the Afghans. The Hazaras would also seem to have held the country from Karabagh to Ghazni but have been in like manner partially expelled (p. 224).

In the east, Pashtun expansion similarly displaced other indigenous communities such as Tajiks who prior to the sixteenth century were the dominant population in the Kabul River valley, Laghman, Nangarhar and Logar. In the same token, the Pashai and *Kaafir* population were pushed from the more fertile regions of Laghman and Kunar to more harsh mountainous areas (Noelle, 1997, p. 161).

The Durrani Empire's taxation system reveals similar trends. While the Durrani tribes enjoyed greater tax exemptions on land and harvests in Qandahar and its environs, non-Pashtuns were subject to progressive tax imposition in a number of ways. Broadly speaking, two different taxation systems evolved for the Pashtun and non-Pashtun lands in the country. Pashtun landholders mostly paid a *jambast* or fixed amount while non-Pashtuns paid under a *kot* system whereby a certain share of the yearly produce was collected by the government (Noelle, 1997, p. 270). The latter discriminated against non-Pashtuns as the *kot* system subjected non-Pashtuns to annual assessment of their produces by the state. Furthermore, Durrani tribal *sardaars* were charged with collecting these taxes from the non-Durrani and non-Pashtun farmers, a role that clearly illustrated the dominant role of all members of the confederation in the system (Farhang, 1988, pp. 139–40).

The amount of tax levied on Muhammad Khwajah, a relatively small Hazara tribe that lived in Nawur, Qarabagh and Sarab areas of Ghazni province, indicates a historical pattern of tax payment by the Hazaras to the Afghan rulers. Given their proximity to Ghazni, they were more accessible to the Afghan rulers and more or less remained under control except for periods of acute crisis. During the Sadozais (1747–1818) they paid the equivalent of 25,000 Kabuli rupees in kind. Under the Muhammadzai dynasty of Barakzai branch of the Durranis, this amount was increased to 30,000 and Dost Muhammad Khan (see below) added another 5,000. Shir Ali Khan (1863–66 and 1867–79) increased it to 40,000 and added taxes on new items such as wheat, oils and bags. Abdur Rahman (1880–1901) demanded additional taxes on every aspect of the life of this tribe, including taxes on marriages and on a certain number of livestock. The total tax paid by the tribe in the late 1880s was estimated to be around 50,000, indicating a twofold increase since the Sadozai periods. This was an extremely high tax from the 3330 families that were estimated to constitute the tribe (Maitland, 1891).

Internalisation of jehad and conquest

How could an empire so short-lived and chronically unstable as the Durrani Empire have such an enduring effect? To understand this, two overlapping aspects of the Durrani Empire are worth exploring here: first a particular relationship between Pashtun tribes and the Durrani rulers and second the political economy of the empire.

Pashtun tribes and the Durrani empire

The empire built by Ahmad Shah was mainly based on the model of its Turko-Persian predecessors. It was heavily influenced by the Nadirid Empire in whose army Ahmad Shah grew to prominence. According to Elphinstone (1842), 'the forms of his court, the great officers of state, the arrangement of the army, and the pretensions of the crown, were exactly the same as those of Nadir Shah.' (p. 282). Although in its form the new empire emulated its predecessors, in practice it was greatly influenced by the particular dynamics of Pashtun society. The Pashtun society that formed the backbone of the empire was organised in complex tribal networks in which tribal and clan interests often competed with those of the empire. Barfield (2010, pp. 67–109) argues that the egalitarian nature of the Pashtun tribal system, characterised by unstable and fluid political allegiance and strong opposition to external authority, stood in stark contrast to the hierarchical system of Turko-Mongolian tribes that for centuries had formed the foundations of enduring hereditary dynasties. As a result, the Turko-Mongolian political and military structure that required a social hierarchy and enduring political loyalties imposed on an egalitarian tribal structure made the Durrani Empire deeply contradictory.

To impose the hierarchical Turko-Mongolian model on the egalitarian structure of the Pashtun society Ahmad Shah, as founder of the empire, relied on war and violence and the distribution of the fruits of his wars of conquests. Violence and distribution of booties of war were central to the founding of the empire because Ahmad Shah hailed from the relatively weak Sadozai clan of the Popalzais, one of the seven major Durrani tribes. In 1747, had they been able to agree on a more powerful ruler, Haji Jamal Khan, the chief of the more numerous Barakzai tribe, could have been an important candidate (Singh, 1977, p. 26).

Contrary to the popular narrative promoted by Afghan historians that claims he was chosen by a 'national *jirga*', his coronation was supported by a narrow section of the Durrani tribes. Jami, a Persian writer and court historian of Ahmad Shah, make no reference to a *jirga* or collective deliberation before Ahmad Shah's coronation as king. To the contrary, his *Tarikh Ahmad Shahi* details the violence and bloodshed that came with the ascension of Ahmad Shah to the throne. According to his account some of the most violent methods such as trampling to death by elephants were used to eliminate some of Ahmad Shah's opponents who refused to pledge allegiance to him (Jami, 2007, p. 66).

According to Jami, the majority of Durrani tribal chiefs initially refused to pledge allegiance to Ahmad Shah as king. Other tribal chiefs supported him because he had a weak tribal base and as a result could not pose a threat. Karim Khan Tarini and Maqsud Khan Beriji, the two powerful chiefs of Foshanj and Shorabak in the vicinity of Qandahar city, militarily challenged the authority of the new ruler. In another indication of Ahmad Khan's precarious position in the first year of his rule, Muhabbat Khan Durrani and Manu Khan, two Durrani chiefs who had been deployed as commanders of Ahmad Khan's troops to force Tarini and Beriji into submission, also joined the opposition. Nur Muhammad Khan, the chief of the Alizai tribe and governor of Qandahar under Nader Shah and Abdur Rahman Khan and Mian Dad Khan, the chiefs of the Ishaqzai and Barakzai tribes were also found to have supported the opposition after they had formally submitted to Ahmad Shah. Before deploying his troops to fight Tarini and Beriji, Ahmad Khan ordered the first two of these chiefs to be trampled to death by elephants. Mian Dad Khan was pardoned, according to Jami, because his involvement in the opposition was not established or more likely because he came from the powerful Barakzai tribe. Tarini and Beriji disappeared after they were taken into custody following the defeat of their forces in a battle against Ahmad Shah, just outside the city of Qandahar (Jami, 2007, pp. 58–72). After having subdued the Durrani rivals in Qandahar, Ahmad Shah turned towards the Ghilzais in Qalat during the first year of his rule. However, once he had established an unrivalled supremacy over the Pashtuns he engaged in a series of wars of conquests that dominated his reign until his death in 1772.

Thus the expansion and stability of the Durrani Empire was largely dependent on the loyalty of the tribal leaders and feudal lords who were bound together by the promises of royal patronage and military conquests and plunder. The dependence of the Durrani rulers on Pashtun tribes can be illustrated by the composition of the empire's army. The empire's army consisted of regular (*Askar-e Munazzam*) and irregular (*Askar-e Ghair Munazaam*) warriors. The regular forces, mostly stationed in the capital, constituted one-third of the entire army. They were divided into *Ghulam-e Shahi* (royal cavalry), *Kashakchian* (body guards) and *Qalawar* (scouts). The irregulars were tribal militias who were mobilised at the times of external wars and military campaigns. Ahmed Shah and most of his successors were dependent on the military skills and loyalty of the non-Pashtun section of the army. These warriors were largely recruited from amongst non-Pashtuns, particularly the Qizilbash who constituted one-third of the royal cavalry. They were part of the permanent and paid fighters who because of their lack of strength were considered more faithful and dependent on the rulers in the events of civil wars and unrests (Singh, 1977, pp. 357–64; Farhang, 1988, p. 114).

This meant Ahmad Shah and his successors needed to maintain a delicate balance between managing and maintaining the loyalty of tribal rivals through the distribution of patronage and keeping their influence within certain limits. In fact, externally a Durrani ruler was recognised as the king (Shah), but in the eyes of many Durrani and Ghilzai power contenders he was the first among equals (Farhang, 1988, p. 141). In other words, for the Pashtun tribes who aligned themselves with the empire, the existential goal of the state was to govern the wars of conquests and distribution of patronage, not its tribal supporters. In short, in agreeing on Ahmad Shah as their king, the tribal chiefs were not ready to cede too much of their power to a powerful king and were more 'setting up a kind of federalism than a centralised state' (Fletcher, 1966, p. 43).

Over time, the central role granted to the Durrani tribes became the chief source of permanent tensions between the state and the tribes and eventually greatly contributed to the demise of the Durrani Empire. In the words of Rawlinson (1841, p. 517):

> Ahmad Shah appears to have hardly been aware of the danger to which he was subjecting the State, in thus laying the foundation of formidable and almost independent Durani power. He considered the Durani tribes to

constitute the true and intrinsic strength of his kingdom, and he believed that the more their power was developed the stronger would be his means for achieving foreign conquest, and the safer would be his bulwark against foreign aggression.

The troubles surfaced with the transition of power to Timur Shah, Ahmad Shah's son and heir designate. At the time of his father's death in 1772, Timur was governor of Herat. Before he arrived in Qandahar, a number of tribal chiefs had declared Solaiman, his brother, as Ahmad Shah's successor. Timur reclaimed the throne and executed the key tribal elites involved in the plot. This was not the end of the troubles. Tribal rivalries and jealousy and competition between tribal *sardaars* remained high. As a more permanent solution to future tribal disturbances, Timur Shah decided to move the seat of the Empire from Qandahar to Kabul where, as described by Elphinstone, he 'gave way to his natural indolence' (1842, pp. 300–1). Furthermore, Timur Shah also attempted to weaken the power of the tribes 'by instituting new offices or altering the duties of old ones so that he could appoint his own officials to the most powerful positions' (Barfield, 2010, p. 106). After the capital was transferred to Kabul, a number of Durrani tribesmen led by Abdul Khaliq, Timur Shah's uncle, revolted against him. To offset the power of tribal chiefs, Timur Shah promoted non-Pashtuns in the ranks of his regular army. The number of Qizilbash and Hazaras increased among his personal bodyguards. According to Fayz Muhammad Kateb (1913, p. 49), the revolt by Abdul Khaliq only increased Timur Shah's suspicion towards the Durrani tribes:

> From that time on, the Qizilbash and the Mongols, (the latter) known as Hazarahs, who were assigned to the Ghulam corps became the people on whom His Highness Timur Shah relied and in whom he trusted. The Durranis, who claimed to be the peers and equals of the shah, fell out of favor.[1]

The death of Timur Shah in 1793 more plainly exposed the weakness of the Durrani Empire. Under Shah Zaman (r.1793–1800), as a result of intense intra-tribal rivalry the role of non-Pashtuns increased further in the army. They constituted the core of the 12,000 royal squadrons.

> The essence and core of the royal forces were the 12,000 troopers of the ghulam squadrons. Most of them were either Mughul (Hazarah) or Qizilbash. A minority were from other ethnic groups....There were

another 12,000 cavalry from these two ethnic groups under the command of other sardars. They always stay with the royal entourage. They guard the private chambers of the shah and the women's quarters, always setting up their camp 300 zarfi from the women's quarters. Most of these 12,000 received all of their salary in cash. (Kateb, 1913, p. 77)

The Durrani rulers turned to non-Pashtun ethnic groups mainly to offset the power and influence of Pashtun tribes. However, this did not disentangle the empire from its tribal base because the relationship between tribes and the state was anchored in a complex set of relations of reciprocal economic and political exchange.

The political economy of conquest and plunder

One major obstacle to the consolidation of the empire in the words of Barfield (2010) was that 'it was a coat worn inside out' (p. 99). Poor and sparsely-populated territories such as Qandahar and Kabul (which became the capital of the Durrani Empire) were meant to integrate richer, extensive and more densely-populated territories such as Panjab, Sindh, Mashhad and Turkestan north of the Hindukush. A key implication of this was that the empire could not collect adequate revenues from within its core territories. The districts and territories east of the Khyber Pass were the primary source of the regular revenues of the Durrani treasury. In the 1790s, before the empire began to decline, the eastern part of the empire, the territories north of Khyber, provided only 25.9 per cent of the total Durrani revenues. This means three-quarters of the revenues came from the districts and regions that were outside the administrative and political centre of the empire (Gankovsky, 1981, pp. 86–91).

To unite internally divided and egalitarian Pashtun tribes Ahmad Shah and his successors needed constantly to organise and lead of wars of conquest. The Indian sub-continent was particularly important. Seven of the ten major military campaigns under him were directed towards India. In 1757, when Ahmad Shah conquered Delhi, the goods plundered by his army were worth 300 million rupees and were carried by 28,000 animals (Farhang, 1988, pp. 114–33; Ghubar, 1997, pp. 360–71).

The fruits of military conquests in the form of plunder bound the otherwise divided Pashtun tribes together as the ruling group in a stratified system. In the words of Elphinstone (1842, pp. 283–4) Ahmad Shah

> relied in a great measure on the effects of his foreign wars. If these were successful, his victories would raise his reputation and his conquests would supply him with the means of maintaining his army and of attaching the Afghan chiefs by favour and rewards: the hopes of plunder would induce many tribes to join him, whom he could not easily have compelled to submit.

Revenues from east of the Khyber Pass were central to Ahmad Shah's ability to coerce or allure his rivals into submission. In 1747 when he was declared king, Ahmad Shah captured a large caravan of 300 camels, carrying treasure of 20 million rupees and diamonds and shawls. These were revenues collected from Sindh and Punjab and were seized by Ahmad Shah in Qandahar after he arrived in the city following the death of Nadir Shah in Mashhad. Among those leading the caravan was Nasir Khan, the governor of Kabul, who was also forced or persuaded to rule Kabul on behalf of Qandahar and pay a tribute of half a million rupees. The timing of the seizure 'did more for his future career than all his private virtues and noble origin' (Singh, 1977, pp. 29–30).

By the early nineteenth century, the Durrani rulers were losing these vast revenues from the Indian sub-continent. At this time, the world around the empire was profoundly changing. During the first half of the nineteenth century, the advent of British colonialism in the Indian sub-continent which gradually took over the former Durrani territories east of the Khyber Pass, and the expansion of the Tsarist Russia north of the Oxus, introduced fundamental changes to the political and military dynamics of the region.

Before the arrival of the Western powers, the Sikh Empire founded by Ranjit Singh in 1799 had begun to take important parts of the declining Durrani Empire including Peshawar, Lahore and Kashmir. The rise of the Sikhs followed by the emergence of European colonialism profoundly altered the regional environment for the Durrani rulers and other traditional forces. These changes shaped the character and nature of the Muhammadzai dynasty. In the face of the Sikhs, Islam gained increased significance as the source of legitimation of political power and mobilisation. During the first half of the nineteenth century, the British gradually made its presence felt closer to the core of the Durrani Empire. The rise of first the Sikhs and second the British induced another fundamental shift in the nature of the Afghan state which became most apparent during the reign of Amir Dost Muhammad Khan. As indicated above, in contrast to the Sadozai rulers who described themselves as Shahs (kings) with secular author-ity, the Muhammadzai rulers assumed the title of Amir-ul-Momenin, indicating a shift towards the religious nature of their authority. While the religious rhetoric was initially employed against these non-Mus-lim enemies to the south of Khyber, as the British became the supreme force, Islam was used as a source of legitimacy for wars of conquest and plunder in Afghanistan. The most important conse-quence of the rise of these powers to the east of the Khyber Pass was that the prospects of wars of conquests and plunder that were central to the political economy of the Durrani Empire diminished. Henceforth, despite the revenues of the Indian sub-continent being reduced, the power of the Pashtun tribes and the need for the Muhammadzai leaders to distribute patronage persisted. Consequently, this did not change the dynamics of relationship between the Durrani rulers and Pashtun tribes. To keep the tribes at bay, beginning with Dost Muhammad Khan, the Muhammadzai rulers turned the direc-tion of conquest and plunder inwards, reconquering and plundering the regions inside the country.

The Hazaras and the Durrani rulers

The Hazaras played an important role in the consolidation, if not the formation, of the Durrani Empire. While claims of Hazara participation in the coronation of Ahmad Shah in 1747 cannot be substantiated, it is clear that initially the Hazaras supported the Durrani Empire. Some Hazara leaders played important roles in extending Ahmad Shah's authority over Kabul and Herat, historically important political and cultural centres of the country. In Herat, Darwish Ali Khan Hazara, the chief of the Hazaras of Badghis, brought down Amir Khan Arab, the governor of the region at that time, and consequently helped to annex Herat to the Durrani Empire. As a reward, Ahmad Shah appointed him as governor of the region and granted him the title of *Beglarbigi*, mean-ing chief of the chiefs (Jami, 2007, pp. 502–6). In Kabul, Ahmad Shah gained control of the city after the Hazaras defected to Durrani (Ghubar, 1997, pp. 361–2).

However, the original concord between the Hazaras and Ahmad Shah did not endure for long. The consolidation of the Durrani authority over these cities began with the appointment and empowerment of Pashtun tribal elders at the expense of local communities. The history of cooperation and conflict of two Hazara leaders with the founders of the Sadozai and Muhammadzai dynasties sheds light on the dynamics of the relationship between Hazaras and the Sadozai and Muhammadzai rulers: Darwish Ali Khan Hazara in Herat during the reign of Ahmad Shah, and Mir Yazdan Bakhsh in the 1830s during the first reign of Amir Dost Muhammad Khan. These two examples illustrate how attempts at expansion and consolidation by the Durrani Empire took the form of expansion and consolidation of Pashtun power over the Hazaras. In both cases, consolidation of state authority over the regions took the form of the appointment of Pashtun officials and the empowerment of Pashtun tribes. Consequently, to the Hazaras, the authority of both Dost Muhammad Khan and Ahmad Shah was represented by Pashtun tribal chiefs, whose economic and political power intersected with the centralisation of power.

Darwish Ali Khan Hazara

We do not have many details of the tension between Ahmad Shah and Darwish Ali Khan. However, the accounts by Jami (2007) and Yazdani (2007) point to a relationship that throughout the 1750s and 1760s was fraught with constant intrigues and conflicts, eventually resulting to the killing of Darwish Ali Khan and his replacement by Timur Shah as governor of the province in 1771. In one instance, which appears to be around 1762, the rivalry between Darwish Ali Khan and Anzal Khan resulted in a conflict in which both sides mobilised tribal warriors. In addition to his own Hazara supporters, Darwish Ali Khan also mobilised Aimaq tribes to fight Anzal Khan, a Pashtun tribal leader who was supported by Qandahar and had found a common cause with the Taimanis of the region. To offset the alliance of Anzal Khan with the Taimanis, Darwish Ali Khan had formed an alliance with the Jamshidis and Ferozkohis, Persian speaking Turkish tribes with a close affinity with the Hazaras. The alliance built by Darwish Ali Khan had extended his influence beyond the Hazaras in the region. Troops dispatched from Qandahar in support of Anzal Khan forced Darwish Ali Khan and his allies to retreat into the city of Merv, presently in Turkmenistan. A deal mediated by Shah Wali Khan, who held a prime ministerial position in the court of Ahmad Shah in Qandahar, allowed Darwish Ali Khan to return to Herat and his title of *Beglarbigi* was reinstated. On two further occasions, Shah Wali Khan intervened in support of Darwish Ali Khan and convinced Ahmad Shah to set him free. However, the underlying power rivalry between Darwish Ali Khan and the Pashtun *sardaars* remained unresolved. In 1771, after tensions resurfaced, Darwish Ali Khan was removed from his position and placed under house arrest. In response, his sons, Islam Khan and Hanzala Khan, rebelled and mobilised Hazara and Jamshidi forces. To suppress the rebellion, fresh forces were dispatched from Qandahar, who, along with Taimani troops raised from within Herat, killed Hanzala Khan and Islam Khan as well as Nayaz Khan, the leader of Jamshidi rebels. These conflicts eventually resulted into the killing of Darwish Ali Khan at the order of Ahmad Shah while in detention (Yazdani, 2007, pp. 95–100).

Another instance of conflict between the Hazaras and Durrani Empire recorded in Jami's account is the rebellion of the Day Kundi Hazaras under the leadership of Enayat Khan Hazara in 1763. The circumstances leading to the rebellion are not recorded and the information available today is mainly based on the accounts of Jami, the official historian of Ahmad Shah. It appears that Enayat Khan, who was also governor of Day Kundi and the surrounding areas, was not fully subordinated to the authority of Qandahar. Upon his return from one of his trips to India, Ahmad Shah deployed a large tribal force to punish Enayat Khan. Jami describes the ensuing battle in an epic manner. He describes a ferocious and bloody battle in which Enayat Khan and his forces were defeated and the local Hazaras were plundered at the hand of Ahmad Shah's forces (2007, pp. 515–18).

It is, however, important to note that like most of other territories conquered by the Durrani Empire until the end of the eighteenth century, the Hazara areas were not integrated into a centralised administrative and political structure. As elsewhere, the authority of Qandahar and Kabul over the Hazaras appears to have been exercised by securing allegiance and the payment of tributes by local Hazara chiefs. The indirect control over the Hazaras appears to have become even more sporadic after the Durrani Empire began to unravel at the beginning of the nineteenth century. However, the instability and breakup of the Durrani Empire into several principalities in the early nineteenth century created a different dynamic, characterised by the emergence of multiple centres of power that were involved in ceaseless competition for the throne well into the middle of the next century. Endless wars of successions and internal rivalries meant that whoever gained the Durrani throne adopted new tactics and approaches towards the Hazaras.

For the Hazaras, the centres of power most relevant were Kabul, Qandahar and Herat, which competed for influence and tax revenues of their territories. On the one hand, this situation allowed a great deal of autonomy for various Hazara chiefs in controlling their own domestic affairs and negotiating the amount and type of the tributes they paid. On the other hand, it reinforced internal fragmentation and rivalries characteristic of the feudal social structure of the Hazaras at that time. The existence of competing centres of power around the Hazarajat region gave the Hazara *mirs* (landed elite) the option of choosing to support whichever one of the Sadozai, or later Muhammadzai, contenders for power they saw fit in view of the internal rivalries in Hazarajat (Temirkhanov, 1993, pp. 145–6).

The Hazaras of north Qandahar and Uruzgan paid tributes to the rulers of Qandahar. The rulers of Herat had an even weaker claim over the Hazaras of western Hazarajat and the Day Ziniat Hazaras of Badghis. In general these tributes were collected in kind or in cash by the *mirs* from their respective territories and tribes and then transferred to the Afghan rulers. The areas deeper into the Hazarajat proper tended to exercise more autonomy and independence from the centres of power. Government influence and control faded out in areas geographically distant from the seats of Afghan rulers. Hence, at some point the realm of influence of the Kabul rulers would extend to cover Day Zangi and Day Kundi regions, which are currently part of Bamyan and the newly established Day Kundi province (Temirkhanov, 1993, pp. 150–66).

Mir Yazdan Bakhsh and Amir Dost Muhammad Khan

The transition from Sadozai to Muhammadzai had particularly significant implications for the Hazaras. Beginning with Amir Dost Muhammad Khan, who founded the Muhammadzai dynasty in 1826, the Afghan state began to establish firmer control over the Hazaras, a long historical process that was completed by Abdur Rahman Khan (1880–1901). In 1826, Amir Dost Muhammad Khan took control of Kabul. Charles Masson (1842) and Mohan Lal (1846), who visited Afghanistan before and during the first Anglo-Afghan War, provide relatively detailed accounts of the extent of Amir Dost Muhammad Khan's reign and his influence and relationship with the Hazaras of Behsud and Bamyan. According to Masson, while the Hazaras of these areas paid some tributes to the Afghan rulers, these were not collected every year and the amount and the types of the tributes were subject to mutual negotiation. He quotes a popular Hazara saying that indicates the negotiating position of the Hazaras with the government of Kabul in the early years of Amir Dost Muhammad Khan. This was *'sang ya buz'* or 'stone or goat' which meant a Hazara chief 'held a goat in one hand and a stone in the other, saying, if the Afghans are willing to accept a goat in place of a sheep we will give tribute, if unwilling, they shall receive stones, or they would resist' (p. 353). Nonetheless, by the 1830s the amount of tax on the Behsud region had increased considerably, indicating greater government control as well as the increased importance of revenues from within the region that became modern Afghanistan. In Behsud, for example, the revenue increased from 17,000 rupees at the time of Sadozai rulers to 80,000 rupees by the time of Amir Dost Muhammad Khan (Harlan, 1842, p. 127).

The key point to note is that the same dynamics of power relations between the state and Pashtun tribes were at work in the centralisation of power by Dost Muhammad Khan. In other words, the very dynamics that had contributed to the demise and disintegration of Sadozai rule were back at work after 1826. After he came to power, Dost Muhammad Khan gave Bamyan as *jagir* to Taj Muhammad Khan, known as Haji Khan, a powerful Pashtun *khan* who had helped Dost Muhammad Khan take control of Kabul. Mohan Lal describes Haji Khan as 'a man of great treachery and hypocrisy' (Lal, 1846, p. 150). Haji Khan's *jagir* was originally fixed at 72,000 rupees per annum of which 55,000 would come from Bamyan and the rest from transit duties in Charikar and the *rabat* or caravanserais between Sir Chashmah near Behsud and Logar. Haji Khan, according to Lal, admitted that he was collecting twice that amount including 100,000 rupees from Bamyan alone. Similarly, Amir Muhammad Khan, a brother of Amir Dost Muhammad Khan, was appointed as governor of Ghazni. At this time he was also responsible for the Behsud region from where he was collecting tributes on annual basis (Masson, 1842, pp. 304–5, 316).

The empowerment of tribal chiefs such as Haji Khan over the Hazaras brought Amir Dost Muhammad Khan into conflict with Yazdan Bakhsh, a leader of the Hazaras of Behsud region. Yazdan Bakhsh happened to be one of the few Hazara leaders who had the charisma to unify and bring an extensive part of the Hazarajat region under his own leadership. In addition to his native Behsud, Mir Yazdan Bakhsh had also extended his influence through marriage and alliances over the mirs of Shaikh Ali and Day Zangi Hazaras. Thus, at a time when Amir Dost Muhammad Khan could only claim to control Kabul and the Kohistan region north of it, Yazdan Bakhsh's expanding influence posed a serious threat to Pashtun rulers since the foundation of the Durrani Empire in 1747. As an indication of his influence, Yazdan Bakhsh ensured security along the Kabul-Bamyan route, one of the principal trade routes, which was previously a 'theatre of forays and depredations' (Masson, 1842, pp. 295–6). In short, according to Charles Masson (p. 296):

> It was evident that a chief of superior ability had arisen among the Hazaras and he became an object of much attention both to the Shias and the government of Kabal; the former congratulating themselves in having a potent ally in case of need, the later apprehensive of his views, and of the effects of a consolidated authority in the Hazarajat.

Amir Dost Muhammad Khan's fears of the rise of Yazdan Bakhsh gained greater strength as he was also largely dependent on the support of the Shi'a Qizilbash community of Kabul in the first years of his reign. The Qizilbash of Kabul, with whom he was related through his mother, were instrumental to his rise to power. He feared that a potential alliance between the Shi'as of Kabul and the Hazaras could pose the most potent threat to his throne (Masson, 1842, pp. 298–300).

To counter the challenge posed by Yazdan Bakhsh with the expansion of his control in Hazarajat, Amir Dost Muhammad Khan first invited him to visit Kabul through the Qizilbash dignitaries of Kabul. However, at the first suitable moment after his arrival, Dost Muhammad Khan ordered him, and his wife who was accompanying him, to be seized and put in prison. According to Masson, he was probably going to be executed but a promise of 50,000 rupees in ransom for an Amir struggling with limited revenues delayed his execution. Yazdan Bakhsh took the opportunity offered by the negotiations over the payment to escape from prison and flee back to Behsud (Masson, 1842, pp. 301–3).

Despite the failed attempt on his life, Yazdan Bakhsh refrained from displaying any open animosity towards Kabul and the security of the road between Kabul and Turkistan was maintained. However, in an apparent show of force Yazdan Bakhsh marched towards Bamyan and several Hazara and smaller Tajik chieftains joined him. In the meantime, Dost Muhammad Khan also waited for another opportunity. Rahimdad Khan, who was appointed as Naib, or deputy of Haji Khan in Bamyan, reached a rapprochement with Muhammad Ali Beg, the Tajik chief of Saighan and a rival of Yazdan Bakhsh who was also increasingly apprehensive of the latter's growing influence. Muhammad Ali Beg was also infamous among the Hazaras for his raids to capture them as slaves for sale in the markets of Central Asia. Thus, an alliance between Haji Khan and the chief of Saighan greatly enraged Yazdan Bakhsh who retaliated by expelling agents and soldiers of Haji Khan stationed along the Kabul-Bamyan road (Masson, 1842, pp. 303–5).

In early 1832, Haji Khan was appointed by Amir Dost Muhammad Khan to collect the tributes from the Behsud region that totalled some 40,000 rupees. Haji Khan was provided with 1,500 horse, two guns and an elephant to carry out the mission. In advance of the mission, Haji Khan attempted to re-establish his friendship with Yazdan Bakhsh through Qizilbash chiefs such as Khan Shirin Khan in Kabul. He 'dispatched no less than seven *kalam-ullahs*, or oaths upon the Koran at various times, as solemn vouchers for the sincerity of his engagements' (Masson, 1842, pp. 314–15).

These gestures, particularly Haji Khan's use of the Holy Quran and his connections to the Shi'a chiefs of Kabul, persuaded Yazdan Bakhsh to welcome Haji Khan and cooperate in the expedition across the Behsud region, including the Jirghai and Borjegai regions of the present day Nawur district in Ghazni. At times, Yazdan Bakhsh accompanied

Haji Khan with his own 2,000 men and at others he simply encouraged Hazara chiefs to pay their tributes. The expedition was successful. At the end, Haji Khan had collected 60,000 rupees worth of revenues. In the words of Masson, 'Hazarah chiefs were full of confidence in the good faith of the Khan, and even two or three leaders of Deh Zanghi had visited his camp at Ghiru Maini and promised the next year to lead him into their country' (1842, p. 371).

In cooperating with Haji Khan, Yazdan Bakhsh was also motivated by the hope of building an alliance with Kabul against Muhammad Ali Beg of Saighan. Haji Khan extensively exploited the widespread resentment towards the chief of Saighan among the Hazaras. Throughout the journey, on every occasion possible he reiterated his intention of eliminating the chief of Saighan. However, once this success was achieved in Hazara areas, Haji Khan accompanied by Yazdan Bakhsh and a few other Hazara leaders moved towards Saighan where, contrary to the expectations of the Hazaras, he reconciled with Muhammad Ali Beg and married one of his daughters. This aroused great suspicions among the Hazara chiefs, one of whom, Mir Baz Ali, left the camp with his 500 horsemen, but Yazdan Bakhsh remained, owing to the oaths of friendship with the Khan. He was, however, greatly mistaken. During a short expedition in the Tatar region at Dasht-e Safid, Haji Khan seized Yazdan Bakhsh and his close companions during a meeting at his camp. Yazdan Bakhsh was taken to Bamyan in chains where he was executed along with a number of other Hazara leaders. Masson (pp. 398–9, 409, 415 and 431) who was also accompanying Khan throughout the journey summed up his own feeling towards the way Yazdan Bakhsh was eliminated:

> I must confess, I was confounded at the Khan's procedure. I had never before witnessed the commission of so flagrant an enormity; and aware of his secret designs, could not conceive why he preferred the alliance of Mahomed Ali Beg to that of so powerful a chief as Mir Yezdanbakhsh. I could not for a moment credit the treacherous intentions imputed to the latter, who, had he been faithless or insincere, could easily have destroyed the khan and his army.

The execution of Yazdan Bakhsh removed the major obstacle that stood in the way of the extension of the control of Kabul deeper into the Hazara territories. Amir Dost Muhammad Khan increased the taxes on the Hazaras. According to Mohan Lal (Lal, 1846, pp. 232–3), towards the end of 1830s the tax on the Behsud region had almost doubled from 40,000 to 70,000 rupees per year. Amir Dost Muhammad Khan also extended Kabul's control over the Hazaras of Shaikh Ali and Day Zangi. However, in the more distant parts of these regions this control was only nominal. In 1842, after Amir Dost Muhammad Khan resumed power after the first Anglo-Afghan War (1839–1842) his control over Hazarajat was far from assured. To resume collecting taxes and re-establish his authority in Hazara areas, he sent an army to Behsud, Day Zangi and Day Kundi (Temirkhanov, 1993, pp. 155–6). Thus, despite periodic control central government presence remained fragile, necessitating conquest after conquest.

The expansion of Kabul's control over the country was disrupted by the first Anglo-Afghan War (1839–1842) which resulted in the occupation of the country by British Indian forces in 1838. The British forced Dost Muhammad Khan into exile in India and installed Shah Shuja, a Sadozai prince, as ruler. In 1842, the British forces were defeated and Shah Shuja was killed in popular revolts. Following the departure and massacres of tens of thousands of British forces, Dost Muhammad Khan was allowed to return and resume his second reign which lasted until his death in 1863. Despite the defeat of the British forces, Dost Muhammad Khan and his successors never managed to extend their authority beyond the Khyber Pass. Deprived of the rich revenues in the Indian sub-continent, the Muhammadzai rulers increased their efforts to collect exorbitant revenues from the territories that became Afghanistan. Mohan Lal (Lal, 1846, pp. 232–3) who accompanied the British forces provides details of two different accounts of revenues: the *Asal* or just revenues and the *Bida't* or unjust revenues that were collected through extortion and other arbitrary ways. The fact that the revenue system officially included an unjust account shows the significance of the shift towards internal plunder in the form of extortion.

Conclusion

In its relatively short-life span, and despite its instability and regular disruptions, the Durrani Empire profoundly shaped the political and social landscape of the territory that became known as Afghanistan. It consolidated old and initiated new political, economic and social changes that placed the Durrani tribes, and the Pashtuns more broadly, in a highly advantageous position. At the core of the relationship between the Durrani rulers and Pashtun tribes was a dynamic of mutual dependence that was responsible for both the rise and downfall of the empire. The distribution of the fruits of wars of external conquest and redistribution of internal lands were the key means through which the rulers allured or coerced the tribes into submission to their authority. After the Durrani ruler's claim over the Indian sub-continent was challenged first by the Sikh Empire and subsequently by the British, land and revenues from inside Afghanistan formed the chief foundation of the empire's political economy. Henceforth, as a substitute for declining revenues from the Indian sub-continent, the Durrani rulers had to impose greater taxes on non-Durranis and non-Pashtuns to fund the state and keep the tribes at bay.

While the distribution of land and revenues to Pashtun tribes at times provided stability, it also prevented the state from gaining autonomy from ethnic and tribal relations and establishing a lasting basis of social contract with its diverse people. The state faced regular rebellion among non-Pashtuns who often experienced intervention from the state through the expansion of Pashtun tribal influence and the empowerment of Pashtun tribal elites in what they considered to be their local affairs. In relation to the Hazaras, two aspects of their encounter with the Afghan state are worth highlighting here: first, the displacement of the Hazaras from extensive territories between Kabul and Helmand by Pashtun tribes; second, the progressive encroachment of Pashtun tribes in what remained of their historical homeland and extraction of revenues in the forms of tributes and taxes from them. The key point to note is that the encroachment of Pashtun tribes in Hazara lands intersected with the ebb and flow of influence of the Afghan state over the Hazaras. In broad historical terms, over the past few centuries, the gradual expansion and consolidation of state authority overlapped with the takeover of Hazara lands by Pashtun tribes. The increased role of Islam under the Muhammadzai rulers had particularly sharp dimensions. As a mainly Shi'a community in a largely Sunni country Hazara challenges to the authority of the Amirs were too easily condemned and more brutally repressed by the Amirs of Kabul. The power of a centralised state clad in the garb of religion turned inwards more fully under Amir Dost Muhammad Khan's grandson, Amir Abdur Rahman. The Hazaras became the principal victims of this shift and we will turn to this in the next chapter.

2

STATE-BUILDING, VIOLENCE AND REBELLIONS

THE PERIOD OF AMIR ABDUR RAHMAN KHAN, 1880–1901

This [Hazara War] is the last of the four great civil wars that took place during my rule, and I consider that the prestige, the strength and power, as well as the peace and safety of my kingdom, have gained more by this war than perhaps any of the others.

Khan (1900, p. 276)

Introduction

Afghanistan as a country with its present boundaries and a centralised state emerged during the reign of Amir Abdur Rahman Khan in the last two decades of the nineteenth century. The centralised state, created through extensive violence and bloodshed, continues to dominate the political imagination of most Afghan political elites and historians. The dominant narrative contrasts the centralised state and its rulers as benevolent agents of order and modern civilisation against ignorant and rebellious people who by standing against the authority of the state also stood against order and progress. This narrative downplays, justifies and legitimates the violence and massacres that were perpetrated by the centralising elites against the people.

In this chapter, I challenge this narrative by revisiting the nexus between state-building, violence and rebellion during this formative period of the Afghan state. I show that the building blocks of the first modern state consisted of British aid, coercion and violence, and a particular interpretation of Islam that justified violence and massacres against the Amir's own people. I argue that Abdur Rahman Khan completed the process of internalisation of the religious doctrine of jehad and the political economy of plunder that began with Amir Dost Muhammad Khan in 1834. The Hazaras became the main target of the internalisation process because they were the archetypal internal enemy against whom the Amir could mobilise the whole population of the country.

This chapter is divided into four main sections. The first section describes the centralised state built by Amir Abdur Rahman Khan, with a particular focus on the roles of Islam and British subsidies in the process. The second section discusses the relationship between the Hazaras and Amir Abdur Rahman Khan during the 1880s. The third section looks at the 1891–93 Hazara War. The final section analyses the aftermath of the final conquest of Hazarajat in 1893 and presents the case that the strategies and tactics of the Amir, during and after the Hazara War, constituted the most significant example of genocide in the modern history of Afghanistan.

State-building and rebellions

Amir Abdur Rahman Khan (1880–1901) is considered by many Afghan historians to be the architect of modern Afghanistan. He is credited with building a highly centralised state in Kabul that extended its direct control over all parts of the country. Kakar (2006) describes his reign as the 'most formative period in the history' of the country (p. 6). In his preface to the Amir's autobiography, which he edited, Sultan Mahomed Khan, the Amir's secretary, describes his most remarkable achievement as transforming Afghanistan 'from a mere barren piece of land full of barbarous tribes, into a consolidated Muslim Kingdom and centre of manufactures and modern inventions' (Khan, 1900, p. VII).

By 1901 when he died, Amir Abdur Rahman Khan had effectively brought the whole country under direct control of his government. He was the second Afghan ruler after Ahmad Shah Durrani to end his reign and transfer the throne to his heir designate peacefully. Beginning with the death of Timur Shah Durrani in 1893, all the Sadozai and Muhammadzai rulers were deposed at least once. The reign of many ended extremely violently, after being blinded, killed or sent to exile. In his twenty-one-year reign, the Amir defeated all dynastic rivals, tamed the previously rebellious tribes and ethnic groups, broke down the resistance of the tribal aristocracy, and deprived the religious establishment of their autonomy, subordinating them to his authority.

Amir Abdur Rahman's reign was also a period of constant war and extensive violence. In contrast to the wars led by the previous Durrani rulers, which were largely directed towards the Indian sub-continent, his wars were entirely directed inwards, and aimed to conquer territories and subjugate the people that constituted the core of the Durrani Empire and of modern Afghanistan. As Afghanistan was squeezed as a buffer state between Russia to the North and the British to the South, the Amir shifted the direction of his wars inwards by focusing his energy on mass internal violence. (Rubin, 2002, pp. 48–52; Giustozzi, 2008, pp. 4–5).

The twenty-one-year reign of Amir Abdur Rahman Khan witnessed some forty separate rebellions (roughly two per year) four of which he himself described as civil wars (Khan, 1900, p. 249). Kakar (1979, p. xxi–xxiv), divides his wars into three broad categories: first, dynastic wars that resulted from rivalries between the Amir and other contenders for power from the Muhammadzai clan; second, rebellions against the imposition of tax by the government; and third wars and rebellions that were provoked by extension of government authority in previously independent areas.

There were two dynastic wars between Amir Abdur Rahman Khan and two of his several cousins. The first was against Ayub Khan, a son of Amir Sher Ali Khan, over control of Qandahar in 1881. Ayub Khan was also a leader of the Afghan forces in the second Anglo-Afghan War and had led Afghan forces in their victory against the British and Indian troops in the famous Battle of Maiwand in July 1880 in Qandahar. As a result, Ayub Khan had greater nationalist credentials as leader of resistance against British occupation. In the summer of 1881, he marched on Qandahar from Herat and took control of the city. He was quickly defeated after fresh troops were deployed from Kabul, and he was forced to flee to Iran and later India. The second major dynastic war was in 1888, led by Ishaq Khan, another cousin of the Amir, who played an important role in establishing his authority and served as governor of Afghan Turkistan at that time. Ishaq Khan was also defeated in the Battle of Tashkurghan, now in the province of Balkh (Lee, 1996, pp. 525–30).

The main focus of this chapter is on the second and third categories of these wars. In important respects, the two categories closely overlap because an extension of government control across the country also entailed the imposition of new taxes and greater intervention of officials in local affairs. Thus both are wars and rebellions that result from the manner in which political power was centralised and the way in which the state was perceived at local levels. Some of the most of important of these wars include the Taraki Ghilzai Pashtun rebellion (1881–1882); the Shinwari Pashtun rebellion (1882–1892); the Mangal and Zurmat Pashtun rebellion (1883–1884); the Ghilzai Pashtun rebellion (1886–1888); the Hazara War (1891–1893); and the Kafiristan War (1895–1896). A quick look at this list shows that the rebellions against state-building often occurred within particular ethnic and tribal frameworks.

Significantly, Amir Abdur Rahman himself attempted to explain the reasons and motivations of the war and violence he organised against his own people. In his own biography, he describes the wars as being between civilised and benevolent state and king, on the one hand, and unruly, ignorant and uncivilised tribes and communities, on the other. He claims that in the past:

> … every priest, mullah, and chief of every tribe and village considered himself an independent king, and for about 200 years past the freedom and independence of many of these priests were never broken by their sovereigns. The Mirs of Turkestan, the Mirs of Hazara, the chiefs of Ghilzai were all stronger than their Amirs, and, so long as they were the rulers, the King could not do justice in the country. (Khan, 1900, p. 217)

The contrast between the civilised and benevolent state and ignorant and unruly people and their chiefs lies at the core of his justifications for the wars:

> There are many prejudiced and ignorant people who blame me for these civil wars, and think that my treatment of the people was very harsh. But even in the most civilised countries of the present day examples are not

wanting to show that they had at the commencement of their history to fight against their own people, who did not at first understand the conditions of civilisation. (p. 219)

The Amir often depicted his foes as uncivilised, ignorant bandits to justify his wars against them. The Amir's justification for these wars are reflected in many of the writings of Afghan historians on this period. For example, Kakar (1971), who like most Afghan historians, credits Abdur Rahman for building a centralised state, states that the Hazaras 'constituted a potential sources of disloyalty to the state, because of their readiness to join foreigners against Afghanistan' (p. 174).

In the case of Hazaras, the Amir stated 'the Hazaras had raided and plundered the neighbouring subjects (of the Afghan confederacy) for about three hundred years past, and none of the kings had the power to make them absolutely peaceful' (Khan, 1900, p. 249). He made a similar accusation against the Shinwari Pashtun tribe in eastern Afghanistan. After defeating the Shinwaris in 1883, the Amir admits to having 'ordered that the heads of all those who were killed in battle should be piled up in the shape of two big towers—one at Jellalabad, and other at the residential place of Shahmad, who had encouraged them in their misbehaviour; so that people, when looking at those towers built with the heads of the rebels, should know that this is the reward for those who kill traveller' (Khan, 1900, p. 238). He then cites a Pashtu poem to describe what he thinks is the character of the tribe.

> You may try gently for hundreds of years to make friends
> But it is impossible to make scorpions, snakes, and Shinwari, friends (p. 238)

To understand the manner in which these rebellions arose and the ability of the Amir to suppress them, we need to explore Abdur Rahman Khan's own state-building strategy and tactics and the role of the British in supporting him.

The role of British India

Amir Abdur Rahman Khan's success in building a centralised state cannot be explained without understanding the nineteenth-century strategic rivalries between Czarist Russia and British India that became known as the Great Game. During the nineteenth century, Czarist Russia steadily expanded its influence southward, subjugating and incorporating the small khanates and kingdoms of Central Asia one after the other. At the same time, during the first half of the century the British also reached the borders of Afghanistan from the Indian sub-continent. It occupied Sindh in 1842 and Punjab in 1849.

Afghanistan remained the only country in the region that was not directly incorporated into the holdings of either of these two vast European empires. After the failure of the first British invasion of Afghanistan in 1838–1842, the British strategy towards Afghanistan fluctuated between 'masterly inactivity' and 'forward policy' (Duthie, 1983). However, a new wave of Russian expansion in Central Asia in the 1860s and 1870s renewed British officials' fears about security of the Empire in India. The British fear of threats posed by Afghanistan towards India also underlined its views of Afghanistan as a fragmented entity lacking unity. In the words of Rawlinson (1875), the country was also seen as one 'lacking political cohesion', in which there was no 'natural or ethnic reasons by Herat and Kandahar' to be attached to Kabul (p. 355).

In November 1878, British and Indian troops invaded Afghanistan after Amir Sher Ali, the then ruler of Kabul, refused to accept a British mission dispatched by Lord Lytton, the British Viceroy in India. Sher Ali fled to the city of Mazar-e Sharif where he died a year later. However, in less than a year, the British occupation faced major resistance, with the most significant uprising erupting in September 1879. As the signs of failure of the military invasion became more apparent, high-level officials of British India intensified the search for a solution to what looked like a quagmire of directly controlling Afghanistan. Sir Lepel Griffin, who was serving as Chief Secretary of Punjab, was sent to Kabul to end the war. Griffin later described the situation he found in Kabul.

> The aspect of affairs was discouraging in the extreme. The country was in the wildest state of ferment. Our army had met with reverses, and in the month of December had been shut up in the fortified cantonment of Sherpur by General Muhammad Jan and a great array of Ghilzai and Kohistani tribesmen and influential chiefs. (1888, p. 247)

It was during this opportune time that Abdur Rahman Khan appeared in the northeast of Afghanistan from exile in Central Asia. He was a grandson of Amir Dost Muhammad Khan and the eldest son of Muhammad Afzal Khan. Afzal Khan was the governor of Balkh at the time of Dost Muhammad Khan's death in 1863. As the oldest son of Dost Muhammad Khan, Afzal Khan had challenged the claim of his younger brother Amir Sher Ali Khan to the throne and had fought against him for four years. In 1869, after the failure of his last insurrection against Sher Ali Khan, Abdur Rahman Khan had fled across the Oxus, first to Bukhara and later to Tashkent. In Tashkent, he was granted asylum by the Russian General Kaufmann.

While Abdur Rahman was still in the northeast of Afghanistan, British officials in Kabul sent envoys to meet and evaluate him as the next ruler of Kabul. He was initially suspected for his ties with Russia but after some exchanges Griffin decided to win him over by 'offering at once more than Russia was in a position to give', hoping that he would ally 'with that power, which could place and maintain him in the most favourable position' (1888, p. 249). On 22 July 1880, while Abdur Rahman Khan was still in Shamali, north of Kabul, British officials found it imperative to announce publicly in Kabul that 'the Viceroy and the Government of the Queen-Empress had been pleased to recognise Sirdar Abdur Rahman Khan as the Amir of Kabul' (1888, p. 250). Five days later, on 27 July, the same day British forces were defeated in the famous battle in Maiwand, Sir Lepel Griffin arrived in Aq Seraj to conduct a three-day negotiation with Abdur Rahman Khan. In August, Abdur Rahman Khan was proclaimed as the Amir in Kabul. In April 1881, the British also handed over Qandahar to him.

In the words of Griffin, after he took Kabul in 1880, Abdur Rahman was 'alone among his enemies' and his main hope was that by his 'selection by England' he 'had acquired great reputation in the world and the eyes of other princes' (Griffin, 1888, p. 257). To consolidate his rule, he insisted that he needed British support in the forms of 'arms, ammunition and treasure' to be able to 'organize a stable administration of a character which would be worthy of the British Government and the opinion they had formed of him' (1888, p. 257).

In return for his cooperation for a dignified withdrawal of British forces, Abdur Rahman received a grant of two million rupees, of which 100,000 were paid for his immediate expenses as he arrived in Kabul, 500,000 after the British troops left Kabul and remainder after they arrived in Jalalabad and Peshawar. In addition, he was also given a large number of field and siege guns, crucial weapons as he began to build up his military arsenal. For his part, the Amir ensured the unmolested retreat of British troops from Kabul and Qandahar and kept key leaders of the anti-British uprising such as Mullah Mushki Alam and General Muhammad Jan under his control in the city (Griffin, 1888).

The smooth withdrawal of British forces was part of a long-term arrangement between the Amir and British India. In return for the flow of British aid, in the words of Leitner, throughout his reign, the Amir's friendship with England, 'never wavered for a moment' (1894, p. 285). The Amir ceded his foreign affairs to British India, which was worried about the fall of Afghanistan under Russian influence. In the early 1890s, he also accepted the borders which were drawn by British and Russian officials, often without consulting him. This included the 2640 km border, now separating Afghanistan and Pakistan, which is referred to by Afghan officials as the Durand Line, after Mortimer Durand, the Foreign Secretary of British India at the time. The line cuts through the Pashtun areas of the North West Frontier, tribal areas and Baluchistan, politically dividing both Pashtuns and Baluch on two sides of the porous border with Pakistan today.

In return for the concessions he made to British India, Amir Abdur Rahman gained significant British financial and military subsidies, and more importantly a free hand to administer the country as he pleased. From 1882, he began to receive an annual subsidy of 1.2 million Indian rupees which was increased to 1.8 million after the formal agreement on the Durand Line in 1893 and to 1.85 million after he accepted the inclusion of the Wakhan Corridor into the territory of Afghanistan. This money was only a small fraction of British aid, which was mostly delivered in the forms of weapons and military hardware (Rubin, 2002, p. 49). In a letter to the Amir in 1889, the Viceroy of India, Lord Lansdowne, reminded him of the following assistance he had received from the Indian Government:

> It has been closely shown to the world that the Government of India was on your side; those who rebelled or intrigued against you have been discouraged; and you have received, in money and military stores, assistance to the following extent: 144 lakhs [one lakh = 100,000 rupees]; 74 guns with ammunition in proportion; 25,000 breach-loading and 11,500

muzzle-loading rifles, with several million rounds of cartridges. You are receiving from my Government a lakh of rupees every month. (Ghani, 1982, p. 391)

For the British, regardless of how he treated his people, the Amir proved to be a reliable ally. In the words of Griffin:

He has thoroughly understood the people he has to govern. He has not given Afghanistan a free press or national congresses but has ruled his people, as he assured me they could be governed, with the stick. In this direction he has certainly shown extraordinary energy and where Amir Sher Ali Khan beat his people with whips, Abdur Rahman has scourged them with scorpions. (1888, p. 255)

Violence and Islam in Amir Abdur Rahman Khan's state-building strategy

Abdur Rahman Khan transformed the Afghan state in other significant ways. He used the annual British subsidies to build the coercive capacity of the state and employed Islam to redefine the concept and nature of state authority. Where the coercive measures and religious legitimation did not work, he extensively manipulated ethnic, religious and tribal divisions to mobilise people against his foes and one another.

To begin with, Abdur Rahman Khan developed a complex religious doctrine to legitimate his claim to political power. The core of the doctrine was the view that as ruler of Afghanistan he derived the right to rule from the will of God and the people as his subjects had an obligation to obey him. He claimed that 'God had made him the shepherd and supporter of his subjects' and 'that kings of religion were the vicars of the prophet, shadow of God, and the shield against unbelief (kufr) and rebellion' (Kakar, 1979, p. 8). The people as subjects had many obligations, the most important of which was participation in *jehad* or holy wars. According to a book written by *ulema* (religious scholars) under government supervision in 1889, 'The Beneficent God has made Jehad so firm and strong as an obligation of all believers that he who denies it becomes an infidel' (Abu Bakr, Dihlavi, & Azim Khan, 1889, pp. 6–7).

The Amir took important measures to subordinate the religious establishment to the authority of the state. He limited the economic privileges of the clerics and brought the *waqf*, religious endowments, under government control. Most importantly, he forced the clerics to align themselves with his policies of centralising power by endorsing and preaching the particular interpretation of religion that was chosen by the Amir (Ghani, 1978).

By elevating religion to the role of the foundation of state authority Abdur Rahman Khan sought to place himself above all tribal, ethnic and dynastic divisions. The central aspect of the new conception of the state was that, by contrast to the Sadozai rulers who claimed a predominantly worldly authority as Shahs, the Amir claimed to have divine rights over the people he ruled. In promoting a particular form of Islam as the religious foundation of the state, Abdur Rahman completed a process that had begun in 1834 when, his grandfather, Amir Dost Muhammad Khan, assumed the title of Amir-ul-Momenin (Commander of the Faithful) in his declaration of jehad against the Sikhs of Punjab. However, he took the divine conception of the state and the religiously-sanctioned wars to deeper levels, but only to employ them in his extensive military campaigns inside Afghanistan. With the internalisation of jehad, Amir Abdur Rahman effectively internalised the wars of conquests and the economy of plunder that were so important to the stability of the Durrani Empire.

The religious legitimation of the Amir's authority was backed by the coercive power of the state, which he steadily increased with British subsidies. Whereas the Sadozai rulers greatly relied on tribal cavalry, Amir Abdur Rahman Khan spent much of his resources on building a regularly paid army. Three years after he took the throne, he had an army of 43,000 which in the last years of his rule reached about 100,000. In addition to the regular troops, he also maintained around 70,000 tribal levies (Kakar, 1979, pp. 98–9). The regular and irregular forces also consumed much of the state expenditure. In 1885 when the army had not yet reached its final strength, the pay of his forces amounted to 7,262,670 rupees, 58.6 per cent of the total state expenditure in that year. As the size of the army increased in subsequent years, the total cost of the army as proportion of the state expenditure is likely to have increased further (Ghani, 1982, pp. 392–3).

The army was backed up by a massive and brutal spy system that was modelled on the Czarist Russian intelligence system to which the Amir was exposed during his long period of exile in Tashkent (Martin, 1907, p. 151). The espionage network included thousands of men and women who reported to him directly from all over the country. It included both known and clandestine operatives, who enjoyed great power and were the only group of people that were immune from the arbitrary use of violence. The information sent by the agents was seen by the Amir personally as he did not trust other officials of his courts to access it. In a footnote to the Amir's autobiography, Mahomed Khan notes that Abdur Rahman Khan's espionage system was one of the most pervasive in the world at that time:

> There is no country in the world, perhaps not even in Russia, where there are so many spies and such a perfect Detective Department as in Afghanistan. Every house is believed to have a spy; a wife is afraid of her husband being set as a spy upon her, and the husband is afraid of his wife. There are not wanting many instances where children report against their parents, as did the son of Sirdar Dalu against his own father; the wife of Mistri Kutb betrayed her own husband. In fact, there are hundreds of cases of this kind every year in which sons, relatives, and dearest friends betray suspected persons, who, being proved guilty, are punished, and the spies are rewarded by the Amir. This is the cause of a general terror; every one fears everybody else. (Khan, 1900, p. 259)

As might be expected, the creation of such an extensive spy system and the condition of 'general terror' that resulted from it also created a pervasive sense of distrust and suspicion at all levels throughout the country. In the words of Ghubar the state established by the Amir was 'founded on the rocks of threat, fear, spying, imprisonment and execution' (1997, p. 652). Tens of thousands of people were arbitrarily arrested and thrown into a series of official and private jails. The number of people held in prisons points to the impact of the espionage network. In June 1882, there were 1,500 prisoners in Kabul but the number quickly rose to 10,000 in 1885, 14,000 in 1890 and to 20,000 in 1896. In 1901, the year the Amir died, the prisons of Kabul alone contained some 12,000 men and 8,000 women. To accommodate the growing number of prisoners, the Amir established a number of new prisons and expanded the existing ones. In 1890, there were sixty prisons in Kabul alone and a few years later the infamous Dehmazang jail, accommodating 9,000 prisoners was ordered to be built (Kakar, 1979, pp. 38–9).

The most notorious of these prisons were called *siachah* or black well because they were built underground and had no light. One of the worst and most dreaded of these was in Bala Hisar of Kabul which was an 'old well … excavated through rock, with the bottom part widened out to some fifteen or twenty feet in diameter, … where … men are imprisoned for life … and live and die there, the bodies of the dead being left where they lie together with the living' (Martin, 1907, p. 149; Ghubar, 1997, pp. 650–7). The Amir also proved to be highly proactive in disposing of the prisoners through executions and poisoning. According to Martin (1907), who worked as Abdur Rahman's chief engineer for several years, the Amir had admitted to having personally ordered the execution of 100,000 people. He was also quite innovative in using diverse methods for torturing his prisoners. Some of the methods of his torture and execution included being hung by the hair, skinned alive, cut into pieces, starved to death in cages, thrown into soap boilers and blown from guns (pp. 142–157).

Abdur Rahman Khan and the Hazaras the during the 1880s

The role of British aid, coercion and a particular form of Islamic legitimation in Abdur Rahman Khan's centralising policies also help to explain the intensity and frequency of violence and rebellion during his reign. However, the military might of the state was not enough to win these wars. The Amir also invested heavily in a divide and rule strategy. He manipulated divisions between tribes and ethnic groups to mobilise sections of the populations against others. During the 1880s, the process of expansion of state control resulted into several military confrontations with Pashtun tribes in the south and east of the country. These Pashtun tribes were subdued one after another in military campaigns that relied on ruthless use of force and manipulation of local tribal and personal rivalries. Having successfully crushed tribal and personal foes among the Pashtuns, the Amir focused his attention on the other ethnic groups, launching a series of campaigns against the Tajiks, Hazaras, Uzbeks, Turkomans and other groups. In the words of Dupree, the expansion and consolidation of the Afghan state authority over the myriad ethnic groups that constituted Afghanistan took the form of 'internal imperialism' (1980, p. xix).

However, a closer look at the manner in which these rebellions arose may show that these revolts were not the product of machinations of unruly and uncivilised tribal and ethnic groups who were bent on opposing the extension of central authority. To the contrary, many of the wars were initiated by the state, and most tribes submitted to the authority of the state and rebelled only after they were subjected to oppression by state agents.

The case of Hazara rebellions clearly challenges the narrative of rebellion of uncivilised people against the civilised state and benevolent king. As the previous chapter showed, by the time of Amir Abdur Rahman Khan, the Hazaras had lost many of their agriculturally-fertile territories between Kabul and Helmand to the Pashtuns and their influence was largely contained to the Hazarajat region. Nonetheless, numerically and geographically, the Hazaras still constituted a formidable force. As Table 2.1 demonstrates, during the 1880s the population of Shi'a Hazaras was estimated to include 132,000 families, who occupied the extensive mountainous region between Kabul to the east, Qalat and Ghazni to the south and southeast, Herat to the west and Afghan Turkestan to the north.

Hazarajat is a mountainous region, consisting of high mountains and deep valleys, mostly with harsh and long winters. Despite its severe climate and environment, the region had particular significance as it connected the transit routes between Kabul and the north, south and west of the country. The roads between Kabul and Afghan Turkestan, north of Hindukush, and Herat in the west went through Hazarajat. Historically, the mountains and harsh climate of the region has had profound implications for the ability of the Hazaras to act collectively. The deep and inaccessible valleys of the area reinforced divisions among feuding Hazara chiefs and tribes who were for the most part unconcerned with the developments outside the region (Canfield, 2004). Isolated from and marginal to the politics of the key urban centres of Herat, Qandahar and Kabul, the Hazara leaders did all they could to minimise external interference in their local affairs.

During his first years on the throne of Kabul, the influence of Amir was limited to the Hazaras closer to the capital and provincial centre of Ghazni but thinned in more remote Hazara territories. As the revenues paid by the Hazara tribes in Table 2.2 show, government revenues from the Hazaras of Behsud and Ghazni who were within the immediate reach of the Amir in Kabul and the governor of Ghazni respectively were much higher in comparison to the more distant areas of Day Zangi and Day Kundi. For example, annually 15,000 Hazara families of Behsud paid 200,000 Kabuli rupees while 11,000 Hazaras of Day Kundi paid 120,000 rupees for the same period.

Table 2.1: The Hazaras 1885–86

Major Tribes	Estimated Population by families in round numbers	Location	Administration
Behsud	15,000	Northeast part of Hazarajat	A district of Kabul province with its own *hakim* (governor)
Day Zangi	13,000	North and northwest of Hazarajat	Mostly under their own chiefs who are subordinate to the governor of Bamyan
Day Kundi	11,000	Western part of Hazarajat	Mostly under the control of their own chiefs who were subordinate to the governor of Bamyan. Some paid revenues to Qandahar
Ghazni Hazaras	22,000	Around Ghazni	Under their own chiefs who were subordinated to governor of Ghazni
Shaikh Ali Hazaras	13,000	Dara Shaikh Ali and Dara Turkoman; Jalmish and Surkhab; Khinjan and Ghori,	Under the Hakim of Shaikh Ali district and governors of Afghan Turkistan

Hazaras of Bamyan	5,500	Bamyan, Duoab and Rui.	Under Bamyan governor
Hazaras of Balkhab and other districts in Afghan Turkistan	8,000	In various districts between Yakawlang and Mazar-e Sharif	Under governors of their respective districts
Independent Hazaras	44,500	Southwest of Hazarajat in and around Uruzgan	Mostly independent of the government with only some paying revenues to Qandahar.
Total	132,000		

Source: Maitland (1891, p. 281).

Table 2.2: Revenues from Selected Major Hazara Tribes in 1880s

Hazara tribes	Annual Tax Paid to the government in Kabuli Rupees
Behsud	200,000
Day Zangi	40,000
Day Kundi	120,000
Ghazni Hazaras	250,000
Total	502,000

Source: Maitland (1891, p. 291).

During the 1880s, before the Amir had built the coercive apparatus of the status, his strategy towards the Hazaras consisted of manipulating rivalries among the Hazara mirs and begs and limited deployments of military force when necessary. According to Temirkhanov (1993, pp. 175–6), many Hazara mirs supported the Amir after he took the throne in Kabul and while he was facing the challenges of dynastic rivals like Sardaar Ayub Khan in Qandahar. The Amir used the state apparatus to dispense patronage among local Hazara rivals, by promoting one against the others. In 1881, the Amir invited all Hazara begs and mirs to Kabul where he greeted them with respect, and officially confirmed their positions in their areas. During this period, the Amir stressed the Islamic bonds that he believed unified the Shi'a and Sunni populations of the country.

However, not all Hazaras had the same attitude towards the Amir. In 1881, the Hazaras of Jaghuri and Jaghatu, who were closely linked to the family of Sher Ali Khan, opposed the army of Amir Abdur Rahman as it marched against Ayub Khan in Qandahar. In the battle that apparently took place in Ghazni along the Kabul-Qandahar route, the Hazaras were defeated and two sons of Sardaar Sher Ali Khan Hazara, perhaps the closest Hazara ally of Amir Sher Ali Khan, were killed. By 1884, the Amir appointed a governor over the Jaghuri Hazaras, thus bringing them under his tight control. At the height of the Ghilzai uprising in 1888, the Jaghuri Hazaras rose again, killing their governor (Kakar, 1971, pp. 161–2).

The only major Hazara tribe that was seriously targeted by the Amir, in this phase, was the Hazaras of Shaikh Ali. There were estimated to be around 3,090 families living on both sides of the southwest end of the Hindukush, in an area currently at the intersection of the Parwan, Bamyan and Baghlan provinces. As with other rebels groups, the Amir accused them of raiding and plundering the caravans on the road between Kabul and Afghan Turkestan that ran through their territories. In 1881 and 1882, the Amir sent three military expeditions to subdue them. With the failure of the military campaigns, the Amir turned to his masterful divide and rule tactics. The Shaikh Ali Hazaras consisted of both Sunni and Shi'a (Ismaili as well as Twelver Shi'a) Muslims. To bring them under his control, the Amir began to exploit the sectarian divisions, promoting and empowering the Sunni clans against their Shi'a rivals. In 1888 at the time of Ishaq Khan's rebellion in the north, the rivalry between the Sunni and Shi'a Hazaras had become a fully-fledged sectarian war. Temirkhanov suggests that the Shi'a Hazaras supported Ishaq Khan while the Sunni clans stood on the side of the government. To punish those who supported Ishaq Khan, the Amir demanded that they disarm and pay 50,000 rupees and large number of cattle in fines. After they refused, the Amir deployed 3,000 regular and 3,000 irregular forces to force the rebellious tribes into submission. After the Shi'a Shaikh Ali Hazaras were defeated, the Amir ordered them to be collectively removed from their lands and dispersed throughout Afghanistan (Temirkhanov, 1993, pp. 182–7; Kakar, 1971, pp. 154, 163).

During the 1880s, the Amir also extensively relied on the Hazaras' support to fight and subjugate his opponents and other tribal communities in other parts of the country. In 1881, the Hazaras of Day Zangi and Day Kundi played a key role in bringing Herat under the control of the Amir. They offered food stuffs and a contingent of 1,000 warriors to Abdul Qudus Khan who used the Western region of Hazara territories to attack Ayub Khan's forces in Herat (Maitland, 1891, p. 36). Two years later, the Amir mobilised the Hazaras to crush the Andar tribes of Pashtuns in Ghazni, and in 1887 he used hundreds of warriors from Day Zangi and Day Kundi to subjugate Sardaar Muhammad Ishaq Khan and his supporters in the Turkestan region in the north. A proclamation sent by the Amir to the *mirs* of the regions reads:

.... It is necessary that you people equip yourselves and plunder his [M. Ishaq Khan's] regions from end to end. You should attack and plunder and slaughter. Don't waste your time because dyeing your beards with henna after the holiday is over is foolish. (Kateb, 1913, p. 405)

The Amir's policy of manipulation of local rivalries and gradual expansion of state authority over Hazaras achieved important successes. By 1886, all Hazaras paid taxes on their land and cattle and even marriage fees. In the following years, the existing taxes were increased and new forms of taxes were introduced. The Hazara tribes closer to Kabul such as the Hazaras of Behsud, Day Mirdad and Shaikh Ali paid between one-quarter and one-tenth of the produce of their land and the more distant tribes such as Day Zangi and Day Kundi paid a fixed amount either on the land or per family (Kakar, 1971, p. 163). Importantly, during the 1880s, the Amir also renovated and partly built a 4-metre wide road that connected Kabul to Herat through the Hazara region. The new road significantly increased the mobility and access of the Afghan government forces to Hazarajat and the regions around it (Maitland, 1891, pp. 282, 285).

The Yaaghi Hazaras

From among the major Hazara regions and tribal groups, the Hazaras of southwest Hazarajat had become known as *Yaaghi* or rebels and the territories they inhabited as *Yaaghistan*, or land of rebels. *Yaaghistan* was an extensive region that included forty-five separate Hazara tribes

Table 2.3: Independent Hazaras of the Pas-i-Koh, or Hazara Yaaghistan

Tribes	Mirs or Chiefs	Location	Number of Families	Remarks
Jirghai Usi Muhammad	Tila Bahadur	Jirghai Pas-i-Koh at the head of Ujaristan	1,000	These are Besuds
Dayah…	Pazai Bahadur	D'ayah Pas-i-Koh, below Jirghai Usu Muhammad.	2,000	
Faol'adi.	No mir	Ujaristan (Ujaristan proper: the lower half of the valley)	5,000	Over 2,000 more in M'alistan, and are ra'iyats (subjects)
Zaoli…	Muhammad Husen Kha'n	Julgai (valley) Zaoli (Ujaristan country)	4,500	Said to be J'aghuris
Sulta'n Ahmad	Kalb-i-Ali Sulta'n	Sar-i-Julaga'I Raoti (Ujaristan country)	3,000	
Urusgan …	Not one chief	Valley and district of Urusga'n, southeast of Ujaristan'n	10,000	Much divided, and have many feuds among themselves
Kalandar …	?	Kalandari-i-Yaghi: the country between Urusga'n and Ja'ghuris (Upper Urghand'ab?)	6,000	Maybe Ja'ghuris, but it is more likely the Ja'ghuri Kalandars are a branch of these
Koli'an …	?	Kolia'n, Sumuk, and Pa'lun. These are said to be Pthree valleys west of Ujarista'n	4,000	This tribe is not mentioned by any other authority

Dai Chopa'n, or Khatai, or Ba'bali.	?	From the Arghanda'b valley along the northern border of the Kandaha'r province (Tirin and Dehra'wat)	5,000	
Da'I Zangi Pitao, or the Southern Dai Zangis	Husen Ali Kha'n and Alizai Kha'n.	On the left bank of the Helmand above the valley of Ghizao, near the ruins of the city of Kurgha'n, which is also on the Helmand.	4,000	These Dai Zangis are said to be of the Sehpai division
Total			44,500	

Source: Maitland (1891, p. 317).

(Kateb, 1913, p. 603). The current province of Uruzgan was its centre and included extensive territories that are currently parts of the Qandahar, Helmand, Zabul and Ghazni provinces. Riyazi Herawi (1907, p. 248) provides a detailed breakdown of some of the tribes and areas in *Yaaghistan*: Ajaristan 6,000 households, Malistan 6,000, Uruzgan 5,000, Mianeshin 1,000, Sultan Ahmed and Palan tribes 1,000, Zawuli 1,500 and the inhabitants of Shira and Banbatan 3,000–4,000 households.

Muhammad Hussain Qizilbash, who was appointed governor of Behsud by Abdur Rahman Khan and was tasked to bring *Yaaghistan* under control, estimated that the total size of *Yaaghi* Hazaras to be around 50,000 families (Maitland, 1891, pp. 345–6). As Table II.3 shows, Maitland suggests the independent Hazaras consisted of 44,500 families.

It is not clear to what extent these Hazara tribes also considered themselves as *yaaghi* or their region as *Yaaghistan*, but fact that the region came to be regarded as *yaaghistan* represented a key transformation that Afghanistan was experiencing under the Amir. While the Amir justified his wars in the name of unification and the protection of the country against the threats posed by the infidel powers (Russia and Britain), his own tactics and strategies became the main driver of violence and rebellion. As shown below, the Yaaghi Hazaras did not pose a threat to the integrity of the Afghan state. On the contrary, they submitted to the authority of the state and even agreed to pay increased taxes.

The Hazara War

Towards the end of the 1880s, Abdur Rahman's gradual consolidation of his authority through the manipulation of local khans had reached its limit. At this point, the Amir was also feeling strong enough to do away with the trouble of repeated Hazara rebellions. He had gained total control of the Pashtun areas in the south, east, and Turkestan in the north. In 1887, Amir Abdur Rahman instructed governors of the regions surrounding Hazarajat to prepare a comprehensive report on the region. The governors deployed a team of informants that included Shi'a Sayeds, Qizilibash and Pashtuns with long-standing trading relations with the Hazaras. Their mission was to gather complete information on the geography, social and political dynamics and the military capabilities of the Hazara tribes. The team spent months travelling all over Hazarajat, collecting information and drawing a detailed map. The map and other information they collected were presented to the Amir in the northern city of Mazar-e Sharif, and he used them to draw a plan for a full military campaign in the region. As a reward, the Amir also gave each member of the team a monthly cash stipend from the state treasury (Kateb, 1913, pp. 462–7, 481).

In 1890, the Amir appointed Sardaar Abdul Qudus Khan as governor of Bamyan, with far-reaching powers and a large number of troops. Qudus Khan was one of the Amir's most trusted military officers who led his major wars. As a result, his appointment indicated the firm determination of the Amir to bring the Hazaras under his direct control. While the preparations for the war were underway, the Amir was communicating with the Hazaras of *Yaaghistan* through letters and delegations. One delegation headed by Sardaar Muhammad Azim Beg, a chief of the Day Zangi Hazaras, who was one of Amir's personal attendants (*pishkhedmat*), convinced the Hazaras of *Yaaghistan* to submit to the Amir's authority and accept a governor appointed from Kabul. Significantly, the *Yaaghistan* Hazaras seem to have accepted the overall authority of Kabul but requested some autonomy for their local affairs and payment of tax to be postponed to the following year (Kakar, 1971, pp. 163–4).

Despite the readiness of the Hazaras of Uruzgan to accept the authority of Kabul, in spring of 1891, 10,000 government troops led by Sardaar Abdul Qudus Khan were ordered to march towards Uruzgan. As the forces advanced into the region, they faced no major resistance. The *Yaaghistan* tribes, the most independent of the Hazaras, did not resist the troops and pledged their allegiance to Kabul. Subsequently, an order was issued by the Amir to disarm the local Hazaras, and bring their leaders to Kabul where he placed them under detention. In Uruzgan, the disarmament process began with relentless abuses, extortion and the dispossession and enslavement of the local Hazaras. The account provided by Kateb shows that government military units were given a free rein in the areas where they were stationed. The looting and plundering went so far that it threatened to undermine the discipline and coherence of the regular troops. Military units fragmented into smaller groups, looting local homes, enslaving men and women and destroying the farms (Kateb, 1913, pp. 611–17, 632–3, 656–7). The most senior military leaders also participated in the loot and plunder campaign. Abdul Qudus Khan, the chief commander of all regular and irregular troops, took several daughters of Hazara *mirs* as servants and concubines. Similarly, other commanders took women and engaged in extensive looting and extortion (Temirkhanov, 1993, p. 196).

Popular uprising of 1892–1893

The consequences of the submission to the government proved to be so grave and humiliating that many Hazaras saw no alternative but to challenge the government troops militarily. The first rebellion broke out after three Pashtun soldiers, pretending to search for weapons, entered the house of a leader of Pahlawans, a Hazara tribe in the Uruzgan region. They raped his wife and tortured him to death after he resisted. In response, the tribe rose up and occupied the military garrison which stored most of the weapons collected from the Hazaras. This was to become the first of a series of rebellions that initially broke out in the *Yaaghistan* region but quickly spread to other Hazara areas (Kateb, 1913, pp. 656–8).

Over the next nearly two years, the Hazara uprising presented the most serious challenge to the authority of Amir Abdur Rahman Khan. According to Temirkhanov (1993, p. 181) and Mousavi (1998, p. 115), this phase of the Hazara uprisings and Amir's military campaigns occurred in two separate periods: April 1892–January 1893 and January 1893–August 1893.

During this period, the Hazara uprising was led by Sardaar Muhammad Azim Beg, the leader of Day Zangi Hazaras who had negotiated with the Uruzgan Hazaras to submit to the authority of Kabul a year earlier. In 1887, he was granted the title of *sardaar* with an annual stipend of 1,660 rupees. Another prominent leader was Qazi Muhammad Askar, the leader of Foladi Hazaras. During 1892, Azim Beg and Qazi Askar attempted to initiate a general mobilisation. In a meeting with other Hazara leaders, they declared a full war, with the aim of overthrowing the monarchy in Kabul (Temirkhanov, 1993, pp. 200–1). This radically changed the nature and strategies of the war on both sides. Both sides mobilised tens of thousands of fighters in a war that perhaps is the first major example of ethnic mobilisation on a high scale in the contemporary history of the country.

The military campaign launched by the Amir in April 1892 was the biggest and most intensive of all wars of his reign. It entailed the most extensive mobilisation of the state and non-state resources, uniting Sunni tribes from all over the country against a Shi'a ethnic group. After the news of the 1891 rebellions in Uruzgan reached Kabul, the Amir sent orders to the Pashtun tribes and leaders of other ethnic groups across the country to mobilise new forces. British writers who reported from Qandahar to British officials in India covered some of the contents of these proclamations.[1] Some 200 notifications were sent to the mullahs and preachers authorised to lead Friday prayers in Qandahar region alone. They claimed that books found in a Shi'a house contained abusive contents regarding companions of the prophet Muhammad and his successors, and that this according to the Sunni clerics amounted to infidelity. The reading out of the notifications for those attending the mosques was made an essential part of the Friday prayer speeches. The notification declared that:

> The fact of their observing such a faith (Shiite) is due to their ignorance of the true religion… but if they persist in their false faith, they should all be put to death, and their property confiscated in accordance with the divine doctrine and the precepts of the Prophet… those Sunnis who will not act willingly in this matter will also be counted infidels. (Taki Khan, 1892).

To encourage popular enthusiasm for the war in Qandahar, on one occasion the Amir sent some 350 families of Shaikh Ali Hazaras from Kabul to be distributed as gifts for the main Durrani tribes in the region. He had instructed 200 families to be given to the Barakzais, and fifty families to each of the Popalzay, Alkozay and Nurzay tribes. These slave gifts were accompanied by massive propaganda campaigns that promised the land and the heads of Hazaras for those participating in the war (Taki Khan, 1891).

Another order was sent to Marshal Ghulam Haydar Khan, who was stationed in the Afghan Turkestan region in the north, instructing him to march towards Uruzgan with two regular infantry regiments, six pieces of artillery and one regular cavalry regiment. These proclamations that were sent throughout the country declared the Hazaras to be *kaafir* or infidels and fighting and eliminating them as a jehad or holy war. According to Kateb (1913) the Amir declared:

> …in order to extirpate these irreligious people so that not a trace of them remains in those places and throughout the mountains and their properties be distributed among the Ghilzai and Durrani tribes, the royal court has approved as policy that a triumphant army made up of regular and tribal forces from every part of the kingdom of the God given government should descend upon the soil of the rebel tribes of the Hazarahjat so that not a soul of those wayward tribes be safe nor escape and that the boys and girls be taken captive (and made slaves) by every member of the tribes of the mujahidin of Afghanistan ….In holy war, repelling and killing infidel evildoers conform to the Pure Noble Law and it is incumbent upon every individual Muslim to make it his own duty to fight them. The quotas for conscription are as follows: Kandaharis responsible for providing 10,000 men, Pusht-i Rud and Farah are responsible for 10,000, Herat for 10,000, Balkh for 10,000, Qataghan for 3,000, Badakhshan for 2,000 horsemen, Kahmard and Siqan for 2,000, the capital and its dependencies of course is responsible for 10,000 and Maymanah for 3,000. (Kateb, 1913, pp. 693–5)

The mobilisation campaign, particularly its propaganda component, achieved a high degree of success. The call for jehad stirred extreme anti-Shi'a feelings which were further reinforced by promises of spoils of war in the forms of land and Hazara slaves. According to Kakar, the Amir mobilised fighters 'on a scale he had never been able to do before' (1971, p. 165). Significantly, Kakar also adds that:

> The Hazara war had all elements of a foreign war. It was for these reasons that for the first time all the Sunni population rallied to the Amir. It increased his power and prestige, and infused sense of unity among his subjects. (p. 175).

The propaganda campaign paid off. Some 100,000 people, including a tribal contingent of 30,000 to 40,000 warriors, were mobilised from all over the country. To make the irregular force more effective, their organisation was significantly improved and stipendiary mullahs were assigned to each unit to preach holy war (Kakar, 1971, p. 166). In the Amir's own words, there were deep hostilities between Pashtun tribes and Hazaras, which he exploited to succeed in his own war.

> Other Afghan chiefs had applied several times to raise a force of country people at their own expense to fight against the Hazaras, whom they

looked upon as enemies to their country and religion. I had not given them permission to do this heretofore, but now I gave a general order that everybody would be allowed to go and help in the punishment of the rebels. The armed forces and volunteers who offered their services, numbering between 30,000 and 40,000 fighting men, started for the country of the Hazaras from all directions, under their respective chiefs and heads. (Khan, 1900, p. 283)

The level of military mobilisation was so high that the general economy of the country was seriously disrupted. For example, because of the rising demand for food supplies for the military campaign in Hazarajat, grain prices rose dramatically. In Qandahar, to regulate the rising prices, the local authorities rationed out grain for the public and required a special permit for its sale. In Kabul, the rising prices came close to causing a general mutiny (Kakar, 1971, p. 167).

The degree of mobilisation was highest amongst the Pashtuns, in general, and the nomad tribes in particular. The nomads had long been vying for the conquest of the summer pasturelands of the mountainous region of Hazarajat. For example, the nomadic tribes of Ghiljai and Mohmand contributed 2,200 fighters, sending one fighter for every fifteen members of the tribes. They also offered 400 camels that were leased on a monthly basis for the transportation of food and other supplies for the regiments in the Hazarajat region (Kateb, 1913, pp. 580–1; Temirkhanov, 1993, p. 208).

Beginning in April 1892, the freshly mobilised forces marched towards Hazarajat, overwhelming the Hazara resistance and pushing the disorganised rebels further high into the mountains. A relentless army of tens of thousands spread throughout the Hazarajat region, killing the rebels and the submissive alike, capturing and enslaving Hazara men, women and children and destroying the houses and livelihoods. The Hazaras of Day Chupan and Chillah Kur, who were loyal to the Amir and whose leaders were serving at his court in Kabul during the war, became victims of the freshly mobilised forces (Kateb, 1913, pp. 678–9).

In the midst of the war, when reports of the fall of Hazara districts, one after another, were being reported to Kabul, the Amir sent an order to the commanders of the regular as well as tribal forces that legitimised the massive campaign of killing and plundering in the region:

...whatever should come into their hands as booty—whether men, women or children, or property and furnishings—they were to understand that one-fifth belongs to the government and should be sent to the throne, in accordance with the custom of the clear religion of the Hazrat, Lord of the Messengers (Prophet Muhammad). Four-fifths could be seized as their own property. (Kateb, 1913, p. 740)

By August 1892, the Amir's forces had gained the upper hand, taking control of key areas from the rebels. Over the next few months, government presence was established throughout the region. However, what happened to the Hazaras of *Yaaghistan* a year earlier was to repeat itself. The Amir issued an order for the destruction of Hazara forts and confiscation of their weapons. Sunni mullahs were assigned to enforce the Sunni interpretation of Islam and an intensive search began for the identification of individuals who had participated in the war (Temirkhanov, 1993, pp. 223–4). In practice, these decrees had the effect of officially licensing and further instigating a systematic process of indiscriminate killing, enslavement and complete dispossession of the Hazaras of their belongings. The troops often did much more than the proclamations called for. The occupation of each village was followed by a methodical destruction of water canals, houses, uprooting of trees and trampling of crops (Kateb, 1913, p. 739).

As a result of these abuses, in spring 1893 the Hazaras rose again. The final phase of the uprising began from Behsud and Day Zangi but quickly spread throughout Hazarajat. However, after subjugating the Hazaras of *Yaaghistan* and creating a generalised climate of terror across the region, the Amir's forces were quick to put down the final rebellion. While the region saw a series of clashes between the Hazaras and government forces from April to August 1893, the Hazaras had lost the morale and the material capability to withstand the government forces for long. In the final phase of the war, a significant number of Hazara leaders sought refuge in Legan, a long and historical cave in the south of what is today Waras district in Bamyan. Towards the end of summer of that year, after a prolonged siege, these Hazara leaders surrendered to Afghan forces. They were detained and sent as prisoners to Kabul. This marked the end of the rebellion by the Hazaras and the final and total victory of the Amir Abdur Rahman Khan (Takki Khan, 1893).

The aftermath of the conquest of Hazarajat

The strategies and tactics the Amir employed during the 1891–93 Hazara War clearly demonstrate that he was seeking to neutralise the Hazaras, politically, economically and socially as a distinctive ethnic group. In other words, the Amir Abdur Rahman's war in Hazarajat went much further than bringing the region under government control. In retrospect, one can argue that the mass killing, enslavement, destruction and displacement that occurred during the war can best be considered as the prime example of genocide in the history of modern Afghanistan. In its ferocity and extent, it is comparable only to genocides such as the Armenian Genocide of 1915 and the Rwandan genocide of 1994.

Raphael Lemkin, the scholar and activist who coined the term 'genocide' after the horrors of the Second World War, defined it as consisting of two key elements: destroying 'the national pattern of the oppressed' and imposing 'the national pattern of the oppressor' (Jones, 2006, p. 11). To assess the effects of the war in these two respects, it is helpful to make a distinction between what happened during and after the war.

Massacres and destructions in the course of the war

Much of what can be described as systematic destruction of the 'national pattern' of Hazaras resulted from the massacres, plunders and destruction that came with the victory of the Amir's army over the Hazaras. In the *Yaaghistan* region, the political, social and economic structures of the local Hazaras were totally destroyed. Many of the forty-five tribes were wiped out and entire valleys were deserted and emptied of their human inhabitants. In the words of Taki Khan, a British News Writer in Qandahar at that time, in October 1892, following the takeover of the region, 'the sole inhabitants of Uruzgan consisted of the army of occupation' (1892).

The extent of the destruction and killing in Hazarajat was also documented by the Amir's own officials. In Uruzgan, from the powerful Sultan Ahmad tribe, who were estimated by Maitland to constitute about 3,000 families, only sixty families survived. According to Samandar Khan and Fazl Ahmad Khan, Amir's newly appointed governor and tax assessor for the province:

All the people of Uruzgan had scattered into the surrounding hills and fled their homes. Their dwelling places are ruined and they have no place to settle and live. Some of the people of Darrah-i Shah Ali, the tribe (Taifah) of Qadam, and the people (qawm) of Bihruz and Bay Timur stayed in their homes while others fled. Of the people of Shirah, all have fled and not one has returned. Sayyid Hasan, one of the Sayyids of Qaq Tabah who was loyal to the government has set out to conciliate and provide guidance in order to get the people of Shirah to return to their homes. Seventy households from Zawuli have returned home but all the rest have fled to Day Zangi, Day Kundi, and Char Shanbah. Sixty households from Sultan Ahmad have come back while all the rest were killed. No one has fled. Of the people of Pashah-I and Shayr Dagh most have returned to their homes. All of the people of Bubash are still (hiding out) in the mountains and won't return because they're afraid. Similarly, 100 households from Darrah-i Pahlawan are up in the hills. The people who have come and sought refuge near the army are picking out (undigested) seeds of barley grains from the piles of camel dung like pigeons and at night make those their sustenance. No one has the means to plant and cultivate the land. (Kateb, 1913, p. 818)

Similarly, Brigadier Abdul Subhan, an Indian official at the Amir's court in Kabul, was sent to survey the land of Hajaristan and other areas around it. This is how he assessed the situation in the district:

The district of Hajaristan is quite extensive and flat.... At this time it is in complete ruin and gives the effect of a mirage. Prior to the advent of the government army it had more than two laks [hundred thousand] of willows and plane trees....and the forts of the district could not be seen because of the profusion of branches and leaves....with the invasion of the army all were cut down and other than the stumps no sign remains of these trees. The crops of its extensive fields are all destroyed or used as fodder for the (army's) animals. (Kateb, 1913, p. 756)

Other parts of the Hazara region, including those that supported the Amir during his 1891 campaign against the Hazaras of *Yaaghistan*, also became the target of the Amir and his forces. In addition to the demands of Kabul, the military commanders in the field also took their own initiative to extract from the local population as much as they could:

Meantime, General Mir Ata Khan on the fifteenth of Rabi al-Sani/ 6 November (1892) forcibly requisitioned 250 kharwaar of wheat and barley, forty sirs by Kabul weight as a fine from each of five hundred households who remained in Hazarah-i Dayah-i Hajaristan. He also ordered that every non farming household which still remained after others had fled and had survived destruction should pay a fine to the government of three rupees cash. He similarly penalized the Hazarahs of Jarghi, Hajaristan district, and Bahadur. He also forcibly requisitioned 600 kharwaar of wheat and barley from the people of Qalandar, Atah, and Maskah without compensation. He imposed damages of 80,000 rupees on the Fuladah, Zawuli, Sultan Ahmad, and Sih Pay tribes of (the part of) Day Zangi which belonged to Muhammad Azim Beg and Gizab for provisions for the army which the Hazarahs had plundered and settled with them that the people of Fuladah should pay 40,000, those from Zawuli and Sultan Ahmad, 20,000, and 20,000 from the people of Sih Pay, Talah, and Gizab. Despite the calamity and disaster which had befallen these peoples, in a short period of time this (amount of) cash and kind was brought in by ruthless collectors and used for the expenses of the victorious regiments. (Kateb, 1913, p. 795)

As a result of the destruction and extortion by the government forces, the local economy of Hazarajat collapsed. The decline in the Hazaras' economic activity was so severe that despite their heavy-handedness, the Amir's governors in Hazarajat could not raise the revenues expected from them in Kabul. In 1896, the Amir wrote to his governors in Hazarajat, inquiring why the amount of revenues had fallen. One of the governors wrote that 'by your highness's orders many Hazaras have been expelled from the country and many have left out of their own accord. A great portion of the country is lying waste' (Mir Khan, 1896).

As might be expected, the Hazara population was greatly reduced as a result of deaths caused by the war and the hunger and famine that followed it as well as slavery and forced migration. According to Temirkhanov, the Hazaras responded in three different ways: a group of 7,000–10,000 families submitted to the authority of the Amir under his terms; another group of 10,000–15,000 families left the country; all others continued to fight until they were defeated (Temirkhanov, 1993, pp. 236–7).

The Hazaras who fled the country generally went in three main directions: the Indian subcontinent in the south, Iran to the west and central Asia to the north. The Hazaras of Quetta city of Baluchistan and other places in Sindh provinces of Pakistan and of Khorasan province of Iran are descendants of those that fled the war and its subsequent destruction and devastation. Many others who fled to central

Asia and other parts of the Indian sub-continent are undocumented, like tens of thousands of others who were sold as slaves (Mousavi, 1998, pp. 139–53).

In addition to those who fled, a large number of Hazaras were sold as slaves in a burgeoning trade that was officially taxed and sanctioned by the Afghan state. The Hazaras who were turned into slaves were not all captured during the war in Hazarajat. Many were enslaved while travelling or fleeing from the war (Taki Khan, 1893). Others were sold into slavery, because many Hazara families could not support themselves during the famine that followed the war. Between July 1892, in the midst of the war in Hazarajat, and June 1894, barely a year after the Hazara uprising was totally subdued, about 9,000 Hazara men and women were sold in the bazaars of Kabul. At the same time, the government had raised 70,000 rupees as tax on the sale of Hazara slaves in Qandahar only. During the same period, 8,755 Hazara prisoners arrived in Kabul (Kakar, 1971, p. 176). Among those brought to Kabul were thousands of Hazara women and girls. The government put 8,000 of them to work in factories in the city (Mousavi, 1998, p. 132).

As might be expected, as a result of massacres and forced displacement during the war and the famine and migration that followed, the population and territorial size of Hazarajat shrank considerably (Kakar, 2006, p. 137). The Behsud tribe of the present Wardak province offers a good example. Because of its proximity to Kabul, in the eastern fringes of the Hazarajat, it was historically under greater control of Kabul. During the Hazara War, the Behsud people did not participate in the rebellion and as a result the area was outside the main theatre of war. In spite of this, 68 per cent of the Beshud people were either killed or forced to leave the country. A survey by the government's own local officials concluded that out of 20,000 households in the Beshud region, only 6,400 remained in their homes after the war; the other 13,600 families were killed or had fled, and their possessions were plundered (Kateb, 1913, p. 1131).

After the war

The destruction of the 'national pattern' of Hazaras and imposition of a new one in its stead continued long after the war ended. Some aspects of the Amir's policies towards the Hazaras are worth highlighting here. First, the Amir redistributed extensive Hazara territories as rewards to new Pashtun settlers. In Uruzgan alone, 12,000 Durrani and 4,000 Ghilzai families were ordered to settle in the formerly Hazara lands (Kakar, 1971, p. 174). A number of officials including Brigadier Subhan, Dost Muhammad Khan and Mawlawi Abdul Shakor were formally designated to administer the distribution of Hazara lands to the new Pashtun settlers. In their various roles, these individuals were issuing land titles and encouraging thousands of Pashtun families to occupy the conquered areas en masse. The government provided protection and economic incentives, such as tax exemption and credit to Pashtuns to settle into these and other fertile areas within the region. The Pashtun nomad tribes, probably the most enthusiastic participants of the war, received decrees for the ownership of Hazarajat's pastureland, which was initially declared state property before being converted to private land (Temirkhanov, 1993, p. 248).

Besides the depopulation of Hazaras from their more known territories such as Uruzgan, the Amir also completed the displacement of Hazaras from the Qandahar region. For example, in 1899, all Hazaras living in Qandahar, except the ill and unmarried, were collectively arrested and transferred under military escort to the direction of present day Behsud region of the Wardak province. With the forced flight of this group of Hazaras, the Amir completed the process of the displacement from Qandahar of its native Hazara communities that had begun with Nadir Shah Afshar and Ahmad Shah Durrani (Ali Shah, 1899).

Second, the central elements of the Amir's campaign to destroy the ethnic pattern of Hazaras was the annihilation or neutralisation of the Hazara elites. During the last days of the war, in August 1893, the Amir ordered his government and army to round up all Hazara elites. These included the *mir* and *beg*, the traditional Hazara landholding elites; and the mullah, *Karbalaye* and *Zawar* (titles given to those who had visited the Shi'a shrines of Imam Hussain and Imam Reza in the cities of Karbala and Mashhad respectively) and Sayeds, the main groups that constituted the religious elites of Hazarajat. Thousands of khans and religious figures were removed from the region with their families; their properties were confiscated and their forts were demolished (Temirkhanov, 1993, p. 245). In 1894, the Amir sent a special team, led by Nayeb Padshah,

Ghulam Khan and Sultan Ali Khan, the latter a son of Sardaar Shir Ali Khan of Jaghuri, whose mission was to identify and arrest Hazara elites who had escaped the arrests of previous year. Within a period of one year, the group arrested and sent to Kabul some 802 Hazara leaders (Kateb, 1913, pp. 828, 841, 846, 919, 926, 928, 931, 934–5, 945). Many of those arrested were charged with treason against the state and executed and others were exiled to other parts of the country.

Third, the efforts to destroy the political, economic and social structure of the Hazara society were accompanied by policies that aimed to impose new cultural and religious forms. Two aspects of the efforts to change the identity of Hazaras and Hazarajat deserve particular attention. One was a policy of de-Shi'atisation which essentially aimed to convert Shi'as, including the Qizilbash, to Sunni Islam. As part of this policy, the Amir ordered several Hanafi Sunni mosques to be built among the Hazaras of Day Kundi which were led by Sunni Mullahs whose job it was to convert the people into Sunni Islam. The Amir appointed Sunni judges and clerics in all Hazara districts to settle legal affairs according to Hanafi jurisprudence (Temirkhanov, 1993, p. 258). The de-Shi'atisation campaign also targeted Shi'a outside Hazarajat. Because of official pressures to convert to Sunni Islam and sectarian animosities in the city of Herat, many Farsiwan Shi'as of the city left for Iran. In Kabul, Sunni mullahs were appointed at two main Shi'a religious centres of Chindawul (Kateb, 1913, p. 806, 1139).

The anti-Shi'a campaign that was initiated during the war against the Hazaras continued throughout the period of the Amir's rule. In 1895 and 1896 reports from British news writers in Kabul and Qandahar indicate that three years after the Hazara uprising was completely repressed, there was no change in language or rhetoric of the sectarian propaganda campaign. Mullahs and preachers of the mosques continued to deliver sectarian messages against the Hazaras, calling them infidels that deserved death or slavery. In 1896, the Hazaras and Qizilbash leaders in Kabul were ordered by the Amir 'to adopt the principles of the Sunni creed, or tie red turbans on their heads like the Hindus, so that others might not mistake them for Sunnis' (Mir Khan, 1896). In a meeting with the Amir, the leaders of these communities were declared to have converted to Islam, but an unassured Amir appointed informants to gather intelligence if the Qizilbash and Hazaras of Kabul were still practising Shi'a Islam

(Mir Khan, 1896). However, there is no evidence to suggest that the Amir achieved any significant success in converting large numbers of Shi'a into Sunni Muslims. It appears most Hazaras and other Shi'as practised *taqiyyah*, a Shi'a principle that allows its followers to conceal their religious beliefs to avoid persecution.

Conclusion

The reign of Abdur Rahman Khan offers important insights into how the people of Afghanistan and its various social groups encountered what became the modern state of the country. The centralised state built by the Amir represents stark changes as well as continuities with its predecessor, the Durrani Empire. In contrast to previous Durrani rulers, Abdur Rahman Khan built a centralised state that exercised direct control over territories with well-defined national borders. By employing Islam as a framework of legitimation of state authority, he took important steps in mitigating the effects of rivalries and demands of Pashtun tribes over the state. However, the underlying relationship between Pashtun tribes and the state did not change. While the British subsidies substituted for the Durrani Empire's revenues from the Indian sub-continent and thus strengthened the position of Abdur Rahman Khan against his dynastic rivals and tribal aristocracy, the Amir maintained a tradition of relying on tribal mobilisation and a policy of divide and rule in his relentless efforts to centralise power. As the ruler, he still needed to organise and administer wars of conquest and distribute fruits of plunder as rewards for tribal warriors, which shows the dynamics of the relationship between the ruler and Pashtun tribes. The only major difference, however, was that the Amir's wars were directed towards people in his own country and thus the religious doctrine of jehad and the political economy of plunder were internalised.

Wars and violence have been common features of the rise of modern nations and states around the world. Wars and violence, particularly if waged against foreign enemies, strengthen national cohesion and solidarity and create symbols of national struggles that binds people together. However, for Afghanistan as an emerging state, if these wars had any effect in developing collective consciousness, it was at the level of particular ethnic groups. For the Hazaras, the 1891–1893

Hazara War had far-reaching consequences, beyond its immediate tragic human costs. The national mobilisation against the Hazaras might be interpreted as an indication of national solidarity of a nation in the making but it produced the opposite effect. Perhaps for the first time in their known history, the mobilisation against Hazaras forced them to mount a collective rebellion against state authority on a national scale. This was a highly significant shift for an ethnic group that was known for its internal feuds and animosities.

Understanding the centralised state built by Abdur Rahman Khan has more than just historical significance. It shaped the course of political history of Afghanistan by dominating the political imagination of most of his Pashtun successors. One of his most enduring legacies is that most Pashtun political elites continue to equate political unification of the country with strong centralisation of power. Decentralisation and, in fact, other forms of political arrangements that might deviate from the model of Abdur Rahman are quickly condemned as threats to national integrity and unity. As we will see, a drive for centralisation has been a key aspect of the state-building process since the international intervention of 2001.

The incorporation of the Hazaras into the Afghan state also profoundly changed the role and influence of Hazara political elites. During the Hazara War, the Hazara political and religious elites were either annihilated or thoroughly weakened. As we will see in the next chapter, those who were left from the traditional Hazara elites were made subservient to Pashtun tribal aristocracy and government officials in the first three-quarters of the twentieth century. Over time, the Pashtuns, as the victorious state-bearing group, and the Hazaras, as a defeated rebellious group, progressively developed a relationship that resembled a social hierarchy in a caste system, with the Hazaras being the lowest caste.

3

THE AFGHAN STATE AND THE HAZARAS, 1901–1978

AFGHAN NATIONALISM AND POLICIES AND POLITICS OF MODERNISATION AND EXCLUSION

Hazaras are spread over the country, and are to be found in every province, village, and town. It is a saying in Afghanistan that they would have had to work like donkeys if it were not that the slaving donkeys of Hazaras do all the work for them.

Amir Abdur Rahman Khan (1900, p. 277)

Introduction

Modern states exist to govern territories and peoples. If states become democratic they govern on behalf of and in consultation with people. Even states that govern in an authoritarian manner offer some services and benefits to the people they expect to follows its laws and regulations. While there is no question that these are important aspects of a modern state, or the idea of a state, there is a darker and messier side to modern states that is often conveniently overlooked. States can turn against their people, and institute and perpetuate unjust systems of governance that exclude, marginalise and persecute some or most sections of their societies. The manner in which the Hazaras encountered the modern state is illustrative of the heavy costs, rather than benefits, that the modern state has imposed on many people. For them, the incorporation into the Afghan state was not an entry into a pleasant and wider economic and social system that could offer pathways towards modernisation and progress. On the contrary, they found themselves at the bottom of a political and socioeconomic system, where, in the words of Mousavi, they lived as a 'nation imprisoned' (Mousavi, 1998, p. 160).

This chapter covers the period between 1901 when Abdur Rahman died and 1978, the year Afghanistan descended into the vicious cycle of war and bloodshed that has continued ever since. It looks at the consequences of incorporation of the Hazaras into the political and bureaucratic structure of the Afghan state. The first section of this chapter provides an overview of the trajectory of the Afghan state between 1901 and 1978, with a focus on the rise and fall of Habibullah Kalakani in 1929 as a critical juncture in this period. The second section discusses the rise and evolution of Afghan nationalism, highlighting the tensions that existed between a national and ethnic conception of nationhood. The third section focuses on relations of the Hazaras with state institutions at the sub-national level and shows how official policies reinforced or at times left untouched informal relations of discrimination and exploitation. The final section looks at changing Hazara responses to state repression and social and economic exclusion and argues that during this period the Hazara response shifted from traditional rural rebellions towards more organised and modern forms of protests.

Continuity and ruptures in the historical trajectory of the Afghan State: 1901–1978

In 1901, the 'Iron Amir', as Abdur Rahman Khan became known, died, leaving behind a highly centralised state. The 'consolidated if terrorized state' (Rubin, 2002, p. 52) became the model that successive Afghan rulers attempted to maintain and emulate. The twentieth century presented the Afghan state and its centralising elites with enormous challenges that would test the capacity and legitimacy of the state as a modern entity. These included reconciling the deep social divisions and healing the trauma that was left behind by Amir Abdur Rahman Khan, crafting and instilling a sense of nationhood among the peoples, planning and implementing social and economic modernisation programmes and responding to demands for political reforms and popular representation in the state. The history of Afghanistan in the twentieth century is a history of struggles and failures in overcoming these challenges.

Meeting these challenges required a fundamental shift in the relationship between the state and the dominant Pashtun political elites, and ordinary Pashtuns as well as other ethno-cultural groups. Thus, a successful transformation of the Afghan state would entail changing its relationships with the non-Pashtun ethnic groups of the country. The link between state formation and consolidation, and the political and economic interests of the Pashtuns (more accurately the Pashtun elites) was so close that one author has described the extension of state authority over non-Pashtuns as 'internal imperialism' (Dupree, 1980, p. xix), and a 'form of internal colonialism by a Pashtun ruling class over the country's many ethnic minorities: Tajiks, Uzbeks, Hazaras, Tur-comen, Aimaqs, Nuristanis, Baluchis, and others' (Hyman, 2002, p. 299). These early encounters of the various ethnic groups with the state set important precedents for the future evolution of the Afghan state.

In evaluating the relationship of the Afghan state with its society over a period as long as the first three-quarters of the twentieth century, it is important to highlight that throughout this period the policies and priorities of the Afghan rulers and the national and international environment in which they ruled varied greatly. Furthermore, between 1901 and 1978, the Afghan state also faced frequent interruptions to its historical trajectory as a result of dynamics within the royal family and domestic politics of the country. During this period, all six Afghan rulers were either killed, overthrown or forced into exile. In 1919, Amir Habibullah, the son and heir of Abdur Rahman Khan, was mysteriously murdered in his tent during a hunting expedition near Jalalabad. His son, Amanullah Khan, who succeeded him and led a most ambitious programme of modernisation during the 1920s, was overthrown by tribal and conservative revolts and forced into exile in 1929. Amanullah was succeeded by Habibullah Kalakani, one of the Tajik leaders of the rebellion, for a period of just nine months. He was overthrown by a counter tribal mobilisation by Nader Khan, who served as a general in Amanullah's army in the 1920s. Nader Khan traced his roots to Sultan Muhammad, one of several brothers of Amir Dost Muhammad Khan. In the 1920s, Nader Khan became Minister of War but after taking Kabul he declared himself king and thus founded the

Musaheban dynasty that ruled the country until 1978. Nader Khan also established the first bicameral national assembly in 1932 that became the first of thirteen successive assemblies until the outbreak of conflict in 1978. Except for the relatively liberal parliaments of 1948–1953 and 1963–1973, most of these assemblies were only symbolic institutions with no real power. Nader Khan was assassinated in 1933 by a high school student in Kabul. He was succeeded by his nineteen-year old son, Zaher Shah, who presided over the longest period of peace that lasted until 1973 when he was overthrown in a coup by his cousin and former Prime Minister, Daoud Khan. Daoud Khan declared the country a republic but was killed along with most of his family members during the PDPA coup five years later in April 1978.

Consequently, the continuities and discontinuities in the approach and policies of the successive rulers must be considered in any historical analysis of the modern state and various social groups in the country. These changes affected some state policies towards the Hazaras. In 1904, Amir Habibullah decreed that Hazaras who were displaced by his father could return to their original land (Farhang, 1988, pp. 298–9). Amanullah also tried to improve the situation of the Hazaras, by legally outlawing slavery (there were still thousands of Hazara slaves in the country), first by a decree in 1921 and second by a constitutional provision in 1923 (Mousavi, 1998, p. 157). Hazaras were also represented in the country's national assemblies. The first assembly under Nader Khan included only seven Shi'a delegates. The number increased to twelve in the seventh national assembly that opened in 1946. Hazara representation significantly increased after the adoption of the 1964 constitution. The new constitutional monarchy, which became the most serious democratic experiment of the country, allowed for a relatively greater degree of equal rights and freedoms for all citizens of the country. During the first parliamentary elections after the adoption of the 1964 constitution, fifteen Hazaras were elected among the 216 members of the Lower House and three others were appointed as members of the Upper House (Nayel, 2000, pp. 450–64).

However, despite the highly significant changes that occurred during this period the Afghan state and the economic and political dynamics that underpinned it show some marked continuities that impeded its ability to transform into an inclusive, effective and multi-ethnic state. The effects of these continuities are evident at the times of crisis and instability of the state, critical junctures that activate the underlying dynamics of Afghanistan's politics and shape the course of political developments for a long period of time. The most significant such critical junctures were the rebellions and counter-rebellions that led to transfer of power from Amanullah Khan, to Habibullah Kalakani and to Nader Khan.

The 1929 rebellion and counter-rebellion

The Afghan state was put to its most serious test by Amanullah Khan who after gaining Afghanistan's independence in 1919 attempted to create a new secular legal basis for the state before attempting to turn it into a vehicle for rapid modernisation. Amanullah declared Afghanistan's independence from British India as one of his top priorities. In May 1919, Afghan forces launched a surprise attack on British Indian posts, just east of the Durand Line, beginning the third Anglo-Afghan War. Exhausted by the First World War and a nationalist agitation in India, the British did not have the wherewithal to engage in another long war and accepted Afghanistan's independence in August of that year. In 1923, Amanullah gave the country its first constitution, which for the first time introduced modern concepts such as universal citizenship and equal rights and obligations among all inhabitants of the country. Furthermore, he passed dozens of laws and regulations that covered different aspects of his complete transformation programme (Poullada, 1973, pp. 99–103).

Amanullah's modernisation programme went in tandem with government policies that aimed to foster a unified Afghan nation state around Pashtuns as the ethno-cultural core of the country. This included resettlement of Pashtuns from the south and east to other regions, historically dominated by other groups, to alter the demographic composition of the country. In 1923, Amanullah Khan promulgated an item of official legislation (*nezamnamah*) concerning the distribution of land to the Pashtun settlers in northern Afghanistan. Among other things, the law required local governors to assist the Pashtun settlers, known as *naaqilin*, by facilitating their settlement and providing them government support in the forms of seeds and agricultural equipment (Government of Afghanistan, 1923).

Amanullah's reforms resulted in the first major rebellion and disintegration of state authority after the death of Abdur Rahman Khan in 1901. The rebellion and counter-rebellion became a critical juncture in the historical trajectory of the centralised state. It put an end to the ambitious programme of modernisation led by Amanullah Khan in the 1920s, brought into power Habibullah Kalakani, the first Tajik and the only non-Pashtun ruler since 1747, and eventually transferred power from Abdur Rahman Khan's direct descendant to the Musaheban, a different family of the Muhammadzai clan. Three aspects of the rebellions and counter-rebellions are worth discussing here.

First, Pashtun tribes played critical roles in the downfall of Amanullah Khan and the coming to power of Nader Khan. While Amanullah's rapid modernisation programme and its consequences for religious legitimation of his authority are often held responsible for instigating the conservative revolts (Nawid, 1999), the main trigger of the revolt was a change in the relationship between Amanullah Khan and the Pashtun tribes. In October 1928, Amanullah Khan abolished payment of what was called *Badraqa* to Pashtuns of Eastern Afghanistan. *Badraqa* was essentially money granted to tribes in return for their cooperation for ensuring the security of the highways between Afghanistan and British India at the time. In November, Pashtun tribes rose in armed rebellion against the government, which then spread to the mainly Tajik areas to the north of Kabul. The rebellion, however, remained largely restricted to the mainly Pashtun eastern and southern provinces without spreading to the Hazarajat or the western, northern and northeastern provinces (Shahrani, 2005). Amanullah's army proved incapable of containing the tribal rebellion, and in January 1929 he fled first to Qandahar in the south before going into exile in India and later Italy and Switzerland where he died in 1960. However, before Pashtun tribes could arrive, rebels led by Habibullah Kalakani, a Tajik from the northern plains of Kabul, took control of the capital where he declared himself Amir Habibullah, *Khadim Din Rasullullah* (The Servant of the Faith of the Messenger of God).

Kalakani ruled for only nine months. As the only non-Pashtun and non-Durrani to claim the throne since 1747, he was seen as a usurper by many Pashtun tribes, including those who had rebelled against Amanullah Khan. In August that year, Nader Khan took the leadership of this ethnic mobilisation to restore a Pashtun to the throne. He returned from France where he was serving as Amanulllah's ambassador.

The circumstances in which Nader Khan came to power show the resilience and continuity of the same dynamics that were at work during Amir Abdur Rahman Khan's reign. Similar to Abdur Rahman Khan, he relied on a foreign power (although to a lesser extent) to buttress his position, and mobilised Pashtun tribesmen with promises of loot and plunder of Kabul and supporters of Kalakani. The tribal mobilisation that was central to his campaign to take Kabul reversed many of the efforts for the creation of modern state institutions. In August 1929, Nader Khan based himself in Waziristan, now in the Tribal Areas of Pakistan, where he began to mobilise tribal *lashkars*, armies from the Pashtun tribes of both sides of the Durand Line. As an incentive for mobilisation, Nader Khan gave the Pashtun tribes the privileged position that they had lost during Amanullah. Lacking the resources to pay the militias, he allowed them to loot and plunder Kabul after they took control of the city from Kalakani in October 1929. After taking control of Kabul, the 12,000 strong militia marched towards Shamali, to the north of the capital, from which Kalakani and most of his supporters came. They captured Kalakani and executed him and most of his aides, and allowed the tribal militias to loot these areas and take young women as booties of the war. The tribes who participated in the takeover of Kabul were exempted from tax and regular military service (Rubin, 2013, pp. 469–71; Rubin, 2002, p. 60).

Second, while Nader Khan proclaimed himself as king and gave important positions to his four brothers, turning Afghanistan into a 'family compact' (Fletcher, 1966, p. 227) he reversed Afghanistan's dependence on the British. In striking similarity to the events leading to the second Anglo-Afghan War (1878–1880), the British were increasingly concerned about the threats to its imperial holdings from the direction of Afghanistan. Amanullah, as the leader of Afghanistan's independence in 1919 and as the first Afghan ruler to open diplomatic relations with many powers, including the Soviet Union, was not seen by the British as a reliable ally. The onset of rivalries between the Soviet Union and other Western powers was reviving the dynamics of the Great Game in the nineteenth century. In view of this, the British Governor of the North West Frontier province allowed Nader Khan to use Waziristan as a base to recruit many Pashtuns from across the Durand Line. Once on the throne, although officially Nader Khan and the Musaheban dynasty attempted to follow neutrality in Afghanistan's foreign policy, Nader Khan remained closer to the British, which provided him 40 million rupees and weapons to consolidate his rule after 1929 (Olesen, 1995, pp. 172–4; Saikal, 2004, pp. 97–9).

Third, beyond its immediate impact on power relations at that time, the rebellion and counter-rebellions produced historical narratives, symbols and figures that are central to ethnic narratives in Afghanistan. The ethnic perception of the events seems to have begun with the fall of Kabul in the hand of Kalakani. For the Pashtun elites he became a 'usurper' of the throne that they believed exclusively belonged to the Pashtuns. The ethnicised narratives are best captured by contestation over the image of Kalakani himself. The official historiography has often described Kalakani as a bandit, *bache saqaw* (son of the water carrier) and illiterate who led a rebellion against modernisation and progress. In more recent decades Tajik nationalists have tried to challenge the view by portraying him as a legendary hero, a Robin Hood-like figure who mobilised the poor against the corrupt government in Kabul (Khalili, 1990; Wafayezada, 2013, pp. 92–3).

The ethnic narrative of the events of 1929 gained particular significance for the Hazaras in 1933, when Nader Khan was assassinated by Abdul Khaleq, a Hazara student at the Nejat High School in Kabul. Khaleq and several members of his family and relatives were executed after they had been severely tortured. Abdul Khaleq was a seventeen-year-old Hazara student who was living with his family at the house of Ghulam Nabi Khan Charkhi, an influential pro-Amanullah figure. During the 1929 rebellion, Ghulam Nabi Khan was Afghanistan's ambassador to Moscow. Like Nader Khan, after the abdication of Amanullah, he returned to Mazar-e Sharif and made an unsuccessful effort to restore Amanullah to the throne. After the fall of Kalakani, Nader Khan, whose legitimacy as the ruler was contested, remained suspicious of Ghulam Nabi Khan. He accused him of promoting Amanullah, who was in exile in Italy, and Russian interests in the country. In 1932, Charkhi was arrested and executed along with several members of his family. Whether Khaleq was motivated to take revenge on behalf of the Charkhi family, or by the persecution and marginalisation of Hazaras is hard to establish today. However, in recent years, Khaleq has been widely admired as a hero in the Hazara narrative of the history of Afghanistan (Dawlatabadi, 2006, pp. 327–55).

Nader Shah was succeeded by his nineteen-year-old son, Zahir Shah, who ruled the country for the next forty years, the longest period of stability in the modern history of the country. Except for the so-called Democracy Decade (1963–1973), through much of Zahir Shah's reign, actual power was exercised by his uncles and cousins who succeeded one another as prime ministers. Hashim Khan (1933–1946) led a renewed drive for consolidation and centralisation of power. He was followed by his more liberal brother Shah Mahmud (1946–1953), whose short experiment with parliamentary politics was abrogated when Zahir Shah's cousin, Daoud Khan, another centralist, became prime minister from 1953 to 1963. In 1963, Zahir Shah promulgated a constitutional democracy that barred members of the royal family from holding executive roles in the government. The reign of Zahir Shah and the experiment with democracy came to an end in 1973 when a marginalised and disaffected Daoud Khan took power in a coup while Zahir Shah was abroad. Daoud Khan's coup became the forerunner of the 1978 coup by the pro-Soviet People's Democratic Party of Afghanistan that ended his life and unleashed cycles of wars and conflict that have continued ever since.

Ethnic and national conceptions of nationhood

The trajectory of the Afghan state in the twentieth century was marked by an attempt to craft and promote a sense of nationhood among its diverse people. The birth of nationalism as an ideology in Afghanistan cannot be explained without looking at the role of the Tarzi family. The Tarzi family, who like the Musaheban belong to the royal Muhammadzai clan and were exiled by Abdur Rahman in 1880s, returned to Afghanistan after spending more than two decades in Damascus, where they were exposed to the modernist and reformist movements that raged across the Ottoman Empire at that time. The most influential member of the family was Mahmud Tarzi who tried to introduce these new ideas to Afghanistan. Mahmud Tarzi became a leading member of what is known as the 'Young Afghans', a small group of modernist elites in Kabul that became the incubator of Afghan nationalism and the country's first constitutionalist movement that became known as *junbesh-i mashrutiat* (Ruttig, 2006; Habibi, 1987).

In 1911, Mahmud Tarzi published the biweekly, *Seraj-ul-Akhbar* (Lamp of News). In its international outlook, the journal was inspired by the dominant ideology of Islamic modernism at that time that emphasised Islamic revival and modernisation as a solution to the problems of the Muslim world in the face of Western colonialism. Gregorian aptly describes the role of the periodical in redefining the nature of the Afghan state:

> The periodical attempted to define for them both the nature and the ultimate aims of Afghan nationalism and to formulate a theoretical basis in order to direct and justify the projected socioeconomic transformation of Afghanistan. (1967, p. 347)

Internally, although Tarzi tried to formulate Afghan nationhood on a geographical and religious basis, formulation of nationalism as a national ideology was complicated by the ethnic mosaic of Afghanistan and very different experiences of various groups with the Afghan state that were supposed to represent and embody a new national consciousness. As a result, nationalism as a national ideology remained weak. In the words of Hyman (2002):

> The theme of 'Nationalism after Colonialism' as far as Afghanistan is concerned begs many questions: with the national or patriotic idea so weak and undeveloped, it arguably makes more sense to analyse rival ideas of the nation held by the country's different ethnic groups than some hypothetical all-embracing Afghan nationalism. (2002, p. 299)

The influence of the Tarzi family and the Young Afghans ended with the abdication of King Amanullah in 1929. While the Young Afghans fluctuated between a geographic and ethnic conception of Afghan nationhood, the Musaheban dynasty chose to move toward a Pashtun-centric conception. These policies that began or were intensified after Nader Khan took the throne in October 1929 aimed at Pashtunisation of Afghanistan's history, culture and society to fit with political domination of the Pashtun elites. The ethnic conception of nationhood had two main dimensions: temporal and spatial.

Temporally, this form of Pashtun ethno-nationalism embraced a new idea of Pashtuns' ethno-genesis as descendants of a greater Aryan race.

The new idea replaced a more popular belief among Pashtun tribes that traced their roots to one of the lost Israelite tribes. The reformulation of Pashtuns as part of the Aryan race became particularly attractive with the rise to power of Hitler in Germany in the 1930s. Afghan historians began to construct a historical continuity between modern Afghanistan and an ancient Aryana that was believed to be cradle of human civilization 'so that it became the recipient of a history reaching back to the very beginnings of ancient time and was in fact elevated to the status of cradle of human civilisation' (Schetter, 2005, p. 8). Abdul Majid Zabuli, who founded the country's first bank in 1933, Bank-e Mill-e Afghanistan, and Daoud Khan and his brother Naim Khan, nephews of Nader Khan, became the chief proponents of such notions. Importantly, both Zabuli and Naim Khan had lived in Germany where they were attracted to the ideology of Aryan racial superiority (Farhang, 1988, p. 427). What followed from such historical construction was that Aryans, the Pashtuns and Tajiks in Afghanistan, were the native inhabitants of the country, not immigrants as the theory of their origin in the lost Israelite tribes would imply. By contrast the Uzbeks and Turkmen were said to be recent migrants from Central Asia and the Hazaras became remnants of the thirteenth-century Mongol army (Wafayezada, 2013, pp. 98–9; Farhang, 1988, pp. 426–8).

The Musaheban form of Afghan nationalism was translated into policies of Pashtun political, economic and cultural supremacy. For Pashtun nationalist historians, Afghanistan's history became essentially the history of Pashtun rulers that was projected into historical continuity through the Aryan reinterpretation of the country's ancient past. In the 1931 constitution, the Pashto language was declared the national language. It was confirmed in the 1964 constitution. Efforts at promoting Pashto were accompanied by a policy of sidelining Farsi, which has historically been the main lingua franca of the country (Farhang, 1988, pp. 426–8).

It is, however, important to note an important continuity in the evolution of Pashtun nationalism between the periods of Amanullah Khan and the Musaheban dynasty. For example, the Pashto Tolana (Pashto Society), which became the main centre of the new historiography was established in the 1920s (Poullada, 1973, p. 73). Under the Musaheban, backed by government funds, the society undertook the task of promoting Pashto over Farsi 'to extreme lengths in inventing new compound Pashto words to replace Persian and other foreign words in common use' (Hyman, 2002, p. 300).

Spatially, throughout the twentieth century successive Afghan rulers adopted and implemented policies that aimed to change the ethno-cultural diversity of the country. First, perhaps the most consistent aspect of this policy was the resettlement of Pashtun tribes from the south and east of Afghanistan to the mainly non-Pashtun regions of the north and northeast of the country. As the previous two chapters of this book showed, occupation of mainly non-Pashtun lands and their distri-bution to loyal Pashtun tribes had been a key feature of the history of the Afghan state from 1747. While some of these migrations or Pashtun expansions occurred voluntarily or without the help of the state, in the twentieth century, beginning with Amanullah Khan, land redistribution schemes became systematic policies of the state. Over time, these set-tlers that became known as *naaqilin*, transferees, formed sizeable Pashtun communities in the Qataghan and Afghan Turkestan regions, which largely overlapped with the northeastern and northern prov-inces of Afghanistan today. Surrounded by non-Pashtuns on whose lands they lived, these communities became dependent on the state (Tapper, 1983; Bleuer, 2012).

Second, consecutive Afghan rulers attempted to level out the ethnic heterogeneity of Afghanistan by breaking up, renaming and redefining geographical units that carried ethnic or others forms of symbolism that conflicted with the official cultural construction of Afghanistan. In the words of Schetter, 'nearly all Afghan rulers until the outbreak of the conflict in 1979 found the cultural heterogeneity of Afghanistan's ter-ritory an annoyance' (2005, p. 7). To overcome the annoyance, admin-istrative, political and cultural reorganisation polices were designed to break up major regions such as Afghan Turkestan, Qataghan, Khorasan, and Hazarajat.

The gradual dissolution of these geographical entities is illustrated by the history of Hazarajat. After the conquest of Hazarajat in 1890s and during the first two decades of the twentieth century, most of Hazarajat was annexed to the province of Kabul. The only major excep-tion was the remaining Hazara districts of Uruzgan that were adminis-tered through Qandahar. The areas annexed to Kabul included two local administrative centres: Badasia in Behsud region of the present day Wardak province and Panjab in Bamyan. Like the rest of the country, a regular system of administration was extended to the Hazara areas and the local offices were staffed by predominantly Pashtun officials who were appointed from Kabul (Ferdinand, 2006, p. 215). In 1921, as part of his reform programmes, King Amanullah promulgated a new statute that divided the country into five main *welayat* or provinces: Kabul, Qandahar, Herat, Turkestan and Qataghan and Badakhshan, and four smaller divisions (*hokumat-e a'ala*): *Samt-e Mashriqi* (eastern region), *Samt-e Jonubi* (southern regions), Farah and Maimanah. Much of Hazarajat continued to be under the control of the governor of Kabul that included the subdivisions of *hokumat-i Kabul, hokumat-i kalan-e samt-e shamali* (Shamali Plains), *hokumat-i kalan-i ghaznain and hokumat-i kalan-e Day Zangi*, the last one being in Panjab Bamyan (Gregorian, 1967; Government of Afghanistan, 1921). An important aspect of Amanullah's administrative system was that for the first time, the provincial and district officials reported to their respective ministers, who formed the Council of Ministers, chaired by the king. Although Nader Shah mainly retained the overall structures of local government under Amanullah, as part of his centralising policies he pushed for greater direct control of the provinces by Kabul (Gopalakrishnan, 1981, pp. 174–83).

In the 1950s, the Bamyan and the Ghorband Valleys were separated from Kabul to become part of the newly created Parwan province. Panjab continued to remain an important administrative centre and was called *hokumat-e Kalan-e Day Zangi* and included Yakawlang, Behsud, Lal-wa-Sarjangal, Shahristan and Day Kundi.

The 1964 constitution completed the break up of ethnic and cultural identities of Afghanistan's regions by creating twenty-eight smaller provinces, breaking up large cultural and historical regions into smaller administrative units. Qataghan in the northeast, and Turkestan in the north, known as Turkestan Afghani, were broken up into smaller administrative provinces. Similarly, Hazarajat was parcelled out amongst its adjacent provinces of Ghazni, Uruzgan, Ghor, Parwan, Wardak, Bamyan, Parwan, Baghlan, Jawzjan and Balkh. Except for Bamyan, which had a Hazara majority population, all other provinces had non-Hazara majorities. In practice, the new division achieved the eventual objective of complete marginalisation of Hazaras by turning them into marginalised minorities in each administrative unit. The new administrative division had two practical consequences for the Hazaras: reduced representation in the national politics and minimal share of national budget resources as the provinces became the unit of national budget allocation and political representation in the country's national assembly.

Third, following the creation of Pakistan in 1947, the spatial conception of Pashtun ethno-nationalism found its most powerful expression in irredentist claims over the Pashtun tribes and territories on the other side of the Durand Line. During the premiership of Daoud Khan (1953–1963), the idea of freeing the Pashtun population of Pakistan to create a separate Pashtunistan or annexing them to create a greater Afghanistan became the main foreign policy objective of the country. The Pashtunistan policy created the foundation of enduring hatred and mistrust between Pakistan and Afghanistan that continues to over-shadow relations between the two countries. Saikal notes that:

> Daoud staunchly believed that the best way to tackle Afghanistan's problems was to embrace the notion of supremacy and unity of Pashtuns, based on their common ethnicity, language, culture and religion, and aimed, amongst other things, against pan-Iranism. Thus, his brand of nationalism was synonymous with 'Pashtunism' and called for the 'Pashtunification' of Afghanistan and reunification of all Pashtuns on both sides of the Durand Line. (2004, p. 112)

As the events of the following decades show, this form of Afghan nationalism created a backlash in the form of resistance and challenges by other ethnic groups against both the spatial and temporal construction of the Pashtun nationalism and more detrimentally Pakistan's policy of interference that aims to keep the Afghan state weak and instable.

The state and ethnic power relations in Hazarajat

At the national level, while the policies of the Afghan rulers fluctuated over time between ethnic and national conceptions of nationhood, the dynamics of the state as an instrument of domination of some Pashtuns over other ethnic groups persisted at the local level. For the Hazaras, the extension and consolidation of state authority had a profound and detrimental ethnic consequence. Canfield summarises the encounter of Hazaras with the Afghan state:

There was the thoroughly effective subjugation of one ethnic group by another, and of one religious sect by another—a situation which, I suggest, progressively appears more like the social distinction between groups in a caste hierarchy. (1972, p. 6)

Between 1901 and 1978, the system of economic exploitation and social and political exclusion of the Hazaras operated on two different levels. First, during this long period, the Hazaras suffered from socioeconomic and political exclusion as a result of official policies, systematically designed and administered by successive Afghan governments. As a consequence of these policies, they were subjected to systematic discrimination in educational institutions, government administration, politics and the economy of the country (Mousavi, 1998, pp. 155–71; Emadi, 1997).

The central government exercised its control over Hazaras in two ways: 'officially through the Hazara *mirs* (whom the government, using the Pashto term, called *Maleks*) and informally through spies and informers' (Canfield, 1972, p. 5). A very important change for the future of the region was the diminishing role of the traditional Hazara landholding elites, known as *mirs* and *begs*. In contrast with the traditional Hazara *mirs*, the *arbaabs* and *maliks* as they became known in the twentieth century, were mostly selected by local government officials to maintain control in their respective areas. They were identified and appointed by the district governors and were paid a regular salary by the central government in Kabul (Mousavi, 1998, p. 132). Thus, they obtained their legitimacy and influence from contact with the government officials, mostly lacking independent sources of power of their own. However, the traditional Hazara elites did not completely wither away. Ferdinand, one of the few Western scholars who conducted research in Hazarajat before 1978, notes that members of the old *mir* families would occasionally occupy this position (of *malik*), but whether they did or not they still 'remained prominent individuals, surrounded by respect and influence that followed from their background and wealth' (2006, p. 202).

Second, these official policies created and perpetuated informal socioeconomic structures that persisted independent of official policies. In other words, formal policies and informal attitudes and socioeconomic relations reciprocally strengthened one another to turn the Hazaras into a large 'underclass'. The ethnic hatred and grievances and sectarian hostilities that resulted from the 1891–93 Hazara War, and the devastating economic impact it had on Hazaras, solidified a social and sectarian boundary between Hazaras and the rest of the country.

The most illustrative example of the formal and informal nature of discrimination against Hazaras was an extremely exploitative and unequal social and economic relationship that developed between the Hazaras and Pashtun nomads in Hazarajat. As the previous chapter showed, as the most enthusiastic participants in the Hazara War, the Pashtun nomads (*kuchi*) found a common interest with the state in extending the state authority over the Hazaras. To reward the *Kuchis*, Amir Abdur Rahman Khan issued a directive to the governors of Hazarajat, banning the Hazaras from grazing in the pastures of the entire region. According to Faiz Mohammad Kateb the proclamation ordered the governors:

> …to forbid the Hazarahs absolutely from grazing their flocks (on the pastures) as they have done in the past and as a result of which they had destroyed those pastures. From this day forward they were not to occupy them and were to consider them all, large or small, as belonging to the government. With the publication of this proclamation, little by little the pastures of the Hazarahjat were turned over to the governors and to individual lessees. They then sold them to Afghan nomads and caused the collapse of herding among the Hazarah people. (1913, p. 1050)

The opening of Hazarajat to the nomads' migration was only the beginning of a complex and highly exploitative social and economic relationship between the sedentary Hazaras and the nomadic Pashtuns. The most significant aspect of this relationship was a close association between the Pashtun nomads and local government officials, who were also mostly Pashtuns and systematically supported the dominant position of the former over the Hazaras (Maqsudi, 1989, pp. 34–42). In the 1950s, when the Danish anthropologist Klaus Ferdinand visited Hazarajat, some nomad chiefs were so confident of their relationship with the state that they still described themselves as a 'standing army that could be called upon when the need arose' (2006, p. 216). Hence, the interests of the central government and Kuchis overlapped to a great extent in Hazarajat.

Central to the preponderant position of the Kuchis in Hazarajat was an economic and trading relationship in which the Hazaras became exceptionally lucrative trading partners. In a bartered system of exchange, the Kuchis would sell clothes, tea and tobaccos, unrefined sugar (*qand*) and numerous other items to the Hazaras. In return, the Hazaras would offer wheat, clarified butter and woven articles such as transport sacks and *gelim* rugs. The value of the exchange was set by the nomads and the local villagers, isolated from the outside world as they were, with little knowledge or power over the actual prices outside the region. The following example of the trade in clarified butter cited by Ferdinand illustrates how the nomads benefited from buying local products as late as the 1960s:

> The nomads might pay 100–150 Afs. (=20–30 British shillings) for one sir (=16 paaw or pounds Kabuli = approx. 7kg) of clarified butter for delivery in the following year. In due course they would resell this, for example in the Logar valley in East Afghanistan for about 500 Afs. (about 100 s.) to be paid a year later. In other words, they obtained about 100 percent gross profits in a twelve-month period, as a purchase of, for example, 125 Afs. within two years would yield about 500 Afs. (2006, pp. 234–5)

Ferdinand also provides another example of how the nomads benefited from the sale of products they sold to the Hazaras:

> Indian and, later, particularly Pakistani cotton cloth was purchased in Peshawar, on their own admission (1960), for about eight annas a yard or metre (=3–3.5 Afs. =7–8 d.) and resold in Hazarajat for between 15–25 Afs. (about 3–5 s.) per meter, to be paid back the next year according to the nomads. (2006, p. 235)

As might be expected, the terms of trade were progressively declining for the Hazaras. Over time they had to sell more and more local produce to buy the same quantity of goods from nomads. The change in terms of trade was so dramatic that the price of a pair of shoes bought by a Hazara, over a period of a few years, equalled the price of over half a ton (1 *kharwaar*) of wheat (Ferdinand, 2006, p. 235). Such trading relationships made the Hazaras indebted to the nomads. As the local villagers failed to service their debt, the nomads offered them another good: cash and credit. They were quite generous in lending money to the Hazaras, which with its attendant interest rates further drowned the villagers in debt and eventually bankruptcy. Hence, a vicious cycle emerged: to service their debts the Hazara had to borrow money which meant more debt; the following year they would have to pay even more, and to do that they needed to borrow more money. Eventually, the indebted villagers had to give more and more of their harvest, livestock and finally their land.

Ferdinand offers the most detailed account of how this debt-credit relationship often resulted into loss of agricultural land by the Hazaras to the nomads. To solve their liquidity problems, the Hazaras would often resort to the last solution that was to give their land to the nomads as *gerawi*, a form of traditional mortgage practised in Afghanistan. The cost of *gerawi* was far below the actual prices of land and could account for only one-fifth of the normal price. The *gerawi* contract was essentially open-ended and could last as long as the Hazaras were unable to repay the loan. Since the nomads had neither the skills to farm the land, nor the intention to settle as farmers, the land would normally be left to the Hazara owners who cultivated it as tenants. The signing of a *gerawi* contract was only one step away from the full transfer of property rights from the local Hazaras to the Pashtun nomads. In some instances, the indebted Hazaras could make a repayment if they found another nomad to lend money with whom they would enter into another *gerawi* agreement. Many were not lucky enough to be able to switch between different lenders and ultimately lost their lands (Ferdinand, 2006, pp. 233–7).

Consequently, across Hazarajat, a significant number of Hazara families were eventually forced into sharecropping relationship with absentee Kuchi landlords on what used to be their own land. Once a year, these landlords would visit the region only to collect their rent, which was usually three-quarters of the harvest. The strategy of land grabbing steadily progressed under King Zahir Shah (1933–1973) and continued up to the Republic of Daoud Khan (1973–1978). Towards the end of the 1960s, the nomads had acquired the ownership of 20 per cent of the farming land and between 60 to 80 per cent of all Hazaras were estimated to be indebted to the nomads (Edwards, 1986, p. 208).

It is also important to note that despite their close association with government officials in Hazarajat, the Pashtun nomads were not integrated into the Afghan state. Outside Hazarajat, Pashtun nomads continued to maintain a high level of autonomy. The contrast in relations of the local Hazaras and Pashtun nomads with the Afghan state can be illustrated by how they responded to the first civil registration process that was launched in the 1930s. During this period, for the first time, the Afghan government began to register all its citizens and distribute a national identity document, called a *tazkera*. The Hazaras showed no resistance and were quickly equipped with the *tazkera* with all its attendant obligations, including military conscription and payment of tax (Maqsudi, 1989, pp. 12–13). By contrast, the nomads saw the registration as a threat to their autonomy and independent way of life. Ferdinand (2006, pp. 216–220) notes that due to resistance, the registration of Kuchis was still not completed in the 1970s, four decades after it was launched.

Shift from Hazara's traditional local rebellion to modern national protest

While at the national level Hazaras were effectively marginalised until 1978, they were not entirely passive and acquiescent about their own political, economic and social exclusion and marginalisation. By 1978 the Hazara strategy towards the Afghan state underwent a qualitative shift with long-term consequences for the politics of the country more generally. Among the Hazaras, the shift entailed a gradual rise of an educated political elite who, in contrast to the traditional landed elites, were exposed to and inspired by modern ideologies of protest and struggles for social and political reform and revolution. At the national level, this shift of attitude also represented a change in locus of Hazara protests mainly from the villages, as in the rural rebellions of the nineteenth century, to more urban and modern forms of protest. Whereas the rural rebellion consisted of localised, and sporadic, incidents of revolt lacking significant ideological and political content, beginning in the late 1940s Hazara grievances and demands began to be expressed in more ideological terms, indicating more sophisticated, political, ethnic and religious forms of consciousness. With regard to the state, the former were largely concerned with limiting state intrusion into local affairs, and mostly emerged in response to localised grievances such as excessive taxation or disputes with Pashtun nomads. By contrast, the urban protests were articulated in the form of broader ideologies, and aimed at influencing and changing state policies in Kabul.

In the longer-term, these changes shifted the focus of Hazara elites towards negotiating and struggling for improved positions within the Afghan state, rather than without it. To illustrate these changes, I look at two incidents that represented two forms of protests against the Afghan state: the November 1945 rebellion led Ibrahim Khan Gawsawar in the Sharistan district of Day Kundi and an attempted coup led by Sayed Ismail Balkhi in March 1950 in Kabul.

Ibrahim Khan Gawsawar: 1945 rebellion against government taxation

As the previous chapter showed, during the 1891–1893 Hazara War, the Hazaras were led by their respective traditional landholding elites who were known as *mir* and *beg*. The eliticide that followed the defeat of Hazaras weakened the traditional Hazara elites and transformed the role of those who survived by making them subservient to the local official in their areas. Nonetheless, the Hazara elites did not completely submit to the authority of the state and at times of great pressure and persecution they were often the only individuals with the resources to take the leadership role. Many of these rebels continue to be remembered as the folk heroes, with Ibrahim Khan being the most prominent of them.

Ibrahim Khan, known as Bache Gawsawar, is probably the most representative of the rural Hazara rebels of the twentieth century. He rose to prominence in a rebellion against the district administration in the district of Shahristan in 1945. Yosuf Beg (also from Shahristan) was another prominent rebel, who gained a Robin Hood like reputation in the 1930s, for successfully resisting the local administration and avoiding arrest for nineteen years. Finally, he was apprehended and executed by the government in Kabul (Edwards, 1986, p. 208).

Ibrahim Khan came from a landholding family, traditional elites who historically led the Hazara rebellions against the state but took a subservient position to state officials after the 1890s. It appears the meaning of his nickname, *bache gawsawar* (the son of bull rider), has led Edwards (1986) to assume that he came from a humble social background. On the contrary, Ibrahim Khan came from an influential and relatively wealthy family of the Shahristan district. Musa Khan, his father who was actually known as *gawsawar*, was an influential local leader. He was also known for resistance against the state and was killed in the early 1930s in a skirmish with the Pashtun nomads (Dawlatabadi, 2006, pp. 357–93; Yazdani, 2007, pp. 61–70).

Ibrahim Khan's rebellion deserves particular attention because it shows the experiences of Hazaras with the Afghan state in one crucial respect: taxation. Following the conquest of Hazarajat in the 1890s, the government levied a series of taxes on the Hazaras. The historical rise in government demands along with the dominant role of the Pashtun nomads were amongst the most important factors prompting Hazara rebellions in the twentieth century. Mousavi describes six of these exorbitant taxes that were collected as late as the 1970s (Mousavi, 1998, pp. 134–5; Maqsudi, 1989, pp. 15–16, 33–4). The particular tax that triggered Ibrahim's rebellion was called *roghan-e shirkat*.

In the early 1940s, the government in Kabul collected clarified butter from the Hazaras. The main reason for the collection of clarified butter was a rapid decline in trading relationships of Afghanistan with the outside world during the Second World War, which significantly increased prices of key commodities in Kabul and other cities. The central government set up the *Cooperative Mamurin* (Cooperative for the Public Servants), with the goal of providing essential commodities at subsidised prices to public servants. One of these supposedly subsidised items was *roghan* or clarified butter, which was due to be purchased from the Hazara producers at the rate of 22 Afghanis per *sir* (7 kg). However, in practice, in Hazarajat, collection of the *roghan* became a new tax, which was collected forcefully and mostly free of charge. The local government officials required every Hazara household to produce certain amounts of *roghan*, in proportion to the amount of *shakh puli*, another tax they were paying for the cows, bulls, sheep and goats in their possessions. As an indication of the usual differences between the official policy and actual practice in Hazarajat, locally the tax became known as *roghan-e kata paawi*; *kata* meaning big as the local official's *paaw* was not the same as the standard *paaw*. According to Yazdani, local officials greatly increased the amount of *roghan* they collected:

> Officially, for every goat and sheep they collected one charak [1800 gr] but in practice it was five paaw [1 paaw = 450 gr]; for every donkey three

charak, in practice one sir [7200 gr], for every cow one sir [in practice five charak], for every horse 1.5 sir but in practice two sir. (2007, p. 63)

Furthermore, the *roghan* was collected on both male and female livestock. By 1945, collection of the *roghan* had created profound discontent across the region. Because most Hazaras were already under extreme pressure to service other taxes, including those on livestock, many families were unable to produce the required amount of *roghan*. It appears most fell in debt to the local government that usually accumulated annually. The local officials began to arrest and torture those who were unable to service their debt.

Among those who were unable to provide the required amount of *roghan* was Ibrahim Khan. This was despite the fact that he was relatively one of the wealthier men of the district. Ibrahim Khan gained the reputation of being a rebel (locally known as *Yaaghi*) first in 1944, when he protested against the flogging of the indebted Hazaras by government officials in Alqan, the district centre of Shahristan. Following a brief armed confrontation with the local government, he mostly stayed in his private residence, occasionally intervening in support of those who were under pressure to service *roghan* and other taxes. However, it is important to note that armed rebellion against government authority occurred after lengthy (often unsuccessful) attempts to communicate local grievances to local officials. In the spring of 1945, Ibrahim Khan travelled to Panjab, the seat of the governor of Hazarajat, to bring to the governor's attention the hardships local communities experienced in producing *roghan-e kata paawi*. Instead of being heard, he was arrested and jailed but released a month later. In the district of Sharistan, in 1945, Abdul Jalil, the Pashtun governor of the district, summoned the indebted villagers in groups, some of whom he ordered to be flogged in public. Yazdani (Yazdani, 2007, p. 63) contends that these beatings were usually accompanied by defamatory language towards Hazaras and Shi'ism.

In November 1945, Ibrahimi Khan led his major armed rebellion against the local administration of Shahristan. After a one-week siege, the district fell into the hand of the rebels, together with arms and ammunitions. The local officials were expelled and throughout the next winter, Shahristan remained under Ibrahim Khan's control. The ability of the central government to respond quickly was constrained by the heavy Hazarajat winter. Rumours also spread that this might be the beginning of a region-wide uprising, with Panjab the next target.

In Kabul, King Zaher Shah adopted a more conciliatory approach. During this year, he also replaced Prime Minister Hashim Khan, who had autocratically ruled the country since 1933, with his more liberal uncle, Shah Mahmud. In comparison to Hashim Khan's heavy-handed centralising policies, Shah Mahmud's reign saw the first, though short, period of experiment with political openness.

In the spring of 1946, Zahir Shah sent a delegation of Hazara dignitaries and religious figures, headed by Ismail Khan Mayar, the governor of Kabul, to Shahristan to negotiate with Ibrahim Khan. The delegation negotiated a peaceful end of the rebellion and persuaded Ibrahim Khan to travel to Kabul. Zahir Shah abolished *roghan-e shirkat* and placed Ibrahim Khan under house arrest in Kabul. A few years later, Ibrahim Khan was allowed to return to Shahristan. In 1949, he was implicated in another rebellion in Shahristan, which was led by another rebel, Qurban Zawar. This time the government deployed a military battalion, which was led by governor of Kabul. Government forces defeated the rebels and arrested Qurban Zawar. The military force also transferred Ibrahim Khan to the capital where he was kept under surveillance and also met Ismail Balkhi.

Ismail Balkhi: the first revolutionary Islamist

Born in 1919, to a religious family in Balkhab on the northern edge of the Hazarajat, Sayed Ismail Balkhi became the 'founder of not only Shi'a but also of Islamic political protest generally in Afghanistan' (Edwards, 1986, p. 214). Determining the exact details of the life of Balkhi is fraught with difficulties. What can one surmise from existing accounts such as a recent edited volume by Shojai (2004) is that at the age of six, Balkhi migrated with his family to the city of Mashhad in Iran, a holy and religious learning centre of the Shi'a world. In Mashahd, at a young age Balkhi was involved in political activities. In 1935, he participated in the famous protest against Reza Shah's radical modernisation policies. He escaped from the ensuing crackdown and returned to the city of Herat. In Herat, he became known for his political speeches and criticism of the government. In the early 1940s, he is believed to have founded *Hezb-e*

Irshad Islami (Party of Islamic Guidance) or *Hezb-e Ittehad-e Islami* (Party of Islamic Unity), a proto political party. The local government exiled him into the northern city of Mazar-e Sharif. In 1948, he moved to Kabul where he gained a reputation as a vocal critic of the government, fervent religious orator and poet.

In Kabul, Balkhi founded another circle that was known as *halqa-e jumhurikhwah* or republican circle (Kazemi, 2004). With the new political group, Balkhi's influence also extended to include prominent Sunnis, including Pashtuns and members of other ethnic groups. Significantly, the group recruited senior police and military officers, including Khwajah Muhammad Naim, a Pashtun who served as the police chief of Kabul, and Yasin Jan Mawlayye, a senior officer of the Afghan army. Ibrahim Khan Gawsawar, who was under house arrest in Kabul, was also a senior figure in the circle (Noktadan, 2004).

On 21 March 1950, the first day of solar New Year, the Republican Circle planned to overthrow the government by a coup and designate the country an Islamic Republic. However, the coup plan was leaked to the government by one of its members, and before the planned coup was launched all fourteen key members of the group were arrested. The government placed them in the notorious Dehmazang prison until 1964, when after the opening of political space with the experiment of a new constitutional democracy they were released. While Balkhi did not succeed in bringing any major social and political change, he influenced a new generation of activists who were inspired by his poems, revolutionary language and thoughts. During his time in prison, Balkhi wrote thousands of poems that introduced ideas of reform, sacrifice, struggle against despotism and most significantly a model of a revolutionary religious figure speaking in the name of poor and marginalised majority. By the time Balkhi was released, new forms of Islamist political ideologies had taken root in the country. After spending more than fourteen years in prison, Balkhi also suffered from poor health until his death in 1969.

Balkhi should be understood as a pioneer of a new generation of educated activists that emerged in Afghanistan and spawned major changes for Hazaras as well as the national politics of Afghanistan. In the internal politics of Hazara society, the educated class became the chief competitor of the traditional elites, the *mir, beg* and *arbaab* as well as the traditional *ulema*. The educated class introduced new concepts and strategies, profoundly shaping the way in which Hazaras began to see their history of persecution as well as their future in the country. While the traditional elites were primarily concerned with defending their local interests against state authorities, the educated class took a more national approach, which among other things, aimed at changing and influencing politics at the national level. Elsewhere, I have discussed the role of the Hazara educated class in articulating a shared history of persecution and marginalisation and developing a historical narrative that is central to the identity of Hazaras (Ibrahimi, 2012a). Here, I will make two general observations before drawing some general conclusions from the chapter.

First, from the introduction of the first modern school in Kabul in 1904 up until 1978, the Hazaras were discriminated against in the modern education sector of the country. Hazaras were particularly underrepresented in modern schools of Kabul where elite schools, the military academy, and colleges of Law and Political Science, and Islamic Law, had almost no Hazara students (Emadi, 1997, pp. 371–2; Jamali, 2002, pp. 94–5). The expansion of modern education beyond Kabul was slowest in Hazarajat. Dawlatabadi (Dawlatabadi, 2006, p. 279) claims in 1952 there were fewer than five formal schools throughout the region. According to Nayel (2000, pp. 77, 99, 130), whose account is based on Afghan government archives, the first school in the Hazarajat region was opened in 1938 in the Raqul area of Behsud, followed by a second school in Panjab district in 1946 and another in Jaghuri in 1953. By the 1960s, when the schools had significantly expanded nationally, the regional contrast was clearly tangible. According to official figures, in 1961 there were some 1,436 schools across the country. If divided by province (there were twenty-nine provinces after the 1964 constitution), there should have been 49.5 schools in each of them. Yet, there were only twenty primary and village schools in the entire Hazara region (Laali, 1993, p. 356).

Because of the official discrimination in the modern education sector, informal education that was dispensed through religious centres of learning such as mosques and madrassahs remained the prevalent and often the only institutions of education among Hazaras. Historically, to acquire an education, large number of Hazaras travelled to Shi'a madrassas in the holy cities of Iran and Iraq. By the 1960s, there were some 1,000–1,500 Hazaras attending the madrassas of Najaf alone (Bindemann, 1987). The number significantly increased in subsequent decades. However, a relatively small number of Hazaras, often from the elite families, attended modern schools in Kabul, whose number increased during the 1960s. As a result, among the Hazaras, despite their great internal tensions, both the ulema, who were trained in the madrassas, and the intelligentsia, who were product of modern schools, contributed to the emergence of modern, ideological and organised protests at the national level.

Second, the small Hazara educated class, including the ulema and intelligentsias, contributed to and were profoundly influenced by the broad ideological struggles that dominated Afghanistan during the second half of the twentieth century. By the 1960s, the relatively small but expanding educated class in Afghanistan was divided between the leftist, nationalist and Islamist ideologies. On the left, two major currents emerged which were inspired by the socialist models of the Soviet Union and China. In January 1965, *Hezb-e Democratic Khalq* (People's Democratic Party) was formed, which was followed by formation of the Progressive Youth Organization (PYO), popularly known as Sholay-i Jawid, a year later. These two organisations became fierce rivals as proponents of the Soviet- and Chinese-style communisms in the country. From the outset, the PYO included a number of prominent Hazaras in its leadership, placing it in a superior position in recruitment of Hazara intelligentsia. Two brothers, Akram Yari, a science teacher at the Habibiah High School and Sadiq Yari, a university lecturer, the sons of a Hazara landholding family from the Jaghuri district of Ghazni, figured prominently in the leadership of the PYO. Together with the family of Abdur Rahman Mahmudi, a well-known figure of the constitutionalist movement in Kabul, the Yaris formed the backbone of the Maoist Movement in the country. Akram was, however, a fervent Maoist ideologue and did not engage in ethnic politics and debates. But by virtue of their social orientation and ethnic origin, they tended to attract more support among their fellow Hazaras (Ibrahimi, 2012b).

By contrast, support for the PDPA remained low among the Hazara intelligentsia. It appears that persecution of Hazaras by the state pushed the Hazara intelligentsia towards more anti-state strategies. As a result, the Maoist strategy of overthrowing the government through a protracted people's war from the countryside was more attractive to the Hazaras compared with the PDPA's approach of working within the system and gradually infiltrating its various agencies. Nonetheless, the PDPA also included some important Hazara figures, most notably Sultan Ali Keshtmand who became a leading figure of its Parcham faction and served as prime minister in 1980s.

The second major ideological current that emerged during this period consisted of various forms of political Islamism. One of the most important Islamist currents was inspired by *Ikhwan-ul-muslemin* or the Egyptian Muslim Brotherhood that was spread into the country by Afghan students who studied at the famous Al-Azhar University in Cairo in the 1950s. The ideology manifested itself first in the *Jawanan-e Musulman* or Muslim Youth, a university-based student organisation that was established to challenge the leftist tendencies. It was led by Ghulam Muhammad Niazi, a graduate of Al-Azhar

It is also important to note here briefly that these early Hazara social and political movements, both leftists and Islamists, were not exclusively oriented towards the Afghan state. They contained the first ideas about what were being conceived as anomalies within the Hazara society. For example, a split was emerging between the younger and politically engaged and the more traditional and apolitical religious elites. Some younger *ulema* also questioned the privileged status of the traditional religious clerics and Sayeds. Similarly, the left-leaning intelligentsia with some radical Islamists also began to question the privileged status of the landed elites in Hazarajat. The traditional clerics who controlled the Shi'a mosques in Kabul largely restricted themselves to delivering religious sermons. Similarly, the Sayeds' claim to respect and *Khoms* (or one-fifth of the annual surplus of a family under Shi'a law) came under severe attacks from politically-minded educated Hazaras, who saw it as another form of unfair extraction from poor Hazaras. Ismail Moballegh, a well-known Hazara intellectual figure, is exemplary of the ideological struggle within the Hazara community. Moballegh was educated at the madrasas of Kabul and became one of the most prominent intellectual figures of the country in his time. He taught at Kabul University and in 1964 was elected to parliament. Moballegh delivered some of the most systematic critiques of the privileged status of the Sayeds in Afghanistan that brought him into bitter conflict with his former teachers such as Ayatollah Waez, who was also a Sayed. He is widely believed to have written *Naqd-e bar sayed garaye* (A Critique of Sayedism), a pamphlet that was circulated by an anonymous author in the 1960s. It has since become one of the most influential texts, questioning the religious premises of privileged social and economic status of the Sayeds in Hazara society.

Conclusion

The centralised state that the Afghan elites inherited from Abdur Rahman Khan was based on a complex coalition of political, religious and economic groups. The coalition included groups that participated in the Amir's centralising wars and excluded others such as Hazaras who resisted and were defeated in the wars. Afghanistan's centralising elites needed to choose one of these two options: restrict the apparatus of the state and selectively distribute the power and resources of the state to the winning coalition that emerged during Abdur Rahman Khan's wars of conquests or make it more inclusive and representative by opening it to all segments of the society. The second option could open avenues for national reconciliation, depoliticisation of ethnic cleavages and gradual development of a popular sense of nationhood. The decision to choose one of these two options was not easy. They entailed risks to the interests of the coalition of elites that benefited from the state at the national as well as subnational level. As the example of Amanullah Khan showed, some Afghan rulers were ready to take great risks to secularise and modernise the country rapidly because modernisation could increase the strength of the state. However, state elites were more reluctant to embrace serious social and political reforms that could make the state and politics more inclusive and representative because such reforms would mean sharing state power and its benefits with larger segments of the society.

The failure of Amanullah's reforms and the rebellions that led to collapse of the Afghan state in 1929 showed the fragility of the coalition of the centralising elites as well as the strength and persistence of the historical dynamics of the stability and instability of the Afghan state. The rebellion against Amanullah began when his modernisation reforms threatened the interests of Pashtun tribes. Even when it reached its full strength and forced the king to abdicate, it remained largely restricted to the Pashtun tribes of eastern and southern Afghanistan. Nader Khan defeated Kalakani and took the throne of Kabul by rebuilding the same coalition of the state and Pashtun tribes that Amanullah Khan's reform had undermined. Like Amir Abdur Rahman Khan, he mobilised the tribes with British support and promises of loot and plunder of Kabul and the Shamali Plain.

The effect of the ethnic relations that were instituted by Amir Abdur Rahman Khan and restored by Nader Khan was felt most at the subnational level. As the trading relations and transfer of land from the sedentary Hazaras to Pashtun nomads in Hazarajat showed, land-grabbing and exploitative economic relations were at the heart of ethnic relations that often existed independent of periodic liberalisation programmes in Kabul.

The rise of Afghanistan's educated class introduced new languages and fresh ways of conceiving, imposing and resisting power relations in the country. While Pashtun educated elites in the state gradually shifted towards ethnic conceptions of state and nation under the Musaheban, the educated Hazaras and, to a lesser extent, educated Tajiks and Uzbeks took the lead in challenging official nationalism in both temporal and spatial ways. The introduction of modern ideologies of protest also changed the Hazaras' response to the exclusionary state from localised, often single-issue, rebellions in the villages to modern urban protests that were framed in broader political and ideological terms and aimed at changing and influencing state policies at the national level. The rise of the Hazara educated class had profound impacts on the internal dynamics of the Hazara society. As will be shown in subsequent chapters, an intense competition between the intelligentsia, the *ulema* and the traditional leadership became a central feature of Hazara political dynamics in the 1980s.

4

THE RISE AND FALL OF A CLERICAL PROTO-STATE

HAZARAJAT, 1979–1984

Introduction

On 27 April 1978 the Marxist People's Democratic Party of Afghanistan (PDPA) seized power in a military coup in Kabul. Since its founding in January 1965 in Kabul, the party had become the most important protagonist of a Soviet-style socialist revolution in Afghanistan. The coup, which became known as the Saur Revolution (Saur because of the second solar month in which it took place) among its supporters, overthrew Daoud Khan, the last ruler of the Muhammadzai dynasty. Some members of the party had helped in Daoud Khan's own successful coup against his cousin, King Zaher Shah in 1973. The second coup pushed the country further towards the mayhem and violence that has continued until the present day.

The PDPA regime announced social and economic reform programmes that they claimed would herald the beginning of a change for the most disadvantaged and marginalised social groups of the country. The party leaders used their newfound power to implement perhaps the most ambitious and wide-ranging socioeconomic and political changes since the time of Amanullah Khan in the 1920s. In the words of Braithwaite the objective of the new regime was to set 'an example

117

to all the backward countries of the world of how to jump from feudal-ism straight to a prosperous, just society' (2011, p. 5). The Outlines of the Revolutionary Tasks of the new government proclaimed these as the main objectives: 'eradication of illiteracy; equality for women; an end to ethnic discrimination; a larger role for the state in the national economy; and the abolition of 'feudal and pre-feudal relationships' (2011, p. 42).

What distinguished the reform agenda of the PDPA was not only its strong socialist goals and rhetoric but also the speed and the scale with which it was planned and scheduled to be implemented. Massive pro-grammes of social and economic change were announced before there was any chance of evaluating their success. These included sweeping reforms of land tenure, gender relations and most controversially the role of religion in the society. In practice, these big ideals of rapid socioeconomic transformation were translated into an attractive and simple slogan for the country's downtrodden majority: *Kour, Kaali, Dodi* (shelter, clothes and food).

Broadly speaking, the Hazaras of Afghanistan optimistically wel-comed the overthrow of Daoud Khan's regime. However, like much of the rest of the country, the initial optimism among the Hazaras was soon shattered as the reform programmes of the new regime were announced locally in the Hazarajat. The programmes of social, eco-nomic and political changes met with local resistance. In response, the Khalq faction of the party, which came to power after the coup, insti-tuted a massive reign of terror across the country, in village and cities, as the regime started arresting landowners, mullahs, nonconformist intellectuals, dissident officers, professionals, and even rival factions of the PDPA itself. Like other parts of the country, Hazara khans, religious scholars, independent intellectuals and other notables were indiscriminately incarcerated, socially humiliated and effectively side-lined at the hands of inexperienced and arrogant party members in the regions. This unleashed a spontaneous and popular rebellion, directed against all state institutions, particularly the public schools which were seen as centres of Marxist indoctrination. In short, the PDPA coup and the unrest and armed opposition it unleashed, were only the beginning of a vicious cycle of bloodletting and violence that has continued ever since.

In the spring of 1979, spontaneously organised uprisings spread across the Hazarajat. By June almost all parts of the region were liberated from government control, allowing Hazara society the first opportunity since the 1890s to reorganise itself free of state control and repression. In September that year a grand assembly of leaders of the rebellion or their representatives from all parts of the region came together in Waras district of Bamyan province where they announced the formation of the *Shura-ie Inqilaab-i Ittifaq Islami Afghanistan* (Revolutionary Council for the Islamic Unity of Afghanistan, referred to as the *Shura* hereafter). The liberation of Hazarajat from government control marked the beginning of years of virtual autonomy for the Hazaras that they lost only to the Taliban in 1998. Just a few months after the formation of the Shura and spread of uprisings across the country, in December 1979, the Soviet Union sent its troops to restructure the PDPA regime, under the leadership of Babrak Karmal from the Parcham faction of the party. The new cabinet included Sultan Ali Keshtmand, a Hazara member of the party, who became the minister of planning and Chairman of the Council of Ministers throughout most of the 1980s. However, in Hazarajat for much of the 1980s, the presence of the central government was limited to the centre of Bamyan and there was only sporadic fighting between the Hazara organisations and the central government and Soviet forces at the fringes of Hazarajat.

This chapter examines the Shura as an attempt to build a proto-state within the broader context of Afghanistan. If we define the key characteristics of the state as a polity having political legitimacy, an administrative system, military control over its territory, providing some services and enjoying official recognition as a state by external powers, the Shura had most of these, at least to some extent or in an embryonic form. The chapter also explains why it nonetheless collapsed after just five years.

The origins of the Shura: *A state within a state*

To understand the *Shura*, it is important to make a distinction between immediate factors such as the PDPA coup and its programmes of rapid change and the longer-term context and history of the Hazaras in Afghanistan. The *Shura* was formed following a series of spontaneous local reactions in the Hazarajat against the radical and hasty modernisation policies of the PDPA regime in Kabul. Thus, opposition to the PDPA was one of the immediate causes of the uprising. In more historical terms, it was also a rebellion of the Hazaras against the historically Pashtun-dominated and Sunni central state. In practice, the effects of PDPA policies were reinforced by historical persecution of Hazaras. A historical perception of injustice and deprivations under the central Afghan government was being reinforced by persecution of Hazara *ulema* and intellectuals under the Khalq faction of the PDPA in cities as well as rural areas, and this gave it its political legitimacy. Thus, the immediate goal of the uprisings was to liberate the region from the control of a repressive and discriminatory central government that had also lost its Islamic legitimacy because of its modernist and communist reform programmes. Once the goal was achieved the rebel leaders concentrated their efforts on defending and securing control of the liberated areas of the Hazarajat until the establishment of an 'Islamic republic' in the country (interview with Jamal Fakuri Behishti, Kabul March 2006). Until that day, the *Shura* was planning to deal with all political, military and judicial affairs of the region and prepare for collective struggle for the rights of the community in future Afghanistan. This was, in fact, the main factor that united rival socio-political groups under the *Shura*, even if they never meant it to be an exclusively Shi'a state or to be hostile to the majoritye Sunni population of the country.

While the *Shura* was meant to be a mini-state, at least temporarily, it was deeply influenced by the experience of Hazara elites with the Afghan state. The founders of the *Shura* designed it to administer the region along the lines of previous Afghan governments. Various agencies were established to provide education, communication and health services to its citizens. The *Shura* introduced taxation and identity cards and demanded its citizens perform military services. It demobilised independent armed groups in areas under its control. Outsiders and foreigners were required to obtain a letter stamped by *Shura* officials to travel through its territory (Farr, 1988, p. 57). The *Shura* armed forces were composed of 'police' groups that would provide security to its citizens against internal threats, and of more organised military fronts that would defend the region against the central government. The latter were required to wear uniforms (Ayatollah Beheshti, 1982).

The *Shura* was meant to be an interim arrangement. There was no ambition to build a permanent separate Hazara state. One can see in the *Shura* literature a high level of emphasis by its leadership on territorial integrity of the country and solidarity with the other Sunni and Shi'a resistance organizations. The first *Shura* declaration, in articles 7 and 8, stated that the organisation would administer the region, 'in solidarity with the other Muslim brothers', until the full establishment in the country of an Islamic Republic[1] that could guarantee 'social justice' and 'equal rights' for all Afghan Muslims (Shura, n.d.).

The *ulema* who dominated the *Shura* shared some important commonalities with their communist rivals. Like the communists who advocated a socialist revolution as a panacea for all problems of the country, including historical persecution of the Hazaras, the Shi'a *ulema* in the *Shura* leadership prescribed Islamic social justice as the ultimate solution. This concept, which was not clearly articulated, implied that equality and mutual social responsibility for the believers would be delivered by the implementation of Islamic laws. Although the region controlled by *Shura* was almost exclusively Hazara, the language and rhetoric of its leaders was mostly religious. Accordingly, the Islamic character of the organization was strongly emphasised internally by appointing the *ulema* to all key and decision making positions and externally in its relations with the other resistance organisations. Historical grievances and demands for a better place for the Shiites in the future of the country were expressed in purely religious terms. Ethno-nationalism was deemed as non-Islamic and divisive in the Muslim country. Past repression and discrimination against the Hazaras were largely blamed on the previous regimes, which according to them were not genuinely Islamic and were influenced by foreign powers. Nonetheless, the *Shura* claimed to represent millions of Afghan Shiites, whose rights they were seeking to promote. One of the main demands was the restructuring of the existing administrative structure of the country. It was strongly believed that the division of the Hazarajat into seven different provinces by the past regimes was an attempt to marginalise the Shiite/Hazara population politically and to minimise their share of political power and national resources. As a first step, they produced their own administrative division of the Hazara areas according to a more local logic, which resulted in the creation of seven provinces and forty-two districts (Ayatollah Behishti, 1982).

The Shura *and emerging ideological and political conflicts among the Hazaras*

The *Shura* reflected on-going social tensions among different Hazara elite groups and the strategies they advocated for improving the situation of Hazaras in Afghanistan. These tensions were apparent in the first region-wide meeting that resulted to the formation of the *Shura* in September 1979. The participants at the first *Shura* meeting represented different socio-political groups of the Hazara society with different and even conflicting ideologies and visions for the future of the region and that of the Hazaras. To many of them the *Shura* was an interim arrangement that could serve as a power sharing mechanism and temporarily fill the vacuum left by the collapse of the government in the region. For the long term, many of them were looking for different vehicles that could better serve their ideological and political objectives. These differences gradually surfaced as bitter internal rivalries that impeded the development of the *Shura* as an effective and cohesive organisation.

Despite the temporary nature of the *Shura* in the eyes of many of its founders, the organisation marked a highly consequential change in the politics of the Hazaras and Afghanistan more generally: the rise of the *ulema* in leadership of war and politics of the country. Among the Hazaras, the *Shura* marked the beginning of a steady rise of a new generation of *ulema* who gradually side-lined the other groups and have since established a monopoly over political leadership of Hazara society. However, the *ulema* also represented two very different lines of religious interpretation that influenced their political behaviours and leadership styles. By the late 1970s there were two dominant theories in the Shi'a world with regard to the role of the *ulema* in the public and political affairs of Muslim countries. Ayatollah Kho'i, top Shi'a *mujtahed* (jurist) of the time, strongly advocated and preached in favour of a non-political role for the *ulema*, who, he believed, should focus on the provision of religious guidance through teaching and preaching. This, however, did not mean that in times of crisis, the *ulema* could not become more active in politics, but politics was generally seen as an unnecessary part of the mandate of the religious establishment. In Afghanistan, this view was represented by Ayatollah Sayed Ali Beheshti, the president of the *Shura*, and other Kho'i followers who had participated in the armed uprisings only after they also became the targets of indiscriminate arrests and persecutions by the regime in Kabul. There was however another strand of thought that was formulated by more activist *ulema* such as Ismail Balkhi in Afghanistan from the late 1940s. Ayatollah Khomeini, the leader of the 1979 Islamic Revolution of Iran, articulated the most advanced version of this line of thinking. He argued that to enforce Islamic laws, the *ulema* needed to establish an Islamic state under their own leadership. Hence, he developed and proposed the doctrine of *Welayat e Faqih* (guardianship of the jurist), which was the core philosophy of the Islamic revolution in Iran. In Afghanistan, Khomeini inspired a new generation of revolutionary Islamists who were not only opposed to the Kabul regime but who also sought to bring radical social, political and cultural changes in society.

In addition to these two groups of *ulema*, the third group in the *Shura* was the secular *mirs* and *begs*, the landed Hazara elites that since the 1890s had become subservient to central government officials in the region. The last group was the Hazara intelligentsia that was the product of modern education both in the country and abroad. This group shared a secular worldview with most of the *mirs* but was mostly attracted to ethno-nationalist and left-wing ideologies.

The election of Beheshti as the leader was a compromise between these groups and their interests. A religious figure from Waras district who had obtained prominence in religious education in Iraq, Beheshti was influential even if he did not command a binding religious authority over other key *Shura* leaders, many of whom were also senior Shi'a *ulema*. In addition to his religiously respectable character, he was believed to be militarily and politically weak and unable to pose serious threats to the interests of other more powerful contending groups. Some powerful Hazara *mirs*, most notably Muhammad Hussain Khan Shahi of Waras, who hosted the first *Shura* assembly, strongly backed him in the meeting as their candidate for leadership. Shahi believed that since Beheshti was from Waras, his district, and had traditionally been dependant on his patronage, he would be able to exercise influence over the organization in the future (Farr, 1988, p. 56; Harpviken, 1995).

The traditionalist non-political ulema

The followers of Kho'i had no desire or interests to engage in politics. Nor they were trained for that. When they had returned from traditional Shi'a learning centres in Iraq in the 1960s, they had concentrated their activities on building centres of religious preaching and teaching in different parts of Afghanistan. They did not advocate any radical social revolution and developed close links to the Shi'a upper classes, who served as their main source of funding. And like most *mirs* after the 1890s, many of the traditionalist *ulema* supported the past governments or at least avoided protesting against their policies (Dawlatabadi et al., 1999, p. 90).

The case of Ayatollah Beheshti, who followed the Kho'i line of interpretation, and his role before and after the April coup of 1978, clearly illustrate a traditionalist non-political approach to the role of the *ulema* in an Islamic society. Beheshti was also a Sayed, a social group that claim descent from the family of Prophet Muhammad and the original twelve Imams of the Shi'as. The Sayeds, thanks to their religious status, enjoyed a privileged social and economic position among Hazaras, received religious donations by their followers, and were closely tied to the Hazara upper class, the *mirs*. Upon his return from Iraq, Beheshti settled in Waras, where in 1963 he built a house and a *madrasah*, a religious school, on plots of lands donated by Muhammad Hussain Khan Shahi. As with many members of this social group, he and other Kho'i students never publicly protested against the central government or its local collaborators. Instead, they appreciated the religious donations of the upper class families and adopted a quietist approach towards the Afghan government, despite the fact that they did not view the central government and its local administrations as Islamic or just towards the rights of the Shi'a community of the country (interviews with Shi'a *ulema*, Kabul December 2005).

After the 1978 coup in Kabul, it was the widespread arrests and persecution of the both the traditionalist *ulema* and the landlords as 'reactionary' and 'feudal' elements that drove them towards opposition activities. Many prominent *ulema* were arrested and persecuted in cities as well as in rural areas. Sayed Waez, a senior representative of Ayatollah Kho'i in Afghanistan, was arrested and killed, allegedly by the government in Kabul. This group of the *ulema* was particularly targeted by the regime as they were closely tied to the upper class families such as the rural landlords and urban businessmen. However, once in opposition, they lacked organisation and even minimal political or military leadership skills. Hence, they largely relied on religious and voluntary support of the population and particularly that of the *mirs*. They were not trained to build military or political organisations and instead assumed that the popular and voluntary mobilisation that brought them to power would continue to exist. Ironically, these weaknesses of the traditional *ulema* also made them more acceptable to the *mirs* and the radical Islamists, as temporary leaders of the *Shura*. Therefore, the paradox of the quietist *ulema* conquering political power was in a sense more apparent than real (interviews with participants of the *Shura* Assembly, Kabul, December 2005).

The long-standing friendly relations between Kho'i's followers and the *mirs* also resurfaced in an alliance between the two groups in the *Shura*. Beheshti as leader of the *Shura* was strongly backed by Muhamad Hussain Khan, his traditional financial sponsor and ally, as well as by other landlords of the region. Hazara *mirs* preferred to exercise indirect influence over the *Shura* leadership. Therefore, the *mirs* rallied around Beheshti as his key allies and provided the basic financial backing and primary military personnel. Many of Beheshti's most loyal commanders were the sons and relatives of the *mirs* who recruited their peasants as the soldiers (interviews with Hazara *mirs* from Day Bamyan and Day Kundi, Kabul, November 2005).

The radical Islamist ulema

As mentioned in the previous chapter, Sayed Ismail Balkhi was the first major Shi'a scholar to engage in a radical Islamist protest in Afghanistan. During the 1960s, radical Islamist politics gained new dimensions as many more began engaging in political activities and in protests against the discriminatory policies of the Afghan monarchy towards the Shi'a and particularly the Hazara community in Afghanistan. Thus, a significant network of activists existed before the April coup of the 1978. Similar to the activists of the Afghan Muslim Brotherhood, the Shi'a Islamists demanded an Islamic state, but one where the Sunni and Shiites would enjoy equal rights and privileges (Edwards, 1986).

In contrast to the quietist approach of the traditionalist *ulema*, the Islamists sought a wide array of radical political, economic, cultural and social changes. They were offering and propagating a new vision for an Islamic society where social justice and equality would be upheld, where all believers both Shi'a and Sunni would be equally respected and where political power and economic resources would be equitably distributed. To achieve their goals, they were prepared to resort to violence against their adversaries. They did not oppose the Soviet-backed regime in Kabul because it persecuted them but rather because it was not an Islamic regime and many of its policies violated and undermined their fundamental ideological values and principles.

The leaders of this group of *ulema* mainly came from the lower classes of Hazara society and believed that the internal structure of the Hazara community was unfair and needed to be changed in favour of the dispossessed. Long before the 1978 coup they attempted to promote their agendas for reforming the Hazara society. Following the collapse of the government in the region and parallel to the struggle against the Soviets and Kabul government, they vigorously started to apply their own social and political reforms in territories under their control. They found a particularly conducive environment for focusing on radical reforms of the Hazara society after the Hazarajat was fully liberated from government control and faced no significant military threat by the government (interviews with former *Shura* and other mujahedin leaders, Kabul, February 2006).

To them, the landlords and the traditionalist *ulema* were reactionary forces and were part of the ruling propertied classes opposed to social and political reforms. As such, Beheshti was seen as an obstacle to long-term revolutionary programmes. In addition to differences in religious interpretation, he was now serving the interests of the landlords who, according to the Islamists, had traditionally been the agents of repressive central governments and had unduly taken control of the scarce resources of the impoverished region. Furthermore, he was also a Sayed, who according to the Islamists had used their alleged ancestral attribution to the Prophet Muhammad's family unfairly to claim a privileged position in the Shi'a community (interview with Ali Jan Zahedi, a former leader of Pasdaran, Kabul, and January 2006).

As a result, the radical Islamists' participation in a *Shura* dominated by traditionalist *ulema* and the *mirs* was inevitably going to be a temporary affair. Many abandoned the *Shura* from the beginning in pursuit of establishing or joining organisations that were more to their liking. One of their key leaders, who had participated in the first *Shura* meeting, stated that he left the *Shura* in the early days because: 'it was dominated by the traditionalists and khans and lacked a conscious political leadership' (interview with Ali Jan Zahedi, Kabul, January 2006).

Sadiqi Nili, a deputy head of the Jehad Commission of *Shura* (see below), is a typical example. In 1963, he established a madrasah in his home district in Day Kundi that was a school of religious training as well as a centre of political activities. Unlike Beheshti's madrasah, Sadiqi used his madrasah to train a generation of motivated Islamists with a radical political ideology and a religious worldview. In 1971, he was designated as *Wakil*, or representative of Ayatollah Khomeini in the country.[2] He preached against the central government as discriminatory, corrupt and most importantly un-Islamic. As far as local politics were concerned, he protested against the role of the landlords, as agents of the central government as well as an exploitative upper class that mistreated the local population. He further undermined the *mirs* and the local administrations by resolving and settling social conflicts and land disputes according to the Sharia (Day Kundi, 1993, p. 35).

The early liberation of the Day Kundi district from government control in 1979 allowed Sadiqi and his like-minded supporters to consolidate their control over the territory and pursue their social reform agendas. They vehemently turned against the *mirs* and applied the harshest methods to punish them for their past and also their continued resistance to the reform programmes. Most khans were jailed or killed and their lands and properties were distributed among the poorer families (interviews with Hazara *mirs* from Bamyan and Day Kundi, Kabul, November 2005).

The secular landed elite

With the fall of central government in Hazarajat in 1979, the fate of the landed elites changed more than any other social and political group among Hazaras. Their social and political status had profoundly changed with the subjugation of Hazarajat at the hand of the iron-handed Amir Abdur Rahman in the 1890s. After the eliticide that followed the

Hazara War in the 1890s, a new generation of Hazara khans and *mirs* emerged, largely co-opted by the central government in Kabul, which in return recognised their privileged status and local influence within the state structure. Their new influence, was however strictly limited within district boundaries and was subject to the endorsement of the local administrations. As most parts of the mountainous region were inaccessible for several months of the year, the government often used the khans to collect the taxes and ensure stability and order in those areas (Canfield, 1972).

The ordinary Hazaras had an entirely different experience under the Afghan state. They remained excluded from economic and social development opportunities within the state and were discriminated against throughout the century. The seizure and distribution of most of the fertile parts of the region to the new Pashtun settlers exacerbated the living conditions of the predominantly peasant Hazaras. The affiliation and collaboration of the khans with central governments, which were seen as discriminatory and repressive by most Hazaras, left them with quite a negative reputation within the community. By 1978, most Hazara landed elites who collaborated with the government were recognised for their wealth, privileged access to the government administrations and betrayal of the long-denied rights and grievances of the Hazaras within the Afghan state (Grevemeyer, 1988).

By refusing to recognise the privileged role of the landed elites, while at the same time failing to attract new socio-political groups, the PDPA regime undermined the only support base of the central government in the region. Declared a reactionary force and symbol of Afghan feudalism by the new regime, the Hazara *mirs* retreated to their past role of leadership of opposition to the central government. In many parts of the Hazarajat, the Hazara *mirs* played an instrumental role in igniting and mobilising the first anti-government uprisings. They provided the basic resources and arms for the fighters because they were the only people in possession of quantities of arms (interviews with Hazara *mirs* from Bamyan and Day Kundi, Kabul, November 2005). The *mirs* were mostly secular in their worldviews and did not share the Islamic radicalism of other Hazara resistance leaders. Many of their children had obtained a modern education, some of them were attracted to different Maoist factions that I will describe in more detail later in the chapter.

Opposition to the government, though probably inevitable, posed new challenges to the continued influence of the *mirs* in the Hazara community. Their connection to the state, which was the main external guarantor of their privileged position, became a liability in the context of liberated Hazarajat after 1979. Their influence was limited to their districts of origin and personal rivalries also impeded their role as regional leaders. Hence, they lacked the necessary legitimacy to emerge as public political leaders and had to rely on 'softer' clerical figures such as Beheshti, who were traditionally their allies. The election of Beheshti as leader of the *Shura* was, nonetheless, a matter of concerns for some of the khans. Muhammad Ali Khan and Muhammad Amir Khan, of the Panjab and Laal districts respectively, expressed their concerns in the first *Shura* meeting that the rise of the *ulema* to political leadership within the resistance might threaten the future role of the khans. However, their failure to agree on a single *mir* as a regional leader and persistent backing of Beheshti by Hussain Khan, as a moderate cleric, resulted in the rise of the *ulema* as leaders of the Shi'a and Hazara resistance organisations and marked the beginning of the marginalisation of *mirs* (interviews with Shi'a *ulema*, Kabul, December 2005).

The intelligentsia

Most modern educated Hazaras in Afghanistan did not support the pro-Soviet PDPA regime in Kabul. They were mostly affiliated to various Maoist factions that originated from the PYO. Akram Yari, a Hazara from the landholding family of the Jaghuri district in Ghazni, was the most prominent Chinese-style socialist revolutionary in the country. The PYO, which became known as Sholay-i Jawid (Eternal Flame) after the periodical it published, was the main Afghan Maoist organisation and a long-standing rival of the PDPA in the 1960s. In its first months in power, the Khalq faction of the PDPA arrested Akram Yari and hundreds of other Hazara members of the organisation, who mostly disappeared into the prisons of the regime. As a result, the organisation lost its leadership and only smaller groups of its members who survived took up arms alongside the other rebel leaders to fight against the PDPA (Ibrahimi, 2012). Many PYO and other independently educated Hazaras had played a role in the overthrow of government administrations in many districts of the region. Some of them participated in the first *Shura* assembly where it was decided that one intellectual from every district would serve as a member of the *Shura*'s central committee (interview with Ustad Babah, a former *Shura* official, Kabul, December 2005).

There was a smaller group of Hazara intelligentsia that espoused a more ethno-nationalistic ideology. This group attempted to promote a secular ethnic identity. They focused on the persecution, exclusion and humiliation of the Hazaras under the Afghan state, including the extensive Hazara lands that were occupied by Pashtun settlers in southern parts of Hazarajat. To them Hazarajat was actually Hazaristan, the land of Hazaras, which was marginalised and broken up under the Afghan state (interview with Jalal Awhidi, a Hazara author and former member of *Ittehadiah*, Kabul, March 2006).

At this point, the *Tanzim-e Nasle Naw-e Hazara Moghul* (Organization of the New Generation of the Moghul Hazaras), based in Quetta (Pakistan), was the main proponent of this ideology. Since its establishment in the late 1960s in Quetta, the *Tanzim* had consistently attempted to promote a secular ethnic identity and had developed contacts with Hazaras in other countries and regions, including many in Kabul. For example, Haji Ghulam Rasul, the head of the delegation that called for the *Shura* assembly, was a businessman in Kabul, where during the 1970s he would receive and distribute the magazines of the *Tanzim* among educated Hazaras in the city (interview with Ghulam Ali Haidari, Chairman of Tanzeem-e Nasl-e Naw-e Hazara Moghul, Quetta, November 2005). The collapse of the government in the Hazarajat and the subsequent migration of local resistance leaders to Quetta allowed the *Tanzim* to engage actively in ethnic politics in Afghanistan.[3] In fact, the delegation that called for the *Shura* assembly in Waras represented the views and aspirations of the Hazara intelligentsia based in Quetta Pakistan. The *Tanzim* leaders sent the delegation to seize the opportunity, after the collapse of the government in the region, to unite and organise Hazaras under a leadership that could defend their interests and promote their rights in the future of the country (interview with Jawad Eisar, Former Secretary-General of Tanzim-e Nasl-e Naw-e Hazara Moghul, Quetta, November 2005). But the assembly environment dominated by the *ulema* was not receptive to the leftists and ethno-nationalists and their secular opinions (Ayatollah Beheshti, 2006).

In fact, the advent of the *Shura* with its conservative clerical leadership was certainly not a favourable outcome for the mainly secular ethno-nationalists and leftists who initially proposed it. Haji Rasul did not join the *Shura* as he thought it was going to be an Islamic organisation that could not serve the interests of the Hazaras. Instead, he returned to Quetta where he became the deputy leader of the nationalist *Ittehadiah Islami-e Mujahedin Afghanistan* (Islamic Association of the Mujahedin of Afghanistan). The *Ittehadiah* leadership included key members of *Tanzim* as well as many Hazaras resistance leaders that had fled from Afghanistan. The *Tanzim* members of the *Ittehadiah* chose to take low profile positions in the organisation, mainly serving as its central committee members and advisors (Gharjistan, 1987, pp. 1–2).

In Afghanistan, educated Hazaras who shared the *Tanzim* style of ethno-nationalism were a minority. For the leaders of *Tanzim* and *Ittehadiah* all Hazaras, regardless of their social and ideological affiliations, were the same. On the other hand, both leftists and Islamists mostly viewed ethno-nationalism with contempt, the former seeking a multi-ethnic peasant revolution and the latter viewing ethno-nationalism as being against the principles of unity and solidarity of the *Ummah*. Shaikh Aman Fasihi, a cleric from Jaghuri district, who had been chosen as the first leader of the *Ittehadiah*, soon resigned from his position and left for Iran in search of organisations with more Islamic leanings (interview with Muhamamd Aman Fasihi, Jaghuri, December 2005). He was replaced by Abdul Hussain Maqsudi, from the Nawur district of Ghazni province who had been a parliamentarian in the 1960s.

Persecuted by both the Kabul regime and the Islamists in Hazarajat, many Hazara leftists joined the *Ittehadiah*, apparently sympathising with the ethno-nationalist agendas of leaders of the organisation and downplaying or concealing their leftist affiliations. They had infiltrated the cultural and administrative offices of the organisation and were clandestinely directing some of its resources towards their own small underground factions in Afghanistan (interviews with former *Shura* and *Ittehadiah* members, Kabul and Quetta, November–December 2005). The penetration of the *Ittehadiah* by the leftists and its secular and ethnic character provoked reactions by the *Shura* as well as the Islamists organisations that were gaining ground in the Hazarajat. *Ittehadiah*'s relationship with the *Shura* was already sour due to differences over its method of distribution of foreign assistance and its persistence in maintaining sole control of the *Shura*'s foreign relations. Eventually, because of its secular and ethnic agendas, the leftists' influence and power competition, the *ulema* declared *Ittehadiah* a Maoist organisation and accused it of being supported by China. In the winter of 1980, *Ittehadiah* activities were officially banned by the *Shura* leadership. *Fatwas* were issued, denouncing the organisation as a *Maoist* and *Mogholist* organisation trying to undermine the Islamic revolution. Its only military and major support base in Jaghuri district of Ghazni was attacked. Various Islamist organisations in cooperation with Sayed Arif, the *Shura* governor of Jaghuri, joined together to attack and take the only base of *Ittehadiah* in the district.

Civil and military structure of the Shura

Before the *Shura* was formed, local leaders of the initial anti-government uprisings had set up district or sub-district committees to deal with local affairs and the defence of the liberated areas against possible government retaliations. These committees were localistic in nature and lacked the necessary vision and leadership for coordinating the mujahedin beyond the district level (interviews with former Hazara mujahedin leaders, Kabul and Ghazni, November–December 2005).

The main challenge for the *Shura* was to replace or integrate these local organisations into a region-wide political and organisational structure. For this purpose, the *Shura* in its central committee established a number of commissions, including a Jehadi Commission, a Judicial Commission, a Finance Commission and a Cultural and Public Relations Commission. The Jehad Commission was tasked to coordinate military activities, which would be financially supported by the Finance Commission that, in turn, would collect the religious dues and taxes. And the Cultural Commission, predominantly run by *ulema* trusted by the *Shura* leadership, was given the task of providing education and communication services and religious propagation and training. The Judicial Commission, exclusively led by the *ulema*, would deal with judicial matters and resolve local disputes. It was planned that the commissions would open offices at all provincial and district levels (Shura Office in Iran, The Shura Declaration: n.d). However, the attainment of these goals was constrained by a number of factors, most notably a lack of resources and professional cadres, compounded by internal rivalries. Furthermore, the clerics appointed to key positions of all agencies were not familiar with the functions of a modern state and methods of providing efficient services.

The Afghan state apparatus, which was overthrown by founders and leaders of the *Shura* was chosen as a model for future administration. The region was divided into seven provinces administered by a provincial governor that would be appointed by the organisation's headquarters, and every province was divided into seven districts. The provincial governors were responsible for coordinating all judicial, educational, financial and cultural institutions in their designated areas whilst a military commander would deal with the military affairs (Grevemeyer, 1988, p. 214).

However, the actual implementation of the plans and consolidation of the centralised agencies proved to be too ambitious. Militarily and religiously, the *Shura* leadership encountered major challenges once it began to expand and integrate the local leaders and committees into a unified organisation. Beheshti's actual influence was limited to Waras and surrounding areas where he was backed by the powerful khan of Waras, Hussain Khan Shahi (interviews with former *Shura* and other mujahedin leaders, Ghazni, January 2006).

Furthermore, some important Shi'a *ulema* were also competing to limit Beheshti's influence. Most notable was Sadiqi Nili, deputy head of the Jehad commission, who controlled most of the Day Kundi district with a significant number of armed forces under his command. Another such religious figure was Muhammad Akbari, the first chief military commander of the *Shura*, who like Beheshti was from Waras. In the spring of 1980, Akbari was replaced as the chief military commander by Sayed Hussain Ali from Nawur district of Ghazni province, known as Sayed Jaglan, and was instead appointed as provincial administrator in the *Shura*'s Behsud and Turkman valley province. Sayed Hussain Jaglan, the second and long-standing chief military commander, also failed to develop a unified military structure beyond Nawur. Akbari, who later became a prominent figure in politics of the region, com-

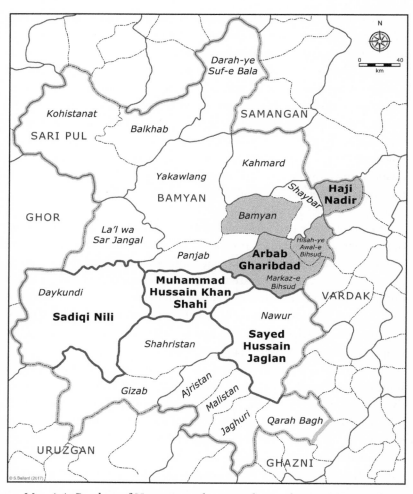

Map 4.1: Borders of Hazarajat and main military players, 1979–1984

manded small organised groups of fighters in Bamyan, Behsud districts of Wardak and Turkmen Valley in Parwan (interviews with former *Shura* and Pasdaran leaders, Kabul and Ghazni, November–December 2006).

Militarily, the *Shura* was a loose alliance of several local strongmen who had established themselves locally by demonstrating leadership and organizational skills in the overthrow of government district administrations prior to the formation of the *Shura*. Each controlled a different part of the region and had independently set up his own local military and administrative structure. Some of the key military commanders were not included in the original *Shura* assembly and had announced their accession after it was formed. Sayed Hussain, the deputy chief military commander of the *Shura*, is a case in point. In spring 1979, well before the formation of the *Shura*, he was chosen as the chief commander of the Ghazni Front, the first mainly Hazara front to emerge after the anti-government uprising. His forces were primarily composed of volunteers, one from every so many households, who would rotate every fifteen days. These forces were mobilised and controlled by 16 subordinate commanders, who were also representing particular localities or tribes. However, despite the widespread popular support of the early months, this system could not work for long. The rotation of the fighters made it difficult for him to build a cohesive and disciplined force and the local populations soon lost their interest and enthusiasm to volunteer the necessary support (interview with Ustad Khadem Nader, a former Shura leader, Kabul, April 2006).

The *Shura*'s relationship with local actors and communities was also complicated by its inability to offer much in return for the demands it was making on local communities. There were very few economic and political incentives for the local commanders to integrate into the *Shura* as an organization. The failure to attract significant foreign assistance (see below) forced it into depending increasingly on collection of religious taxes from its citizens, who were among the poorest in the country, as the main source of its revenues. It planned to build its military force through involuntary conscription, and lacking its own resources, it usually demanded local communities to provide food and accommodation for its military forces. *Shura* forces deployed outside their districts of origin often coerced the local population to pay for their food, accommodation and other expenses. These measures appear to have alienated most of the local communities soon after the Shura was formed. For instance, *Shura* military forces deployed from other districts to Jaghato district in Ghazni and Turkman valley of Parwan provinces were increasingly unpopular locally. Local commanders of the two strategically important districts used this to justify their own hold over the districts and call for the withdrawal of *Shura*'s forces (interviews in Ghazni, December 2005 and in Kabul February 2006).

Given the significance of military strength in the resistance activities, many of the commanders had already begun to play political roles as well. The majority of these leaders already enjoyed legitimacy deriving from the endorsement of committees representing local and tribal identities.[4]

In many ways, the *Shura* leadership underestimated or failed to acknowledge its internal limitations and the imminent ideological and political splits in the region as well as in Iran, where factional splits within the Islamic movement would soon begin being reflected in Afghanistan. Attempts at expansion and consolidation of the *Shura* beyond its headquarter resulted in tensions and conflicts with the local leaders who were not prepared to compromise their autonomy by fully integrating into the organisation. The *Shura* leadership could only appoint governors for the five out of its seven provinces. And most of those appointed faced opposition and were challenged by local leaders (interviews with a former senior *Shura* leader, Kabul, March 2006). At the same time, domestic and foreign political dynamics were undergoing changes, with serious implications for resistance organisations such as the *Shura*, which did not have foreign sponsors and ideological alignments. The foreign ideological and material assistance that came from the West and the Arab countries was increasingly channelled to the new and more radical Sunni groups that were emerging on the Afghan political stage and were prepared to fight the regime in Kabul and its Soviet sponsor.

The idea of building an Islamic state was also fraught with challenges given the limitations and weakness of Beheshti as a leader and the obvious lack of military and financial resources to exercise the key functions of the state. Beheshti was a religious figure only and his chief military commander, Sayed Jaglan, lacked the necessary strength to force other commanders to comply with the *Shura*'s orders. He was only one of several strong military commanders of the *Shura*, who were competing for territorial control and political leadership at the local level. And his predecessor, Muhammad Akbari, continued independently to run his own small organised groups in various parts of the region (interviews with former *Shura* and Pasdaran leaders, Kabul, February 2006).

Generally speaking, the *Shura*'s military commanders limited their military activities within the Hazarajat region. They did not pursue a proactive and aggressive strategy in its relations with the government in Kabul. Their main mission, overthrowing the structures of an undesirable state in the region, had already been achieved. In the early 1980s, there were just three main military *Shura* fronts that that were directly in contact with government and Soviet forces in the strategically more important parts of the region. The first front was in Ghazni which was directly commanded by the *Shura*'s chief military commander, Sayed Hussain Jaglan. Arbaab Gharibdad, who had emerged as a significant field commander, was commanding another front in Behsud districts of the Wardak province. The other major military front was in Turkmen valley of Parwan province and was commanded by Haji Nadir Allahyar, a former Hazara parliamentarian. The internal rivalries, which were soon to turn into violent conflicts also forced many of the *Shura*'s front line commanders to divert their resources to counter the emerging Islamist groups. For example, all three main frontline commanders Haji Nadir Allahyar, Arbaab Gharibdad and Sayed Jaglan had soon to stop anti-government activities to fight the internal challenges to their authority. By limiting their activities within the Hazarajat region, the *Shura*'s commanders also did not pose a threat to the areas controlled by the government in other regions. As a result, the government of Kabul largely disengaged from most of the Hazarajat during much of the 1980s.

The Shura's diplomacy

Although the *Shura* never aspired to gain full recognition as an independent state, it did seek to develop rudimentary diplomatic relations in the form of unofficial links with Iran and Pakistan. Nonetheless, this was an area where the *Shura* leadership failed completely. Between 1979 and 983, in its effort to attract foreign assistance, the *Shura* shifted between Iran and Pakistan. Unlike most of the other main mujahedin organisations, the *Shura* failed to attract any significant and sustainable amount of either the foreign material assistance or the political backing it needed to further its goals. Because the organisation was led by the Shi'a clerics, the newly established Islamic Republic of Iran was expected to be its main foreign supporter. Despite the differences between the clerical leadership of the *Shura* and that of the Iranian Islamic Republic over matters of religious interpretation, the former chose to follow Iran in international affairs by adopting the Iranian slogan 'neither West nor East' (Ayatollah Beheshti, 1982). And despite the continued refusal of the *Shura* leadership to recognise Khomeini as the supreme religious leader, the official slogan of the *Shura* was: *Allah Akbar, Khomeini Rahbar, Beheshti Rahbar*, God is Great, Khomeini Leader and Beheshti Leader (Beheshti, 2006). There were pragmatic reasons for doing so. In its first few years after the Islamic Revolution in 1979, the Islamic Republic of Iran, with its internationalist revolutionary agenda, was seen as the major potential foreign sponsor for Shi'a resistance organisations in Afghanistan and elsewhere in the Islamic world. Consequently, many Islamist Shi'a resistance leaders of Afghanistan were expecting significant Iranian ideological guidance and material assistance. However, the Iranian assistance came with significant conditions. Although the *Shura* was officially listed as a receiver of Iranian assistance by Sayed Mahdi Hashimi, a radical Khomeinist and the coordinator of the assistance of the Iranian Revolutionary Guards to Afghanistan, in reality only a little of what was expected materialised during the early 1980s (interview with a former *Shura* leader, Kabul, December 2005). Iran, the only Shi'a-majority country actually governed by Shi'as at that time, did not see the *Shura* as favourable to its interests and policy goals in Afghanistan. Despite the *Shura*'s desperate need for Iranian assistance, Beheshti refused to recognise Khomeini as the supreme religious leader and acted as an independent follower of Kho'i's line of thinking (interview with Ustad Nader Ali Mahdawi, former *Shura* representative in Iran, Kabul, February 2006). Furthermore, Beheshti's self-assertion as Khomeini's equivalent in terms of religious prominence in Afghanistan had serious implications for Iran's relationship with the *Shura*. It was particularly important in the context of the ongoing internal power struggle between moderate and hard-line *ulema* in post-revolution Iran, which resulted into effective sidelining of the Kho'i followers and other moderate scholars. Thus, Beheshti was not an ideal choice for the hardliners of the Islamic regime that were trying to export their style of revolution towards Muslim countries such as Afghanistan. Most of the Ulema in the *Shura* leadership were Kho'i students and followers and as a result most of the ordinary Hazaras were also his followers (Farr & Lorentz, n.d).

The *Shura* hardly did better on the Pakistani side. With the arrival of the new mujahedin groups based in Pakistan and Iran, the jehad lost its popular and spontaneous character and began to experience a process of radicalisation that was polarising the fighters along ideological, political and ethnic lines. This process was further intensified by the Soviet invasion of the country on 25 December 1979 that prolonged and escalated the conflict by adding a nationalist legitimacy to the resistance against the PDPA regime. Subsequently, the vast majority of western and Arab assistance was then channelled through Pakistan to a limited number of resistance organisations that were judged ideologically suitable, motivated and prepared for a long-term fight against the Kabul regime and its Soviet sponsor. This had serious consequences for the poorly organised *Shura*, with weak international connections. As a result, sectarian divisions were further deepened and the Shi'as were largely excluded from international aid (Harpviken, 1998, p. 185).

The *Ittehadiah* remained, therefore, the largest channel of foreign military assistance to the *Shura*. The badly needed assistance they distributed was not substantial enough to help *Shura* achieve its goals. Moreover, this very assistance turned to be a major impediment for the development of the *Shura* as a unified organization. The assistance was provided on a quota basis, directly to every district or sub-district commander, strengthening them locally vis-à-vis the *Shura*'s central leadership. This meant Sayed Jaglan was only one of several commanders listed by the *Ittehadiah* for assistance. This method of distribution turned to be a major source of contention between the two organisations. The *Shura* leaders wanted to take control of the distribution of assistance, which would give it greater bargaining power in its relations to the field commanders. But the *Ittehadiah* leaders insisted on the direct supply of arms to every individual commander, giving them no incentive to comply with the directives of the *Shura*'s leadership. It is clear that the relationship between the two organisations was poorly defined. The *Ittehadiah* leadership in Quetta was determined to take sole control of the *Shura*'s foreign relations. In the words of one of its leaders, the organisation was created to serve as the 'foreign affairs agency' of the *Shura*. On the other hand many of the *Shura* leaders did not recognise this role for the organisation, which they were increasingly viewing as ethno-nationalist and leftist and therefore unsuitable for close cooperation (interviews with former *Shura* and *Ittehadiah* members, Kabul and Quetta, November–December 2005).

In an attempt to attract Iran's confidence, the *Shura* leaders progressively banned the distribution of western assistance through the *Ittehadiah*. The *Shura* leaders began to argue that Western aid was suspicious, and likely to pursue goals that might undermine the Islamic nature of the resistance (Ayatollah Beheshti, 1982). A number of *Shura* delegations travelled to Iran to present a more favourable image to the Iranian authorities and solicit a higher level of assistance. The delegation opened offices in Qom and Tehran and launched publications which lobbied for Iranian assistance and defended themselves against the propaganda of radical groups which labelled the *Shura* as a reactionary, khan-dominated and corrupt organisation. Nonetheless, Iran's disregard and indifference towards the *Shura* was stated even more explicitly by the authorities. It was implied that provision of Iranian assistance was conditional on the *Shura* leadership switching from Kho'i's to Khomeini's line of thinking (interview with Ustad Nader Ali Mahdawi, former *Shura* representative in Iran, Kabul, February 2006).

Dismayed by Iran, the *Shura* leaders concentrated their efforts on lobbying Pakistani officials directly for assistance. Abul Samad Akbari, a known religious scholar, was appointed as the *Shura*'s representative to Pakistan (he was described by many as minister of foreign affairs). In Pakistan, Akbari attempted to wrest the control of the *Shura*'s relations with the authorities away from the *Ittehadiah*. However, the *Shura*'s request for Western help through the Pakistani government was not very successful. For a short period, what had been the *Ittehadiah*'s share of foreign assistance was evenly divided between the two organisations. Yet this happened at a time when the Pakistani government was already scaling down their assistance to *Ittehadiah*, the only Hazara/Shi'a organisation that received some Western aid. It is widely believed that the leaders of the Sunni resistance organisations based in Peshawar, many of whom were Pashtuns, strongly lobbied the Pakistani officials to stop aiding *Ittehadiah*, due to its vocal Hazara nationalism.

Furthermore, the rising Iranian influence in the Hazarajat led to suspicion and distrust of the Shi'a organisations by Pakistan and its Western allies. It was feared that provision of assistance to resistance organisations in the region might result in the strengthening of the pro-Iranian elements in the country. In early 1983, the Pakistani authorities removed both *Ittehadiah* and the *Shura* from the list of resistance organisations endorsed for assistance. Future aid was conditional on the approval of one of the major seven Sunni organisations based in Peshawar. The radical Sunni organisations, which attracted the largest share of foreign resources, were not friendly towards the *Shura* and refused to endorse it. Only moderate Sunni organisations agreed to endorse the *Shura* representatives in Pakistan for assistance (interview with a former *Shura* delegate in Pakistan, Kabul, March 2006).

The failure of the *Shura* leadership to attract external support, combined with internal, ideological differences and factional and personal rivalries in *Shura* led to its failure as a proto-state by 1984. These internal conflicts and external support for the more radical Islamist groups resulted in a series of civil wars first between the *Shura* and other groups and later among the groups that emerged victorious in the war against the *Shura*.

Conclusion

The rise and fall of the *Shura* illuminates many aspects of the complex dynamics of war, politics and foreign influences in Afghanistan. As an indigenous proto-state, the *Shura* achieved some significant success. It provided services to the people under its control, although they were very limited and not very efficient. It exercised some degree of control over its territories, although indirectly and through local strongmen. It built a military structure that was weak and dependent on the charisma of a few semi-independent military commanders. Despite these shortcomings, the organisation somehow managed to function even in the absence of substantial external support, which had been a key historical feature of the Afghan state since the reign of Abdur Rahman Khan (1880–1901).

The *Shura* might well have survived much longer had it not been for its greatest shortcoming, the failure of its diplomacy to attract foreign assistance. In this respect, it was badly outclassed by its radical challengers. The decision of Iranian and Pakistani officials to channel their assistance to the more radical Shi'a and Sunni organisations was probably by far the most important single cause of collapse of indigenous organisations such as the *Shura*. The *Shura* ended up having to rely on the collection of religious taxes, which contributed to weakening its legitimacy.

Besides the conflicts and rivalries among various Hazara elites, the *Shura* also demonstrates the role of ethnicity in the early years of war and violence in Afghanistan. While in its rhetoric the *Shura* emphasised Islamic and national solidarity, the fact that it became an almost exclusively Hazara organisation demonstrates the role of ethnicity as a major fault-line of Afghanistan's politics before neighbouring countries such as Iran and Pakistan could exploit such social divisions. Thus, foreign influences in radicalisation and ethnicisation of Afghanistan's politics in subsequent years must be seen as an additional layer of a complex web of Afghanistan's own past and new problems in subsequent years.

In the internal politics of the Hazaras, the *Shura*'s withdrawal from Waras, its headquarters, in autumn 1984 marked the collapse of the *Shura* as the Interim Islamic state, the marginalisation of the traditionalist pro-Kho'i *ulema* and the khans, and rise of the Islamist groups to power. The destabilisation that followed resulted in a protracted civil war among the competing Hazara mujahedin organisations, which is the subject of the next chapter.

5

AT THE SOURCE OF FACTIONALISM AND CIVIL WAR IN HAZARAJAT, 1981–1989

Introduction

For much of the 1980s, the Soviet army and the Kabul government refrained from large-scale military offensives in Hazarajat. Militarily, these mountainous areas would have been difficult to control without investing a significant amount of manpower and military resources. The government of the People's Democratic Party of Afghanistan in Kabul backed by the Soviet forces focused on securing and defending its control over major urban centres, provincial towns and the main highways of the country. In Hazarajat, the government maintained control of the provincial towns of Bamyan, Chaghcharan and Ghazni and conceded the mostly mountainous and rural districts to the Hazara armed opposition. Sporadic clashes between the Hazara mujahedin and government or Soviet forces only occurred around provincial towns and at the fringes of Hazarajat, such as in the Pishiband area of Doshi district in Baghlan, in Dawlatabad in Balkh, in the southern parts of Behsud in Wardak and in the Jaghori and Qarabagh districts in Ghazni which border strategic areas and highways.

The vacuum created by the almost complete state withdrawal did not lead to the creation of an idyllic stateless environment but rather to a series of bitter struggles over re-establishing some form of polity in

Hazarajat. As the previous chapter showed, the first such attempt took the form of a region-wide inclusive organisation in the form of *Shura-ye Inqilaab-e Ittefaq Islami*, in September 1979. The conflict which led to the dissolution of the *Shura* as a region-wide organisation by 1984 was underpinned by a combination of local and intra-Hazara tensions and external support for the more radical and better organised group. Among the Hazaras, the conflict brought four main elite groups against one another: the Hazara *khans* and *mirs*, the traditionalist *ulema*, the Islamist *ulema* and the Hazara intelligentsia. The rival mujahedin organisations that were backed by these four groups engaged in endless competition and hostility as they began to establish and secure territorial control over the region throughout the 1980s. The Islamist *ulema*, which enjoyed greater external support and better organisational skills and networks weakened these other groups but fell short of gaining complete victory in the armed conflicts. They established their dominance over the region only after opting for a more inclusive forms of politics.

This chapter examines the conflict by presenting and evaluating its main players, local and external influences and finally evaluating its outcome. The first section looks at the first major phase of the war between the traditionalist *ulema* and the khans, on one side, and the Islamist *ulema*, on the other. The second section describes the fragmentation of the Islamist networks that began a new phase of armed conflict in the region. The third section describes the emergence of a new group of competitors for the leadership of Hazaras, a network of military commanders and warriors that emerged during this period. The final section explains why no single faction in the civil war succeeded in emerging victorious and imposing a new order in Hazarajat.

The first civil war within the clergy: Islamists versus traditionalists

As the previous chapter showed, state collapse and the absence of other organised social forces provided a unique opportunity for the Shi'a *ulema* to rise as a dominant political and military force in the Hazarajat area. Deriving their legitimacy from their ability to speak in the name of and as interpreters of Islam, as well as from having been the source of ideological inspiration for the rebellion against the PDPA government, the *ulema* effectively marginalised the khans and the weak intelligentsia. At this point, one might have expected a stable Hazarajat to emerge, as all power was concentrated in the hands of the clergy. However, the *ulema* also suffered from deep rivalries among different networks. Power rivalries were in turn strengthened by disagreements over matters of religious doctrine, particularly with regard to the role of the *ulema* in public life, and by the different social backgrounds of various groups of *ulema*. Revolutionary enthusiasm, inspired by the success of the 1979 Islamic Revolution in Iran, reinforced this trend. The inexperienced factional leaders and the almost-as-inexperienced patrons supporting them in Iran held inflated expectations about what they could achieve in terms of expanding their influence and even becoming the sole power in Hazarajat. External Iranian support and the continued radicalisation of the political and military environment created the conditions for the bid by the Islamist component of the clergy for absolute power.

The role of clerical networks

One major factor in the emergence of the clerics as a dominant player in Hazara politics was the existence of widespread *ulema* networks throughout the region, which allowed sections of the clerics to act as relatively more cohesive political groups in comparison to the khans.[1] The central nodes in the *ulema* network were the centres of religious learning, usually known as *madrasah*. Since the 1960s, the number of students attending these educational centres in Iran and Iraq had substantially increased. A growing number of these students began to return to Afghanistan, with a higher level of religious education and new ideas regarding matters of religious interpretation. They built new mosques and madrasahs in cities as well as in rural areas, which further expanded their network and amplified their ideological reach.

The main centres of learning such as those in Najaf in Iraq and Qom in Iran continued to maintain the linkages between smaller networks that were developing inside Afghanistan. Members of different networks in Afghanistan would meet abroad and sometimes find that they had the same patrons among Shi'a ayatollahs. This, together with the polarisation and mobilisation created by the coup of April 1978 and by the Iranian revolution, helped different clerical networks, at least temporarily, to coalesce into solid entities. This wider network could then spread its influence throughout the region and major urban centres, and was vertically connected to like-minded religious authorities in Iraq and Iran.

After the Islamic Revolution of Iran in 1979, which brought the Iranian *ulema* to power, the clerical networks became channels of access to significant financial and military assistance by the revolutionary regime in Iran to like-minded groups in many countries. The state support helped the *ulema* networks to transform into political and military organisations. By contrast, the other two main social forces within the region, the khans and the intelligentsia,[2] were in a disadvantageous position. The khans, who were known for their internal feuds and rivalries, had no regional network and had previously maintained vertical relations with the central government and local alliances with members of the traditionalist clergy. As a result, they suffered from bitter regional, tribal and personal rivalries. The communities that gathered around them through patronage were segmented at the regional level (Harpviken, 1998, p. 185). Lacking education, they were unable to produce a cohesive political ideology or long-term plan for the future of the region. The intellectuals, on the other hand, had the resources to produce a plan for Hazarajat, but they were divided into two main groups: Maoists and nationalists. They were also few in numbers and unevenly distributed, with very little influence in the villages. Their networks were smaller and more limited geographically than those of the clergy.

In sum, in 1979–80 the clergy was the closest thing to a region-wide force in Hazarajat. In 1979, this placed them in an advantageous position for competition for leadership of the *Shura*. However, after the defeat of their common enemies, the khans and the intelligentsia, the clerics started to fragment again into rival networks. As the previous chapter showed, initially, these were grouped into two opposing alliances: the traditionalists and the Islamists. Those described here as 'traditionalists' were the followers of what had once been the mainstream view in Shi'a Islam, that the clergy should not directly take a political role or assume power in society. They were also followers of Ayatollah Kho'i, the most prominent religious figure of the Shi'a world at that time. By contrast, the Islamists advocated extensive social and political reforms, which they argued, required the *ulema* to take active leadership roles in Muslim societies. While this group of activist *ulema* was greatly influenced and inspired by the thoughts and leadership of Ayatollah Khomeini during the 1980s, one should not see political Islamism in Afghanistan as products of Iranian revolution. As Chapter IV showed, social protests and agitation for political change led by *ulema* began by Ismail Balkhi in the 1940s.

However, it appears that until the 1970s, the Islamists were still mostly junior clerics with a small social following in Hazarajat. Their role in the alliance of clerical networks, which dominated Hazarajat from 1979 to 1982, was modest. Nevertheless, they proved to be more dynamic and better organised than the traditionalists. In particular, they invested considerable energy and resources in strengthening their networks by, for example, creating new madrasahs for the ideological training and recruitment of new mullahs.

The importance attached to the madrasahs throughout the 1980s resulted in a sharp rise in madrasah enrolment rates across Hazarajat. Historically, the madrasahs filled a gap created by discriminatory educational policies towards Hazaras. The significance and number of madrasahs increased further after the collapse of the formal educational system in 1979. In these new madrasahs, students were exposed to both a highly politicised Islam and to ideas and methods of armed struggle. In many cases, they were located inside or close to military bases. The military base of Nasr (see below) in the Sholgarah district of Balkh, named Paaygah-e Al-fat'h, serves as a good illustration. This base, established by Abdul Ali Mazari, who became the most influential of Hazara mujahedin leaders in the 1990s, included a mosque, a medical centre, a prison, a madrasah and several weapon depots. Militants and madrasah students were required to attend daily religious, ideological and military training (Samangani, 1994, pp. 102–11). Abdul Ali Mazari was an emerging leader and his military base served as a model for leaders of other organisations. In Jaghori and Malistan districts of Ghazni province, Nahzat-i Islami (see below) established and supported similar madrasahs, where instructors also played the role of political and military leaders. However, ideological training was not limited to the madrasahs. Young and well-indoctrinated activists from different organisations often travelled to bases throughout the region to ensure

the acquaintance of militants and rank and file members with the ideological directions of their organisations (interviews with former Hazara
mujahedin, Bamyan, July and Kabul December 2006).

The role of external influence and support

The success of the Iranian Islamic revolution in 1979 held enormous
implications for the Shi'a resistance organisations in neighbouring
Afghanistan. By establishing the Islamic Republic of Iran under his leadership as supreme leader, Ayatollah Khomeini provided a role model
for the politically active Shi'a clerics around the world. He transformed
Shi'a Islam into a mass political ideology and spoke in the name of the
downtrodden against the corrupt governments and indifferent upper
classes and traditionalist religious elites. He articulated a wide range of
reforms in all spheres of society, which he argued were essential for the
revival and re-establishment of an Islamic society based on the example
set by the Prophet Muhammad in the sixth century. Most importantly,
for the purposes of our discussion here, he argued that the *ulema* had
an obligation actively to engage with and lead the processes of Islamic
reform and revival (Khomeini, 1978).

Iran under Khomeini's rule also opened up its borders for Afghan
refugees, allowing an estimated 2 million people, mostly Hazaras, to
settle in various cities within the country. The influx of refugees into
the country provided a unique opportunity for ideological indoctrination and recruitment, both for the Iranian authorities and the Shi'a
militant organisations who were based in the country. Across Iran,
several training centres were set up where the trainees would mix with
participants from other parts of the world and be exposed to the ideas
of an expanding Islamic revolution, centred around and led by the
Islamic Iran. An indication of the internationalist character of this brand
of Islamism was the fact that often many non-Iranian militants, including Afghans, were being recruited from among the refugees and
deployed to fight for Iran in the front lines of the 1980–1988 Iran-Iraq
War (Emadi, 1995).

In its foreign policy, exporting a Khomenini style revolution to
other parts of the Muslim world became a key foreign policy objective
of Iran, particularly in neighbouring countries like Afghanistan. Shi'a

activists from around the world looked to Iran for ideological inspiration as well as military and financial assistance. Less than a year after the Iranian revolution, Islamist Hazaras had established contacts with various agencies within the Islamic regime, which started to provide them with financial and military assistance. By early 1980, groups of militants trained in Iran began to arrive in several areas of Hazarajat. These revolutionaries had not played any significant role in the overthrowing of the PDPA government apparatus in Hazarajat in 1979, but thanks to their ideological inspiration, higher spirits and better military equipment they quickly asserted themselves across the region. They began to articulate and spread revolutionary ideas. Soon, their influence expanded to the extent that adherence to the Islamist political Islam became the major determinant of credibility of a person's standing at home and abroad.

However, compared to Western and Arab assistance for the Sunni mujahedin, Iranian support for the Shi'a resistance organisations in Afghanistan was limited and cautious. From 1980, Iran was busy defending itself from neighbouring Iraq in a war of huge financial and military cost to Iran. Furthermore, the Iranians did not want to antagonise the Soviet Union by actively sabotaging the PDPA government in Kabul. Instead, they were trying to improve relations with Moscow, which was supplying arms to Iraq in its war against Iran. Thus, external support for Shi'a resistance activities was by and large limited within the boundaries of Hazarajat. Priority was placed on staging an internal revolution in that region (Harpviken, 1995, p. 66).

The role of ideology and legitimacy

Islam and its various interpretations were not the only source of ideological conflict. Even after the collapse of government in Hazarajat in spring 1979, the legacy and history of the Afghan state and the prospects of re-establishment of its control over the region deeply influenced the dynamics of conflicts among the various Hazara organisations. In liberated Hazarajat, the Islamists attacked the legitimacy and credibility of the khans and of the traditionalist *ulema* for their historical association with an Afghan state which had long been perceived to discriminate against the Hazaras. What followed from the historical view was a challenge against the traditional elites' claim to political power and leadership of the Hazara society. The challenging group, known in the 1980s as *pairawan-e khatt-e imam* or 'followers of the path of Imam', labelled the khans and the clerics as reactionaries, backward and thus ill-suited for the leadership of an 'Islamic revolution'. Though Islam was invoked as a source of legitimacy and was equally used to mobilise fighters by the khans and the traditionalist *ulema*, the new revolutionaries questioned both the traditionalist interpretation of Islam and the figures representing it. To the revolutionaries, Islam not only provided legitimacy for the resistance against the communist regime in Kabul but was also a comprehensive and dynamic political ideology that required constant change and reform across all spheres of the individual and social life of a believer. They introduced new criteria for a legitimate political leader and a new vision for an Islamic society. Their religious revivalism was in stark contrast with the locally accepted religious values and practices. For the khans and the traditionalist religious elites, the collapse of the state in the region and its defence against future penetration by the Kabul regime was the ultimate goal of the rebellion, but for the Islamists this was just the beginning. Their revolutionary ideas were not only directed against the communist regime in Kabul, but more immediately against the local notables, traditionalists and folk religious practices and values.

In a way, the reform agenda of the Islamists was similar to the reform packages of the PDPA regime, which provoked the rebellion of the conservative traditional society in 1979. Both Islamists and the PDPA activists were predominantly rural youth of humble social backgrounds who were disenchanted with the injustice, class inequality and slow pace of development of the country. Members of each were also returning to their villages after spending years in education, where they embraced new ideas and lost contact with their social and cultural backgrounds. Upon their return to the villages, they wanted both to shake up society in favour of the *mostaza'fin* or the 'dispossessed' (the Islamists) or the 'proletariat' (PDPA) (Khomeini, 1978, p. 43; Dawlatabadi, 1992, pp. 300–12). Although the atheism of the PDPA revolutionaries was fundamentally opposed to Islam, both ideologies promised to deliver the masses from oppression and injustice and to establish a utopian society. The Khomeini style synthesis of elements of

Islamic tradition and modern political ideologies undermined any potential influence that educated Hazaras with Maoist inclinations or secular outlooks could have exercised. Thus, the Islamists no longer faced competition in mobilising the semi-educated and dislocated youth, whom they turned into the core component of their militias.

The legitimacy of the political ideologies held by the Islamists would also soon be undermined. During the second half of the 1980s, the role of the *ulema* in instigating the infighting that claimed thousands of lives and allegations of corruption against those appointed as judges at the *hawzahs*, contributed to the undermining of their credibility and of the ideologies associated with them. By then, however, the khans and intelligentsia had been completely marginalised and no longer represented a serious challenge. Hence, the *ulema* continued their unchallenged domination of all spheres of public life in Hazara society.

The defeat of the traditionalists

The civil war in Hazarajat in the 1980s occurred in two different phases. In the first phase, the Islamists, backed by Iran, fought against the khans and the traditionalist *ulema*. Small scale armed conflicts began as early as 1981 and continued until roughly 1984 when the traditionalists and the khans were largely defeated. Central Hazarajat experienced the worst of the first phase of the civil war and of the power struggle between the Islamists and traditionalists. The reason was that the *Shura*, under the leadership of Ayatollah Behesthi, was headquartered in Waras and enjoyed the backing of the most powerful khans in the region. As a result, the Islamists' attempts at expansion met with greater resistance by the khans and the traditionalists. Conflict broke out as ideological warfare. The Islamists' propaganda campaigns against the khans and the traditionalist clergy in 1980 had provoked the *Shura* into arresting and restricting activities of the young Khomenist leaders of the Nasr and Pasdaran groups in Yakawlang and surrounding areas. The *Shura* crackdown forced many activists to flee into northern districts of Hazarajat where they were protected by like-minded clerics who enjoyed relatively greater influence far away from the reach of the *Shura* headquarters (interview with Ustad Muhammadi, a former Nasr local leader, Yakawlang July 2006). However, the situation changed drastically in favour of the Islamists after two key *Shura* leaders, Mohammad Akbari from Waras and Sadiqi Nili from Day Kundi, split from the *Shura* and became key leaders of Pasdaran after short trips to Iran in 1982. They returned with greater military assistance and fresh revolutionary enthusiasm, rapidly outclassing the *Shura* and eventually altering the balance of power in favour of the Islamists. In autumn 1984, Pasdaran and Nasr forces jointly attacked the poorly organised *Shura* commanders in their bases in La'al, Panjab, Yakawlang and Waras districts. They captured these districts and forced the *Shura* leadership to flee into Nawur district of the Ghazni province (interviews with former Hazara mujahedin, Kabul, December 2005 and Bamyan July 2006).

The southern province of Ghazni itself was also the theatre of much bitter fighting, due to its high strategic value for all the organisations involved: it was one of the major supply routes of the *mujahedin* for their northern bases. All were trying to maintain bases in the province that could ensure security for the movement of their personnel and military supplies between Pakistan and central and northern Afghanistan. For example, Hezb-e Islami, a predominantly Sunni and Pashtun organisation, was trying to expand into the Hazara area of the province in order to open routes to supply and support their commanders in northern Afghanistan, whilst Pasdaran and Nasr were desperate to connect to their strongholds in the central and northern districts of the region. The Nawur district of Ghazni became the only major of base of *Shura* after it lost control of Waras in Bamyan in 1984. Because of the hostilities between *Shura* and the Islamists in Ghazni, the former entered into an informal alliance with *Harakat-e Islami* of Sheikh Mohseni, the only other significant pro-Kho'i organisation in Afghanistan. Like Beheshti, Mohseni was a follower of Kho'i, and initially had difficult relations with the Iranian authorities. But contrary to the *Shura*, Harakat was mainly led by urban educated non-Hazara Shi'a elites, even if it managed to gather some support among rural khans opposed to Nasr in northern Afghanistan and in southern Hazarajat. The alliance of Harakat and *Shura*, though not officially announced, proved important in containing the Islamists, at least for a while. This was particularly true of Ghazni, where the fighting started in 1981 after Sayed Qasim, a Shi'a commander of Hezb-e Islami, attempted to expand his territory and exert his supremacy over the local commanders of both Harakat and Shura.

5.1: Northern Hazarajat in the second half of the 1980s
Source: Author's research and interviews with participants of the conflict.

In response, *Shura* and Harakat joined forces to defeat Sayed Qasim, and Nasr and Pasdaran clandestinely supported Hezb-e Islami, hoping that this would weaken the *Shura*. Instead, *Shura* and Harakat emerged victorious and drove Hezb-e Islami out of most of the Hazara areas. Nasr itself was forced to retreat from its base in Qarabagh into the neighbouring Jaghori district (interviews with former Hazara mujahedin, Ghazni, January 2006).

Weakened by this development, Nasr and Pasdaran had to delay their confrontation with the *Shura* and spend another two years building up their organisations. In 1982, Jan Ali Zahedi of Pasdaran returned from Iran with better weapons and established a base in the Ala'a-uddin valley of Nawur, while Nasr's small group of about fifty trained cadres in the Naiqal'ah area of Qarabagh grew into the hundreds. By 1983–

5.2: The conflict in southern Hazarajat, 1983–84

Source: Author's research and interviews with participants of the conflict

84, the Islamists had developed into a force capable of taking on the *Shura* and Harakat simultaneously. Coincidently, at this time senior cleric Ayatollah Wahidi in the Qarabagh district also withdrew his support from Harakat in protest against the presence of alleged Maoists among the *Shura* commanders who fought Nasr in the district. Wahidi's departure effectively weakened the support base of Harakat in the district and a year later a more organised and better equipped Nasr drove Harakat out. Simultaneously, Nasr and Sepah were advancing into other parts of the province. Harakat became mostly limited to the Torgan and Kakrak areas, although the *Shura* managed to survive frequents attacks by Zahedi and other commanders.

Similarly, in the northern provinces, ideological differences and attempts at expanding at the expense of rival groups led to low scale clashes and assassination tactics in the early 1980s. Here, Harakat alone had to face Nasr and other smaller Islamist organisations. The first major conflict broke out in the Charkent district of Balkh between Abdul Ali Mazari of Nasr and Din Mohammad Khan of Harakat. By the mid-1980s, the conflict had turned into a bloody civil war. Thanks to Din Muhammad's social influence, Harakat pushed Mazari out of Charkent. Mazari moved into the Sholgarah district, which was becoming the main stronghold of the organisation in the northern region. Muhammad Muhaqiq, the provincial leader of Nasr, had already defeated rival organisations in Shulgarah. Darra-ye Suf, the predominantly Hazara district of Samangan, remained a battleground between the two organisations. The capital of the district was fiercely fought over. In September 1987, Qarayadar Talib of Harakat and his forces overran the central bazaar and killed several members of Nasr. A year later Nasr mobilised forces from Sholgarah and other surrounding districts and captured most parts of the district. Thereafter, Nasr emerged as the dominant organisation in the Sholgarah and Darra-ye Suf districts whilst Harakat maintained control of most of Charkent district (Samangani, 1994, pp. 368, 411).

In the end, key factors in the defeat of the traditionalists were the lack of external support to match that given by Iran to the Islamists and their weak capabilities in terms of organisation and mobilisation. However, it is important to point out that the Islamists were never able to completely wipe out the traditionalists, both in terms of military presence and in terms of social influence. Similarly, in Hazarajat as a whole the *ulema* had never been able to eliminate the khans and the secular intelligentsia completely. Some khans even maintained a role in the conflict by becoming local commanders of the *Shura* or of Harakat, while some intellectuals infiltrated the various political factions and continued to play a role in the shadows. Hence, it can be argued that although Iranian patronage allowed the Islamists to expand their influence and power, after the first two phases of civil strife and war in Hazarajat large sections of Hazara society had already been excluded from any political system that could have emerged at the end of each phase of conflict. When the Islamists decided to stabilise Hazarajat in 1984–85 and establish a working political system, this could not be very inclusive and its chances of confining political competition to non-violent means were limited. What made things much worse, of course, was the fact that such an attempt was internally flawed and collapsed rapidly.

The second civil war: Islamists versus islamists

From 1984, the pro-Kho'i school was effectively marginalised. Loyalty to Khomeini's form of political Islam was ensured mainly by making Iranian assistance conditional on allegiance to the authority of Khomeini as supreme leader. In Iran, militants and activists, who were trained in several training camps, were required to sign letters stating their firm belief in the leadership of Khomeini and condemning the enemy of the day (significantly, the enemies included General Zia-ul-Haq, the Pakistani military dictator who supported the Sunni *mujahedin*). Those refusing to sign such statements were rejected; this included independent-minded clerics and organisations (interview with a former Hazara refugee in Iran, Kabul, December 2005). Apart from the *Shura*, this also happened to the other main pro-Kho'i organisation in Afghanistan: Harakat-i Islami. Mohseni's close ties with the Iranian religious authorities helped him to attract significant assistance from the Iranian Islamic regime in the first few years when Harakat actually deployed one of the first group of militants trained in Iran. However, in the aftermath of the Iranian revolution the radical Khomeinists swiftly marginalised moderate scholars in Iran, including followers of the Kho'i line of thinking. Moshini's relationship with the Iranian authorities soured to such an extent that in 1984 he had to leave Iran for Quetta in Pakistan, where he established his headquarters and began to develop closer ties to Pakistan and Peshawar-based *mujahedin* group. As the post-revolutionary internal ideological battles subsided and the Islamic Republic became more pragmatist in its foreign policy in the 1990s, Mohseni's relations improved with Iran. In more recent years, Mohseni has forged the closest ties with Iran.

Fragmentation of the Islamists networks

While Iran's discrimination against the traditionalists might have secured the influence of its Islamist clerics among Afghanistan's Hazaras, it did not pacify Hazarajat. The conflict between Islamists and traditionalists was just the first in a series of civil wars that devastated Hazarajat in the 1980s and 1990s. The Hazara Islamits' social reform agenda was particularly polarising because of its direct threats to the privileged status of the traditional religious and landholding elites, including the Sayeds who were accused by many of taking illegitimate privileges disguised as religion. The reform agenda ranged from changing relations in the family, to overhauling the socioeconomic structure of the Hazaras, to transforming inter-ethnic relations at the national level. For instance, Nasr's constitution rejected all forms of patriarchy in families and called for the elimination of the feudal and khan-dominated system in the country (Dawlatabadi, 1992, p. 309). In short, they were aiming to transform the local folk version of Shi'a Islam into a modern political ideology, and equip the largely hereditary Muslims with a rational understanding of Islam and its history. Attempts to implement such wide-ranging reforms polarised the communities along hard ideological and factional lines, involving almost all sections of the society in the infighting in one way or another. Consequently, in the absence of a working political system, the victory of the Islamist groups was not going to stabilise Hazarajat. Although for most of the 1980s, the Islamists had no intention of recognising a role for the defeated but not annihilated khans, intelligentsia and traditionalist clergy, they could not even agree on a framework for lasting cooperation within the Islamist tendency itself.

Table 5.1: Major Shi'a Mujahedin Organisations in the 1980s

	Organisation	Leadership	Place / Date of Formation	Ideological Tendency	Areas of Operation
1	Harakat-e Islami Afghanistan (Islamic Movement of Afghanistan)	Ayatollah Asif Mohsini	Qom, Iran 1979	Pro-Khoi/ Pragmatist	Ghazni, Kandahar, Wardak, Parwan, Bamyan and Samangan provinces
2	Shuray-e Ittefaq-e Enqelab-e Islami Afghanistan (Unity Council of the Islamic Revolution of Afghanistan)	Sayed Ali Behishti	Bamyan, September 1979	Pro-Khoi/ Traditionalist	Hazarajat region but restricted to parts of Nawur district of Ghazni and Panjab and Waras districts of Bamyan after 1984
3	Sazman-e Nasr-e Afghanistan (Victory Organisation of Afghanistan)	Central council of 10 members	Iran 1979 (circles existed in Afghanistan before 1979)	Islamist/ Nationalist	Kabul, Wardak, Ghazni, Bamyan, Ghor, Samangan, Baghlan, Balkh and Uruzgan provinces
4	Pasdaran-e Jihad-e Islami Afghanistan (Guardians of the Islamic Jihad of Afghanistan)	Council of leaders	Iran, 1983	Islamist	Wardak, Ghazni, Bamyan, Ghor, Uruzgan and Parwan provinces
5	Hezbullah (Party of God)	Sheikh Wusuqi and Qari Ali Ahmed Darwazi	Iran, 1981	Islamist	Herat and Jaghori district of Ghazni

6	Nahzat-e Islami Afghanistan (Islamic Movement of Afghanistan)	Council of Leaders	Iran, 1979	Islamist	Jaghori district of Ghazni and Herat
7	Jabhe Muttahed-e Inqelab-e Islami Afghanistan (United Front for Islamic Revolution of Afghanistan)	Council of Leaders	Iran, 1981	Islamist	Jaghuri district of Ghazni and Saripul province
8	Hezb-e Da'wat-e Ittehadi Islami Afghanistan (Party of Invitation for Islamic Unity of Afghanistan)	Council of leaders	1986	Islamist	Qarabagh district of Ghazni
9	Sazman-e Nairoy-e Islami Afghanistan (Organisation of the Islamic Forces of Afghanistan)	Sayed Muhammad Zahir Muhaqiq	1978	Islamist	Behsud and Herat

Source: Author's interviews; Dawlatabadi, (1992; 1999).

Having defeated their common enemies by 1984, the Islamists' network started to fall apart quite rapidly. Many of those I interviewed, including former Islamists who now critically assess their past, blamed the officials of the Iranian Islamic regime for the unbridled factionalism. They alleged that Iranians encouraged and supported multiple organisations in order to have multiple channels of influence on the Hazara mujahedin. While there is some logic to this statement, the division of the Shi'a *mujahedin* seems to have been more a result of internal power rivalries within official and clerical circles of post-revolution Iran, which manifested itself in contradictory and disorganised policies abroad. Soon after the victory of the Iranian Revolution in February 1979, many Afghans, both Hazara and non-Hazaras and mostly clerics, travelled to Iran after the revolution in search of patrons in various agencies of the regime. As a result several organisations sprang up in Afghanistan and Iran, often based on pre-existing clerical networks. However, to make their existence felt and their organisations politically relevant, they all started to establish bases and claim control of territories. This had already been a major factor of the conflict between the khans and the traditionalists, organised into the *Shura* (Farr & Lorentz, n.d).

As Iranian political infighting was being reflected in Hazarajat, the success of an organisation largely depended on its ability to claim territory and on the degree of influence of its patrons in the changing context of power rivalries within Iran. The size of territories controlled by each organisation was seen as an indication of its strength, capability and political relevance, and as a result the basis for attraction of Iranian assistance. Once associated with a particular patron, however, the Afghan organisations were exposed to the side effects of the on-going factional struggle in Iran. The weakening of a patron in Iran could result in the reduction of the level of financial and military supplies. For instance, Nahzat Islami, mostly supported by Ayatollah Montazeri, then the official successor of Ayatollah Khomaini, significantly declined after the marginalisation of Montazeri in Iran in the mid-1980s. Pasdaran-e Jihad-e Islami remained a powerful player thanks to the lasting backing and influence of the Iranian Revolutionary Guards.

Although the intended or inadvertent role of Iranian factions in stimulating violent competition among Islamist factions was crucial, the dynamic of the intra-Islamist civil war was also affected by the different nature and composition of some of the factions. Politically, militarily and ideologically, Nasr was one of the best organised of all *mujahedin* groups in Afghanistan. Its political and military activities were pursued in conjunction with ideological and educational programmes through mosques and madrasahs as well as libraries that it had set up in areas under its control. It published eight magazines both within and outside of the country, giving it a preponderant soft power in relation to its competitors. Whilst in their coverage of international affairs these magazines were influenced by Khomeini and the Iranian Revolution, they articulated a native narrative of the history of Afghanistan, discussing internal reforms of the Hazara society, the history of the Islamist *ulema* in the country and the persecution and marginalisation of the Hazaras. Furthermore, the influence from Iran did not entirely come from the clerical or official networks. Many leaders of Nasr were influenced by the Iranian activist and sociologist Ali Shariati, who sought to construct a revolutionary ideology, combining elements of Islamic thought and history with socialism.

The ideas and practical agendas of Nasr for social reform unleashed such a reaction from conservative and privileged sections of the Hazara society that rival groups such as the khans, the Sayeds and the traditionalist *ulema* began to label it variously as a left-wing, Hazara nationalist and non-Islamic organisation. What made the backlash inevitable was the fact that all of the key Nasr leaders came from humble social backgrounds. Despite their modernist interpretation of Islam, none of the Nasr leaders could claim prominence in matters of religious interpretation. The only exception might have been Sadiqi Parwani, who claimed the title of Ayatollah, but could not provide independent religious interpretation and commentary. Moreover, there were only two Sayeds in its Central Council. The criticism of Nasr on ethnicist grounds did have some foundation. Indeed, Nasr stood out among the Islamist groups, and in particular in comparison to Pasdaran, in its combination of Islamism and Hazara nationalism. As the next chapter shows, the increasingly evident ethnic tendency in Nasr's ideology became the chief source of trouble in its relations with the Iranian authorities.[3] The criticism of Nasr from the conservative side would soon also be picked up by competitors within the Islamist movement.

Compared to Nasr, Pasdaran was less cohesive and functioned more like a network of local mullahs and military commanders, evenly spread across the region. It was, however, the most radical of all the Shi'a Islamist organisations. It was so closely associated with the Iranian Sepah-e Pasdaran (Revolutionary Guards) that it is still better known as Sepah-e Pasdaran rather than by its actual name, Pasdaran Jihad-e Islami Afghanistan. This reputation did not help it to attract the support of more moderate and nationalist Hazara *mujahedin*. At the leadership level it was composed of radical mullahs, but its rank-and-file was characterised by the strong presence of young militants with a comparatively lower level of education than the other Islamist groups. As a result, Pasdaran's cultural and propaganda activities did not get much attention. It did not publish any significant magazines in Afghanistan or abroad. Militarily, it was the most aggressive and violent and, thanks to greater Iranian military assistance, it operated with better military equipment. As a result the organisation quickly asserted itself as a key political and military player both in the factional infighting of 1984–1988 and after the victory of the mujahedin in 1992 (interviews with former Hazara mujahedin, Bamyan, July 2006).

After 1984, when the *Shura* was dislodged from its headquarter in Waras, Nasr and Pasdaran emerged as the most powerful of the Islamist organisations. During these years, the two organisations received the highest levels of Iranian military and financial assistance. For instance, in 1984–85, Nasr alone deployed around 4,000 militants who were recruited from among the refugees in Iran and trained by the Iranian agencies. During the same period, the organisation also bought more than 5,000 Kalashnikovs and some heavy weapons from East Germany (interview with a former senior member of Nasr, Kabul, July 2006). Pasdaran commanders in different parts of the region were directly supplied by the officials of the Iranian Revolutionary Guard who frequently travelled to the Hazarajat and monitored the activities of Pasdaran.

Nasr and Pasdaran formed the core of the Islamists alliance. After the last major defeat of *Shura* in 1984, in an assembly of Nasr and Pasdaran leaders from Waras, Panjab, Yakawlang and Laal wa Sarjangal districts, the political and military structure created by the *Shura* was dissolved. Instead, a new *Shura* called *Shuray-e Chaharganah*, or council of the four, was announced. The new *Shura* formalised the alliance of Nasr and

Pasdaran leaders in the four districts dominated by the two organisations. Muhammad Akbari of Pasdaran acted as de facto leader of the alliance. The two organisations had reached an agreement on the distribution of positions of power based upon the relative military strength and size of territories controlled by each organisation in the four districts (interviews with former Pasdaran and Nasr leaders, Bamyan, July 2006). This was the first significant effort to establish a political system to manage intra-Islamist competition in a non-violent way. Indeed, it was successful in containing violent conflicts between the two organisations in those four districts. They introduced a new administrative and military structure. The district centre of this structure was called *'hawzah'*, instead of the commonly used term *'wuluswali'*. The head of the *hawzah* would usually be appointed by the dominant organisation in the district. However, there was no attempt to establish a monopoly of armed force for the new *Shuray-e Chaharganah*: each organisation was allowed to maintain and establish its own base, called *Qarargah* or *Paaygah*, in areas under their control in the district.[4]

The limited inclusiveness and the internal flaws of the *Shura-ye Chaharganah* as a political system for Hazarajat resulted in on-going civil strife in most of the region. Where the Nasr-Sepah alliance was better able to hold together, it was mainly because it still faced the opposition of the remnants of Harakat and the *Shura*.

- Shura commanders had maintained a stronghold in Nawur district, from where they posed a continuing threat to the central districts of Panjab and Waras by conducting hit and run operations on Pasdaran and Nasr bases, which therefore had a strong incentive to cooperate effectively;
- Nasr, Pasdaran, Nahzat and Nairoy-e Islami had to join forces to contest Harakat's strong base in the Siasang area of Behsud district (Wardak);
- In the Hazara part of the Ghazni province Nasr, Nahzat, Pasdaran and Jabhe Muttahed were helping each other in the fight against Shura, Harakat and later Hizb-e Islami. Following the defeat of Harakat in Qarabagh of Ghazni (1985) at the hand of Nasr, the Islamist organisations united to contest Hizb-e Islami's supremacy in the districts of Jaghori and Malistan.

5.3: Factional control over Hazarajat by the late 1980s

- In the north, Jabhe Mutthahed and Nasr were allied against Harakat in the districts of Darra-ye Suf and Charkent.

Elsewhere, in the absence of an external threat, the common revolutionary ideology and the *Shura-ye Chaharganah* framework failed to hold the Islamists together. Shahristan and Day Kundi, where no significant common threat existed, became the battlegrounds of Islamists' infighting. Pasdaran emerged as the most powerful group in these areas mainly due its leading role in the overthrow of the *Shura* and its stronger emphasis on military activities. By contrast, Nasr had tried to establish itself in these areas through ideological and cultural activities, but had been confronted by the intolerance of the military commanders of Pasdaran. In 1985, Nasr's ideological campaign, centred in a local school in Shahristan and run by a former teacher, provoked Commander Afkari of Pasdaran to attack the school, execute the teacher and throw the organisation out of the district. For many years, Nasr was not able to return to Shahristan. Following this incident, the leaders of Nasr realised the need to build up their military strength in order to survive in the two districts. Whilst Nasr failed to compete with Afkari in Shahristan, it managed to establish military bases and cultural centres in parts of Day Kundi. It took control of areas such as Dare Khodi and Shakardarah, while Pasdaran controlled Nili, Sangemom and Lazir. Other areas such as Khidir, Sang-e Takht, Bandar, Ashtarlai, Charqol and Baghal-e Kando were turned into battlegrounds. Attacks and counter-attacks between the two rival organisations became routine in these areas for many years (interview with an aid worker from Shahristan, Bamyan, July 2006).

Similarly, once Harakat was effectively weakened in Jaghori and Qarabagh, tensions developed between Nasr and Nahzat commanders who had initially collaborated in weakening Harakat in those areas. Nahzat's initial dominance of eastern and northern Jaghori and southern-western parts of Malistan was challenged by Nasr's commanders, who accused Nahzat's local commanders of corruption and deviation from ideological principles. Similarly Nasr and Pasdaran did not feel it necessary to cooperate with Hezb-e Islami in the Jaghori and Malistan districts, even if they were allies in other districts of Jaghori. In these areas, during the second half of the 1980s, local Hezb-e Islami commanders became the real enemies, despite the fact that the two organisations had clandestinely cooperated with Hezb-e Islami in its conflict with the *Shura* and Harakat in other parts of the province in the early 1980s (interviews with former *mujahedin* leaders, Ghazni, September 2006).

The merging of political factionalism and segmented society

Given the segmented character of Hazara society and the dislocation caused by civil war, an overwhelming military superiority or a sophisticated and inclusive political system would have been needed to pacify the region. The inexperienced leadership of the Islamist groups, by contrast, did not know how to handle societal tensions, nor how to prevent them from affecting the Islamists themselves. Without a political system able to absorb such tensions and translate them politically, the fault lines between Islamist factions were only going to be reinforced. In many areas, tensions among local communities threatened to hijack the Islamist movement.

As the conflict prolonged and rivalries intensified, ideological rhetoric lost the pre-eminence of the early days. Local hostilities and growing frustration about the endless infighting required many local leaders to adopt more pragmatic approaches, suitable to local contexts. Some Islamist leaders in their interviews acknowledge that by the mid-1980s they had to recognise the need to slow down their ideological campaign in the face of growing local sensitivities (interview with Ustad Yosuf Waezi, a former senior member of Nasr, Kabul, July 2006). Furthermore, as they expanded the territory under their control, the incompetence and ineptitude of the *ulema* in effectively administering the 'liberated' areas became more evident. They failed to manage social tensions and created even more tensions through their insensitivity towards local norms and traditions. Being trained in religious madrasahs, where only holy texts and Islamic and Arabic literature were taught, they had not graduated with the practical skills to resolve and manage complex social issues. In addition to this, overpopulation and scarcity of resources in most parts of the region, compounded by social tensions and displacement as a result of the war, created formidable challenges for the clerical leadership.

In many cases, the *ulema* themselves indulged in activities that were incompatible with their early ideological rhetoric. For example, the *ulema* who were appointed as judges were rapidly embroiled in allegations of corruption and misconduct. In many cases, bribery became a common aspect of solving land disputes. Furthermore, the declarations of jehad against similar Shi'a groups, which were supported by a different cleric, eroded public confidence in the future role of the *ulema* as political leaders. Cases of land disputes involving members or sympathisers of two different groups could spark violent conflicts dragging whole organisations into armed battle. As associates of many unpopular and ruthless military commanders, the *ulema* provided a religious justification for the infighting, seriously undermining their credibility in the long run. It was not only the Islamist factions that were drawn towards civil society and its contradictions; the contrary was also true. In the chaos caused by infighting, ordinary Hazaras had to join an organisation in order to protect their properties and lives. By joining, however, they would in turn encourage local rivals to join an organisation hostile to their own. Such alignments had significant implications for members. For example, the defeat of one's organisation would result in the loss in a land dispute. This vicious cycle gradually affected all sections of society and pushed them into one organisation or the other (interviews with former Hazara mujahedin, Bamyan, July and Kabul December 2006).

Not surprisingly, the increasing inclination towards adapting to local contexts produced different results on the ground. In some contexts, political and military rivalries reinforced existing social rifts and tensions while in some other situations they crossed traditional socioeconomic boundaries. For instance, in southern parts of Hazarajat such as Ghazni and the Behsud area of Wardak, where the population were exposed to urban lifestyles as a result of migration to the cities, the different factions mostly recruited across tribal and local identities, including in their ranks members from all tribes, sub-tribes and villages. By and large in these areas, political alignment and factional affiliation were mostly determined on the basis of individual interests and ideological inclinations.

In parts of Hazarajat less exposed to the influence of urban life, tension among groups tended to reflect social and tribal cleavages. Local communities tended to use the factions for their own purposes, in the same way that the factions used communities. This was true in the more remote parts of southern Hazarajat too. A good example is the conflict between Pasdaran and the *Shura* in Nawur. Here Pasdaran was predominantly represented by the Ala'a-uddin community and region of the same name. The community is locally believed to be descended from the army of Sultan Ala'a-uddin Hussain, one of the strongest of the Ghorid dynasty who invaded Ghazni and overthrew the Ghaznavid kingdom in the second half of the twelfth century. They have settled in two valleys in eastern part of Nawur and are estimated to number around 3,000 families. The community, also known locally for their war-like characteristics and for their relatively poor economic conditions in a generally poor district, had traditionally been at odds with the khans of Khawat, a landed and more prosperous local community. The ideological conflict between the *Shura* and the Pasdaran reinforced these old tensions. The Ala'a-uddin people, organised by Ali Jan Zahedi of Pasdaran, were frequently attacking the Khawat area, which was defended by the joint resistance of the *Shura* and the khans. After the defeat of Pasdaran, the opportunism of Khawat's alliance with the *Shura* became clear once community resistance drove out the unpopular militias of the *Shura* (interviews with former mujahedin from Nawur, Ghazni January and Bamyan July 2006).

In some parts of Hazarajat, identities were even more tribal and local than in Khawat. However, they did not necessarily reinforce rivalry. Sometimes they could have the opposite effect. The Hazaras of Turkman valley in Sorkh Parsa district of Parwan provide a good example. Despite substantial migration to Kabul, where they gained the reputation of being successful businessmen, the Turkman valley Hazaras maintained a strong tribal identity and their affiliation to jehadi organisations was mostly decided at tribal and sub-tribal levels. For instance, Nasr predominantly recruited from the Khidir, Pasdaran from Ali Khani and Harakat from Dawlatkhani branches of the tribe. The association of the mujahedin organisations with the branches of the Turkman Hazaras was so strong that local mujahedin groups were called 'group-e ali khani', 'group-e khidir and 'group-e dawlatkhani', after the names of the sub-tribes. Despite the local tribal character of the organisations operating in the valley, infighting was largely contained by shared local interests and community pressure on local commanders (interviews with former mujahedin from Turkman Valley, Kabul, June 2006).

However, in the absence of such shared interests or dominance by one particular organisation, disastrous conflicts could emerge. In villages where several organisations competed for influence and none exerted dominance, petty personal, familial and local disputes determined the affiliation of an individual. For instance, in Patmasti, a village in the south of the provincial centre of Bamyan, Harakat and Nasr activists, who were members of the same clan, even cousins and relatives, indulged in one of the bloodiest conflicts. The number of deaths caused by shooting, assassinations and armed battles in this small village has been estimated at more than eighty (interview with a human rights activist, Bamyan, July 2006).

The rise of the military class and its destabilising role

Origins and mutation of the military class

Tensions among local communities were not the only factor threatening the complete implosion of the Islamist movement in Hazarajat. The prolongation of the war resulted into the rise of a military class as well as of a culture of militancy throughout the country. Thus in a society where traditionally age, property and family lineage determined the social standing of individuals, a Kalashnikov and affiliation to a militant organisation (both easily accessible) now paved the way for the rise of a formerly repressed ambitious youth who became known as *qomandaan*, or commanders. A commander could have hundreds of armed men, usually referred to as *nezami* in Hazarajat, stationed at military bases. The commander's control over the fighters was exercised through '*sargrups*', or group leaders, who would in turn be in charge of ten to twenty men. The group leaders earned their reputation and authority by demonstrating their fighting skills and bravery and were the key agents of mobilisation. They were also instrumental in achieving tactical superiority in battle (Monsutti, 2008). The growth of this new generation of local leaders increased the vulnerability of the khans and traditionalist elite. Militancy became a new and easy way of elevating one's social standing.

The growth of the military class conferred significant advantage to the Islamist organisations. By virtue of their role as local military-political leaders, the military class represented a societal change in opposition to the traditional leadership of the khans. The anti-government rebellion in 1979 was successful because of the spontaneous mobilisation of fighters under the leadership of local notables and traditionalist clerics. However, following state collapse and the ensuing disappearance of an imminent external threat, the spontaneity of the social mobilisation evaporated. Many fighters returned to their farms and privileged khans and traditionalist clergy preferred to avoid the risks of direct involvement in military activities. This allowed ambitious and underprivileged individuals to engage in long-term militancy as a way of life. What further encouraged this trend was the way the new Islamist organisations recruited, trained and equipped dedicated militants. The emergence of several competing organisations strengthened the role of these militant individuals.

However, the relationship of the military class with their political leaders was not always unproblematic. The prolonging of the civil war and the associated militarisation of society increased the weight of the commanders in comparison to political leaders. Unlike the political leaders, who were either based in Iran or frequently travelling, the military commanders were mostly based in their districts and as a result had a better grasp over local political and military affairs. Many political leaders were aware of the rise of their commanders throughout the 1980s. One of them described this process after 1985 as a trend towards anarchy and alleged the commanders had a tendency to indulge in corrupt practices that were at odds with their stated political ideologies (interview with a former Nasr leader, Kabul, June 2006). A good example is provided by the local leadership of Nahzat-e Islami in Ghazni. Most of the rank-and-file of the party led by Ghulam Sakhi Waseq, a cleric-turned-military-commander, gradually lost their initial ideological enthusiasm and direct relationship with its leader, Ali Yawar Eftekhari. Under the local leadership of Waseq and other military commanders, the organisation became one of the main parties to the bloody armed conflict in the district of Jaghori. Attempts by Eftekhari and other leaders based in Iran to preserve the ideological character failed to produce any results and ultimately the organisation fell completely under the control of various local commanders (interview with a former Nahzat official, Kabul, October 2006).

The local strength of any organisation initially depended on a group of activists who had mostly received ideological and military training at home or in Iran. These core groups were mostly dedicated militants committed to their ideological principles, which demanded disciplined and decent behaviour towards the ordinary population as well as an obligation to fight against rival political and ideological groups. However, to broaden their base of support, the different organisations tried to attract other followers as well, who were collectively known as '*muttahedin*' or allies. The allies were not required to volunteer as full-time militants or play a very active role. They were only expected to support their respective organisations when needed in times of conflict and offer accommodation for the troops that would pass through their areas. In return, the organisations would promise protection, security and often support in local disputes.

The main point is that throughout the 1980s, the military class would play an important role in prolonging the conflict and preventing a political settlement. As long as its interests were not taken into consideration, the military class would continue to wage local wars and to consolidate its hold over portions of Hazarajat.

The characteristics of civil warfare

Multiple sources of support from within the Iranian Islamic regime and religious circles allowed many organisations to continue to exist even when they fared badly on the battlefield. This meant that even the most powerful players, such as Pasdaran and Nasr, were unable to gain sufficient political credibility and military strength to dominate the entire region and take the lead in an effort to build a strong political system. However, this was far from being the only important factor impeding political consolidation: the mountainous terrain and harsh climatic conditions were another important one. Timely coordination by the senior leaders and organisational communication, were nearly impossible tasks in a context of conflicts and shifting alliances that required quick communication and decision making. In the region's long winters, most of the districts are cut off from the rest of the region due to heavy snowfalls. The intensification of conflict and rivalries, and control of territories by hostile opponents, often made it impossible for local leaders of an organisation to communicate with senior leaders across the region. In the absence of effective radio equipment, the only means of communication between different units of an organisation in different districts were letters carried by trusted messengers. These letters would often take weeks and even months to reach their destination. Hence, most decisions about war and peace, alliance and hostilities, had to be made in the local context. This meant that local commanders, though affiliated to larger organisations, had to adapt and cope with the local political, military and social conditions.

As a result, rather than a single civil war, the armed conflict in Hazarajat consisted of series of local conflicts that were only loosely connected to one another. Most of the fighting was also limited to local affairs, like control of the districts and villages, with little concern for region-wide conditions. Whilst some districts were dominated by a single organisation, others remained areas of conflicts. Where a single organisation gained supremacy, the situation was mostly stable. For instance, the district of Yakawlang in Bamyan was entirely dominated by Nasr, and Shahristan, presently in Day Kundi, by Pasdaran. Neither of these experienced the reciprocal slaughter that occurred in Patmasti village. In these areas, opposition activities were not tolerated and members of other organisations were effectively subdued or even forced to flee. Afkari, the Pasdaran commander of Shahristan, established full control over the district after he successfully ousted the activists of Nasr and Hezb-e Islami in 1984. Khans and local notables, affiliated to the *Shura*, had already been defeated a year earlier. Afkari was assisted by Sadiqi, Pasdaran's ideological and clerical leader in the district, in gaining ultimate control. Khans, Nasr activists and Hezb-e Islami members were not permitted to operate. He applied the most severe measures against the khans. He forced them to leave and distributed their lands to their previous farmers. These farmers were then required to provide one fighter per family as human tribute to Afkari. These fighters, numbering more than 1,000, joined the ideological cadres in ensuring that nobody could challenge the dominance of Afkari in the district (interviews with former mujahedin from Shahristan, Bamyan, July 2006). Despite their ruthless tactics and intolerance, Sadiqi and Afkari introduced important reforms and development programmes that boosted economic and social development in the district. They encouraged or forced people to build roads, rehabilitate schools and water canals. More importantly, they required farmers to plant a certain number of almond trees every year or otherwise risk the transfer of land to another farmer.[5]

The parties involved in the conflict were using and developing a range of tactics and approaches suitable to the mountainous terrain of the region. These included fully-fledged battles, assassinations, ambushes and forced displacement of the opponents. The military-political bases were usually located high in the mountains in order to control and monitor the surrounding valleys. The bases served as more than a simple military unit. The prolongation of the conflict and the increasing importance of mountainous areas at the expense of bazaars and valleys turned the bases into public authorities that would administer justice by settling land disputes and punishing offenders, including collaborators with the enemy. To serve these purposes, the commander of a base would usually be assisted by a judge, normally a cleric, and would have at his disposal a rudimentary prison where he would incarcerate and torture the opponents. Control of strategic and unassailable mountains was essential for the survival and dominance of an organisation in a given district. As a result, many bloody battles took place to ascertain their control. For instance, in the Hutqol and Patu areas of Jaghori and Pashi valley of Malistan, mountain bases were established by the district Hazara commanders of *Hezb-e Islami* to ensure control of the valleys and villages throughout the southern parts of Jaghori and western parts of Malistan. An alliance of Nasr, Pasdaran, Nahzat and Jabhe Mutaahed frequently launched attacks at these bases, but they were never taken. These bases ensured the dominance of *Hezb-e Islami* until 1990, when *Hezb-e Wahdat* was formed (see below). Flat valleys and bazaars such as the main bazaar in Sangimashah, the district capital, and Angori, the second main trading post in Jaghori, were constantly the object of fighting. At times, hostile parties would dig trenches in and around the bazaar with machine guns and RPGs pointed at one another. The control of bazaars was essential for raising funds, collecting taxes from villagers, shopkeepers and obtaining fees from travellers.[6] During the war, Angori bazaar boomed as the major transit point connecting Hazarajat to Pakistan through the Pashtun provinces. Its control by *Hezb-e Islami* was ensured by a base right below the bazaar on the edge of Hazarajat.

The absence of an effective political system was the ultimate cause of the prevalence of local commanders and their petty interests. However, once these became established, they turned into one of the main causes of delay in the development of such political system, as it emerged during the inter-factional negotiations of 1985–89. As the next chapter will show, rapid changes in politics at the national level became the main driving force of a major push for unification of Hazaras.

Conclusion

The turbulent history of civil war and factionalism in the Hazarajat was a predictable and natural consequence of state collapse in an oppressed and closed society where experience of inclusive and tolerant politics was almost non-existent. Furthermore, the forced incorporation of Hazarajat into the Afghan state in 1890s and its subsequent control by coercive power and exclusion of the Hazaras from political participation and socioeconomic development had important bearings on the politics of the region in the 1980s. For almost a century, the Hazaras had been denied the opportunity to participate in state politics and develop the ability to manage and administer their society. Their socio-economic affairs were handled by the central government without much involvement of their own. Historically, the Hazara khans mainly dominated the social and economic affairs of the community but under the Afghan state their role was largely reduced to district or village agent in a vertical relationship with the central government. As a result of exclusionary policies towards the region, the Hazara intelligentsia took its first steps and only the clerics had some potential for regional political leadership. In addition, historical frustration and grievances led sections of the intelligentsia and the clerics to embrace imported radical ideologies such as Marxism and Islamism. Both groups sought to establish an idealised society to address all social ills before obtaining their political credibility or developing legitimate tools for doing so. The ethno-nationalism of a tiny section of the educated class failed to compete successfully with the two revolutionary ideologies. The impact of competing imported ideologies in Hazarajat's nascent phase of political development inevitably polarised and fragmented society into violent and hostile factions. The polarisation deepened to the extent that it triggered and transformed existing social cleavages into incessant violent conflicts.

As demonstrated, all social forces in the region failed to articulate a viable vision for an inclusive and acceptable form of political system. In the absence of peaceful mechanisms of power sharing and a system of control, they attempted to define their status and to play a role in crafting a polity by resorting to violence and eliminating their adversaries. The intelligentsia were the first to vanish as a competitor to be reckoned with, followed by weakening of the khans and the traditionalist clergy. By the mid-1980s the Islamist clergy rose to power in most parts of the region. They too fragmented further along clerical networks and still had to compete with the khans and the traditionalist clergy in territories controlled by the *Shura* and Harakat. Thereby, a political and military stalemate emerged in the region that, despite continued military confrontation, created an increasingly conducive environment for negotiations for political settlements. The desire for political settlement was further enhanced by the UN-led process that provided for the Soviet Army withdrawal in 1989. What further prompted the Hazara political leaders to concentrate their efforts in building a more forceful political organisation was their exclusion by the Sunni organisations from interim governments in Pakistan. The exclusion renewed the historical sense of exclusion and deprivation that necessitated the urgency of collective political presence in the national arena. It was such an environment that brought the different political leaderships together to impose peace on the field commanders and then unify in Bamyan in 1989 under the name of *Hezb-e Wahdat*. Hazarajat finally had its own political system, although it would soon be confronted with the issue of finding its place in a dramatically changing Afghanistan.

6

THE SHIFT FROM INTERNAL WARS
OF DOMINATION TO NATIONAL STRUGGLES
FOR RECOGNITION

HAZARAS AND ETHNICISATION OF POLITICS AND WAR
IN 1990S

Introduction

During the second half of the 1980s, a stalemate emerged in the civil war in Hazarajat that convinced the leaders of the warring factions that a full military victory over their rivals was not achievable. The impact of the war on the credibility of the Hazara mujahedin factions was also becoming evident. Thousands were killed in local armed conflicts, and the political leaders of the factions were losing control over a rising military class that was closely linked to the armed conflict. A growing demand for an end of the infighting in Hazarajat was being reinforced by rapidly emerging trends in war and politics at the national level. In 1988, the Soviet Union declared that it was withdrawing its military from the country, raising serious questions about the survival of the PDPA regime in Kabul. After the departure of Soviet troops in 1989, the PDPA government faced a highly uncertain future. These factors became the driving forces behind a radical move towards creating a single and inclusive Hazara political party that became the Hezb-e

Wahdat-e Islami Afghanistan (Party of Islamic Unity of Afghanistan, Hezb-e Wahdat hereafter) in 1989.

On 28 April 1992, the PDPA government in Kabul collapsed, marking the end of a war that had claimed the lives of roughly a million people and had forced millions of others to flee to the neighbouring countries (Khalidi, 1991). Henceforth the importance of Islam and Communism as unifying ideologies of the war declined. The mujahedin organisations that emerged victorious in the long and bloody conflict tilted towards their ethnic, regional and sectarian constituencies. Unable to agree on a national government, these groups engaged in a civil war that destroyed much of Kabul, and killed tens of thousands of people between 1992 and 1996. In 1994, the Taliban emerged in the southern province of Qandahar with a proclaimed mission to end the anarchy of the mujahedin rule. In reality, it became another deadly force in the more deadly phase of the civil war between 1996 and 2001. During the civil war, the Afghan state institutions collapsed, tens of thousands of people were killed and millions were displaced or forced to flee into neighbouring countries.

For the Hazaras, the civil wars had particularly strong ethnic and sectarian consequences. The political autonomy that Hazarajat had gained from 1979 and the experience of a new generation of Hazara elites with modern forms of political organisation and military warfare had emboldened the Hazaras to assert their claims for a share of power at the national level. Yet, as Afghanistan's most persecuted ethnic minority, they had profound fears that a reconstituted centralised Afghan state would turn against them and push them back to their historically marginalised and subordinate status. To protect their rights, the Hazara elites demanded a share of power in the central state institutions in Kabul and Hezb-e Wahdat became the main vehicle through which they engaged in political bargaining and armed conflict with other ethno-political players of the country. In the process, the Hazara civilians became the victims of the most ethnically targeted atrocities of the war, most notably the February 1993 massacre of civilian Hazaras by the *mujahedin* militias in the Afshar neighbourhood of west Kabul, and the August 1998 genocidal killing of civilian Hazaras by the Taliban in Mazar-e Sharif.

This chapter offers a broad overview of the key trends in the Hazara politics as they pushed for national recognition and political representation during this tumultuous period. The first section explains the background and the process that led to the formation of Hezb-e Wahdat. The second deals with the Hazaras and the mujahedin government, beginning with the exclusion of Hezb-e Wahdat by the Sunni mujahedin in Pakistan in the late 1980s. The third section looks at the strategies and tactics of the Taliban towards the Hazaras as they attempted to subjugate them between 1996 and 2001. It will highlight some of the similarities between the Taliban's approach towards the Hazaras and Amir Abdur Rahman Khan's campaign to conquer Hazarajat in the 1890s.

The shift from internal Hazara politics to national politics: 1989–1992

Throughout the 1980s, several attempts were made to end the conflict in Hazarajat and build more inclusive political alliances. Several such alliances and agreements were crafted and dismantled one after the other. The most important and effective of these were the Shuray-e Eatelaf, an alliance of eight major organisations that was formed in Tehran in 1985. However, while the alliance provided the Hazara mujahedin with a common political voice in negotiations and bargaining with the Sunni organisations based in Peshawar, it failed to tackle the incessant infighting on the ground. To stabilise the region a more radical move was required (Dawlatabadi et al., 1999; Erfani, 1993).

The push for an end to the factional wars in Hazarajat gained greater momentum at the national level. In January 1988, the Soviet Union declared it was withdrawing its troops from Afghanistan, raising serious doubts about the viability of the government in Kabul, which was heavily dependent on Soviet military and financial aid. Uncertain about their future political prospects, most of the elite in Kabul began to shift or diversify their political allegiances, setting in motion a reconfiguration of power relations that became more evidently ethnic and subsumed the ideological divide between the mujahedin and the Afghan communists.

The ethnic and sectarian tensions first surfaced with the formation of a government in exile by the Sunni mujahedin organisations that were based in Pakistan. The first such government was formed in 1987 and the most serious attempt was made in early 1989. The Interim Islamic Governments largely excluded the Shuray-e Eatelaf, the main coalition of Shi'a mujahedin groups based in Tehran. It offered token representation to the Shi'a mujahedin after it was formed but excluded them from the actual negotiations concerning distribution of power. The combined effect of these developments among the Hazara mujahedin was greater awareness of the need for more collective and assertive bargaining with their Sunni counterparts if they were to be taken seriously.

Locally in Hazarajat, the drive towards unification gained greater momentum with the collapse of the local government in Bamyan at the hands of the Hazara mujahedin in August 1988. The military operation that resulted in the collapse of the government in Bamyan's provincial centre was coordinated by Sazmaan-e Nasr but also included other active mujahedin organisations in the province (interview with Ustad Qurban Ali Erfani, a founding member of Nasr and Hezb-e Wahdat, Kabul, July 2007). The liberation of Bamyan also marked the end of any central government presence in the entire region. Henceforth, Bamyan became the political centre of Hazarajat, injecting a new stimulus into the on-going unification process among the mujahedin organisations in the region.

It was against this background that a more radical demand of unification and merger of all existing politico-military organisations into a single party dominated the politics of the region. Several meetings were held throughout the region in which the nature and composition of the new party and the role of existing organisations in it were extensively debated. The two main organisations, Pasdaran and Nasr, which were the most exposed to the threat of delegitimisation as a result of their loss of control over their military commanders, took the lead in coordination of the process. An assembly of leaders of the two organisations in La'al district of Ghur province in September 1988 decided on a merger into a single organisation and continued efforts for the negotiation and inclusion of other organisations. This was followed by a number of gatherings in other parts of Hazarajat which aimed to broaden the appeal and participation in the process. Parallel discussions in several districts of the region led to a regional congress in Bamyan in July 1989 that resulted in the declaration of the misaq-e wahdat, or the unity treaty, the founding document of Hezb-e Wahdat-e Islami Afghanistan (Erfani, 1993; Hezb-e Wahdat-e Islami Afghanistan, 1990).

Before describing *Hezb-e Wahdat* in greater details, it is important to note that the negotiation process for the formation of *Wahdat* was essentially a process initiated from within the Hazarajat region. It was instigated and informed by the realities of war, factionalism and loss of control of the political leaderships over military commanders within the region and the growing concerns of the Hazaras about their fate at the national level. By contrast, the previous coalition-building efforts such as Shuray-e Eatelaf were mostly initiated in Iran and were often under the influence of the Iranian authorities. Consequently, after it was formed a key challenge of the Wahdat founders was to convince the officials of the Shuray-e Eatelaf in Tehran to support the locally driven process of unification.

The fragmentation of the Hazara mujahedin had given the Iranians effective leverage to control small organisations, often tied to various religious authorities and government agencies in Iran. The Iranians feared that a single party based inside Afghanistan could weaken their influence over the movement. Furthermore, the increasingly evident ethnic discourse among founders of the new party was seen unfavourably by the Iranian authorities who had for years tried to promote a more pan-Shi'a political Islamism. Husain Ibrahimi, the representative of Ayatollah Ali Khamenei, the Iranian supreme leader, is alleged to have tried to prevent the formation of Hezb-e Wahdat in order to maintain his influence.[1] Eventually, once the party was announced in Bamyan the Iranians could not sabotage the process. As will be seen further below, the initial tensions between the party and the Iranian policy in Afghanistan became more evident over time. The party pursued a rather independent political strategy, often in conflict with Iranian policies and interests in the country.

Hezb-e Wahdat, a party of unity

As the name *Wahdat* indicates, the main objective of the party was to unify all Shi'a mujahedin organisations under a single political leadership. The quest for inclusiveness and unity had important consequences for the organisational structure of the party. In its hierarchy, the party included a secretary general and the following key structures:

- Shuray-e Aali Nezarat, or Supreme Supervisory Council, a supervisory mechanism that included high-ranking religious figures and experts. In its supervisory role, the council was tasked to monitor

181

all levels of the party and serve as the highest leadership and control mechanism over all activities and policies of the party. In practices, it remained weak.

- The next and most important body within the party was its Central Council. This organ was the most powerful deliberative and decision-making authority within the party. Because of the importance attached to it, its membership expanded in a most dramatic manner. Originally, it was planned to include thirty-six members, but the growing need for expansion and inclusion of other figures and groups into the party resulted into constant increase in its size. The first congress of the party in September 1991 urged the party leadership to facilitate integration of other Shi'a groups and figures into the party. As such it was also resolved that the central and supervisory councils could be expanded as needed (Erfani, 1993, p. 271). At its peak, the body included more than eighty members representing nearly all religious and political groups and influential figures of the region, as well as influential Hazaras from the cities. It was through membership and division of power through this council that the party managed to hold the previously fragmented and hostile Hazara political groupings together.
- The Wahdat manifesto also provided for the formation of provincial- and district-level councils that would report to their relevant committees at the headquarters in Bamyan.

As a party led by clerics, Hezb-e Wahdat can be credited for its exceptional openness and inclusiveness in a conservative society like Afghanistan. In an exceptional move among the Afghan mujahedin, the party included ten women members in its central council and had devoted an entire committee for women's affairs that was headed by a university-educated Hazara woman.

However, the signing of the party declaration was only one step in a painstakingly long and complex process, because each faction sought to maximise its role in the process. This turned out to be a major contentious issue throughout several rounds of negotiations in the run up to the formation of the party. Smaller parties pressed for equal representation of all groups while the more powerful ones demanded greater power and share of the positions in the unified party in proportion to their military strength and control of territories. Eventually the latter argument prevailed; *Nasr* and *Pasdaran* persuaded other organisations to concede to proportional representation.

After the two main organisations agreed to a unification process, many groups had no other choice than to join it: the cost of standing outside would have been unbearable. The following two examples provide insight into the complexity of the process. Harakat-e Islami, led by Shaikh Asif Mohseni, was the main Shi'a party that refused to join *Wahdat*. The party was dominated by non-Hazara Shi'as. It was represented in the initial negotiations, but Mohseni, a prominent controversial cleric from the Shi'as of Qandahar, presented a number of conditions to be met. His conditions were interpreted as an unwillingness to join a party in which historical Hazara grievances and political aspirations predominated. Mohseni and most of Harakat could resist the pressure to join mainly because it was located outside the region. However, it did lose a substantial section of its Hazara following *to Hezb-eWahdat, a* fact that underlined the growing importance of ethnic identities in the aftermath of *jehad* in the country.

The military class that had flourished during the civil war posed one of the main obstacles to unification. Nahzat-e Islami is a good example of military commanders refusing to unite in spite of the agreement of their leaders. Its senior leaders participated in the unification process and hosted one of the meetings in their stronghold in the Jaghori district of Ghazni. However, Ghulam Sakhi Wasiq, Nehzat's main military commander in the district, refused to dismantle his military structure and continued to operate under the name of Nahzat. This resulted in a military confrontation with the former Nasr commanders who were fighting on behalf of Hezb-e Wahdat. The conflict resulted in the defeat of Nahzat and other smaller organisations in this district in 1993. As a result, Wahdat in Jaghori and most other parts of Ghazni established itself through the military victory of the former Nasr forces (interviews with former Wahdat officials, Kabul, December 2007).

Eventually, at least in the short term, the formation of the Wahdat was highly successful. Except for Harakat, officially all the previous organisations were dissolved and their military structures were dismantled. A relatively stable political order was restored in the areas under Wahdat control. One after another the smaller parties were pressured or coaxed to join the process. Significantly, in November

1989, the remnant of Beheshti's Shuray-e Ittefaq also joined. His decision to participate in the unification process was a turning point in the development of clerical leadership in the Hazarajat, as it symbolised the recognition of Islamists' hegemony by the traditional *ulema*. However, by the time Hezb-e Wahdat was in the making, Beheshti's Shura was reduced to a small faction in Nawur district of Ghazni.

The emerging tension between ethnicity and ideology

Ideologically, most Hezb-e Wahdat leaders were political Islamists. Like other Islamists around the world, they sought to establish an Islamic political order as a panacea for all sorts of social, political and economic problems. In a way, the formation of the party was the culmination of a process of Islamisation of the Hazara anti-Soviet resistance groups in Afghanistan. In fact, the party marked the final victory of the clerical Islamists who continued to adhere to important Islamist political objectives. The Wahdat manifesto emphasised the continuation and intensification of efforts for the creation of an Islamic government based on the Quran and Sunnah.[2] Importantly, it called for further efforts to incorporate all other genuine Shi'a groups into the party, and to act in solidarity with all Sunni Islamic organisations. The language of the manifesto clearly indicates that *Wahdat* was meant to be, at least predominantly, a Shi'a organisation, but one that would work in cooperation with the Sunni organisations.

The main point, however, is that gradually the organisation shifted towards its ethnic support base. The result was a fusion of Islamist ideology with the fears, aspirations and vulnerability of the Hazaras as a historically persecuted and excluded ethnic group. As such it became a champion of the rights and status of Hazaras against threats of renewed marginalisation. In fact, ideologically, Nasr's trademark combination of ethnic nationalism and Islamism increasingly became the ideology of Wahdat, an ethnic discourse dominated by, and expressed through, Islamic language.

During this period, Hezb-e Wahdat articulated a number of substantive demands for the inclusion of the Hazaras in the national politics of the country. First, Hezb-e Wahdat consistently stressed that general elections were the best means for forming a parliament and government in Afghanistan. Second, the party demanded that political representation be in proportion to the size of population of each region or province, rather than be based on administrative divisions which was used before the war to delineate electoral constituencies. The Hazaras believed that the pre-war administrative division of provinces and districts was deliberately designed to marginalise them. Third, the party demanded that the Shi'a *fiqh*, or religious jurisprudence, be accorded the same official recognition as the Hanafi *fiqh*. Fourth, the party insisted that Hazaras be included in the actual processes of decision-making in the central government. As such, throughout the 1990s they demanded that the ministry of defence, security or finance be given to a Hazara. Finally, the party became one of the earliest proponents of a federal system or at least a form of decentralisation of power in Afghanistan (Hezb-e Wahdat Islami Afghanistan, 1990; Bunyad-e rahbar-e shahid, 2000; Arwin 2012).

Abdul Ali Mazari, a former member of Nasr and the first secretary general of *Wahdat*, was the main agent of the explicit transformation of the party into a platform for the rights and political demands of the Hazaras. When the party moved to Kabul after the fall of Najibullah in April 1992, Mazari further opened the door of the party to Hazaras of all social and ideological backgrounds. A group of former leftists and government bureaucrats joined the inner circle of the party leadership, challenging the fragile arrangements among the clerical elites. This was a real test of political tolerance of the more conservative section of the party. While the party was created to unify the predominantly Islamist and clerical organisations, in Kabul it confronted groups of educated Hazaras much larger than had been the case in the provinces; these were also mostly leftist and relatively well organised. The question of whether the party should accept these individuals divided the party leadership. The *ulema* needed the knowledge and experiences of these educated Hazaras to help the party adjust to an urban political setting. The party suffered from a chronic shortage of members who had benefited from a modern education. Furthermore, most of the clerics, who were trained in religious centres of Iran, Iraq or Hazarajat, had little familiarity with the politics of Kabul. Militarily, Wahdat fighters lacked the skills suitable to an urban environment. Despite that, many key figures in the Central Council opposed the inclusion of the educated Kabulis in the party, viewing them as godless communists (see below).

Hezb-e Wahdat and the Mujahedin government

The idea of building an Islamic political order, which had become the main declared ideal of the anti-Soviet mujahedin in the 1980s, ran into serious difficulties. Actual efforts to explain how such a system might work or could be formed in the country opened a number of thorny questions. The nation-wide solidarity of the early days of *jehad* faded as ethnic, sectarian, regional and factional fault-lines gained greater prominence among anti-Soviet Afghan resistance organisations. As the importance of ideologies (Islam vis-à-vis communism) after the Soviet withdrawal declined, ethnicity gained greater currency. None of the dozens of mujahedin organisations that were established during this period offered a platform that could genuinely appeal to all communities of the country. The existence of a Soviet-backed government in Kabul, as the common enemy, meant that important cleavages among the mujahedin were dormant, at least temporarily, during the 1980s. But negotiations over the nature, composition and system of future government towards the end of 1980s revealed major contradictions and inconsistencies in the politics of Afghan resistance organisations (Dorronsoro, 2005, pp. 223–37).

One of the main challenges facing the mujahedin leaders was whether they could depart from exclusionary politics of the past and agree on an inclusive mechanism for governing the country. Hezb-e Wahdat's stance as the representative of the Hazara mujahedin was not welcomed by the Sunni organizations in Peshawar. To the contrary, it was effectively excluded from the negotiations over the formation of the Interim Islamic governments (IIG) that took place in Pakistan towards the end of the 1980s. Some of the Peshawar-based organisations had strong sectarian prejudices and viewed the Shi'as with contempt. In 1989, Wahdat sent a delegation, headed by its Secretary General Abdul Ali Mazari, to Peshawar, to negotiate a possible inclusion in the process. The group returned to Bamyan badly disappointed. Some of the major Peshawar-based organisations had basically ignored the Shi'a claims of any form of effective representation in a future government. In response to Hezb-e Wahdat's demand of a one-quarter share in a future power-sharing arrangement, some of the Sunni parties stated that the Shi'as did not count as a significant community, deserving to be included in the negotiation process (interview with a member of the delegation that travelled to Peshawar, Kabul December 2005).

Among the Hazara mujahedin, the vocal disregard of their demands by the Sunni counterparts, most of whom were Pashtuns, reinvigorated fears that the historically Pashtun-dominated and repressive central state would probably be restored. In view of this, Hezb-e Wahdat devised a new strategy that aimed to unite non-Pashtuns in a coalition to prevent the revival of Pashtun domination. In a Central Council meeting in Bamyan, the delegation that returned from Peshawar raised the issue of a new political strategy. Three days of deliberations in the party's central council in Bamyan produced a new strategy: working out an alliance of the country's historically marginalised ethnic communities. This new strategy was to be pursued with the military commanders of various communities in the provinces rather than with the leaders in Peshawar. Government officials of various ethnic communities were also contacted to join or support the new alliance. The new strategy was communicated to various political and military players in the country through delegations and individual representatives. Fifty delegations were dispatched to several parts of the country, including Panjsher valley, the stronghold of Ahmad Shah Massoud, and the northern province of Balkh. Massoud was the most prominent military commander of Jamiat-e Islami and leader of the Shuray-e Nazar-e Shamal or Supervisory Council of the North (SCN), a group of Jamiat commanders from the northeast region that he established in 1986. Members of the Wahdat delegations were given the task of exploring a common political strategy for collectively bargaining over the rights of minorities in future political arrangements (interviews with former Wahdat officials, Kabul March 2007; Dawlatabadi, 1992, p. 246).

The delegations to Panjsher and the northern province of Balkh reached important agreements with Massoud and the future leaders of the emerging party that became known as Junbish-e Milli Islami Afghanistan. These initial contacts resulted into a new political agreement that became known as Paiman-e Jabal- Seraj, or the Jabal-seraj agreement, a short-lived alliance named after the area in Parwan province where one of the final negotiations took place in early 1992. Massoud was chosen as head of the alliance's council, Muhammad Mohaqiq from Hezb-e Wahdat as his deputy and General Dostum, the leader of Junbesh, as commander of its military affairs (Waezi, 1999).

The fall of the PDPA government

However, the durability of the *Jabal-seraj* agreement was put into question during March 1992 when the government in Kabul began to disintegrate rapidly as several mujahedin forces began to advance from all directions. During the month, Massoud took much of Parwan including the strategic air field in Bagram. Hekmatyar, the leader of the mainly Pashtun Hezb-e Islami, and one of the most organised of the Sunni parties based in Pakistan, took positions to the south and east of the city and Hezbe Wahdat infiltrated from the western side of the capital to take positions in the predominantly Hazara areas of the city. Dostum had substantial forces that were already inside the city.

In April 1992, Afghanistan experienced one of the most fundamental changes in its history. President Najibullah's PDPA government collapsed in Kabul, the state institutions unravelled and for the second time (after the abdication of Amanullah 1929) in nearly three centuries the Pashtuns lost control of Kabul (Ahady, 1995). Much of Kabul fell into the hands of Wahdat, Massoud and the forces of General Dostum. The SCN, led by Ahmed Shah Massoud, dominated the key government institutions and emerged as the most powerful in the capital. Gulbudin Hekmatyar was defeated by Ahmad Shah Massoud in the first armed battle for the control of Kabul. The capital, like much of the rest of the country, was divided among several political and military organisations, with increasingly evident ethno-linguistic, religious and regional constituencies. The ethnic character of the new configuration of alignments is clearly described by a Human Rights Watch report:

> Most Pashtun officials and police officers in the interior ministry (mostly from the Khalq faction) now sought to build alliances with Hekmatyar, while Tajik officers in the military and government (mostly Parcham) were defecting to Massoud. Turkmen and Uzbek officials were siding with Dostum. (Human Rights Watch, 2005, p. 17)

Hezb-e Wahdat, as the most powerful and united Hazara organisation, offered protection and a role for the Hazara members of the disintegrating PDPA regime who, in return, played key roles in establishing its control over the strategic western section of the capital. Military depots and weapon caches were handed over to the Wahdat commanders that later proved to be vital in the ensuing civil war. Control of almost half of the capital placed Hezb-e Wahdat in a position to be reckoned with and enabled the organisation to play an important role in all major conflicts and political and military alignments of 1992–1995. What followed was universal civil war. Hezb-e Wahdat had established a similarly strong presence in other major cities. For example, in Ghazni, its leaders had persuaded the local Pashtuns to concede 50 per cent of the provincial positions to the Hazaras (interview with Ustad Fekrat, a senior Hazara mujahedin leader, Ghazni, March 2007).

The pace of development in Kabul forced the mujahedin in Peshawar to agree on what became known as the Peshawar Accords. The Accords had divided key ministries among the Peshawar-based mujahedin organisations, and with regards to Hezb-e Wahdat they only said that 'ministries for Hezb-e Wahdat' and 'Maulavi Mansoor and other brothers' would be determined by the Leadership Council (Article 11). On 28 April 1992, a large convoy of mujahedin headed by Sebgatullah Mojaddadi, the leader of the moderate and relatively weak Peshawar-based *Jabh-e Nejat-e Milli* (National Liberation Front) took control of Kabul. The mujahedin government reported to a fifty-one-member strong leadership council (Shuraye Qiadi). During the two months of his rule, Mojaddadi was severely constrained as head of the state. Militarily and politically, his Jabh-e Nejat was one of the weakest parties, and consequently his main challenge was to maintain a delicate balance among several much larger and more powerful political and military organisations.[3]

In late June 1992, Mojaddadi was replaced by Burhanuddin Rabbani, the leader of Jamiat-e Islami and a Tajik from the northeastern province of Badakhshan. Initially, according to the Peshawar Accords, Rabbani took the office for a period of four months. As his term expired in October that year, Rabbani's presidency was first extended for forty-five days, by the Leadership Council, and then for eighteen months by a grand Islamic council (Shuraye- Hal Wa A'aqd) in Kabul. The circumstances in which his terms were extended were highly controversial.

Hezb-e Wahdat had reached some agreement with Mojaddedi during his two-month presidency. As part of this agreement, Wahdat was offered four ministerial posts and eight seats in the leadership council. One of the main sources of controversy between the Wahdat and the Mojaddedi and Rabbani governments was the former's demand of one of the key ministries: interior, defence or national security. Towards the end of his term, Mojaddedi offered the Ministry of National Security, or the national intelligence agency of the country. When Rabbani took over, he downgraded the ministry to a department for national security. Furthermore, he also turned down General Khodadad, a former Hazara PDPA official who was nominated by Wahdat for the post (Dawlatabadi, 2006, p. 492).

In relation to Hezb-e Wahdat, the Rabbani government rejected the demand for a quarter of the cabinet positions, and instead relied on a combination of negotiation and military attacks on Wahdat positions in Kabul to force it to reduce its demands. Nonetheless, Hezb-e Wahdat continued to retain control of most of the western half of the city and insisted on its demands.

The key point to note is that such negotiations among political leaders miserably lagged behind the actual political fragmentation and collapse of the city. Amidst an environment of flux and uncertainty, ethnic and sectarian tensions resulted in bloody street battles within days of the fall of the PDPA government. During the months of May and June 1992, Wahdat forces clashed with those of Ittehad-e Islami, a predominately Pashtun party aligned with Rabbani. Ittehad was led by Abdur Rab Rasul Sayaf, a known proponent of Wahabi Islami that views Shi'a Islam as heresy. In July, Jamiat commanders' efforts to expand control over the city after Rabbani took power in June resulted in armed clashes with Wahdat. These were the first in a series of wars between *Wahdat* on one side and Ittehad and Jamiat on the other. Massoud and other Jamiat commanders claimed to fight on behalf of the Islamic State of Afghanistan, a claim that was contested by other groups that did not recognise the state before an acceptable political settlement was reached. Between May 1992 and March 1995, the western part of the capital dominated by the Hazaras was the scene of at least twenty-seven battles, making it the main battlefield of the country's civil war.

The strategy of Rabbani's government towards the Hazaras illustrates some aspects of the complexity of Afghan politics. On the one hand, Rabbani vowed to put an end to the Pashtuns' tribal monarchy and ethnic hegemony and called upon the country's other ethnic groups to support his government (Muradi, 2006, p. 112). This slogan resonated well across the non-Pashtun communities who threw their support behind his government in the first few months. On the other, Rabbani's government failed to negotiate mutually satisfactory agreements with factions that claimed to represent the major ethnic groups. As a result, the Rabbani regime itself was open to accusations of ethnic monopolisation, the key players within it all being Tajiks. In particular, members of Jamiat refused to share control of the powerful security, interior and defence ministries with its allies as well as with its arch-rival, the predominantly Pashtun Hezb-e Islami of Gulbuddin Hekmatyar. Thus, despite brief alliances with many other organisations and the symbolic presence of figures from other ethnic groups, it essentially remained a Tajik-dominated government and the forces that fought to protect and defend it in Kabul were primarily the former mujahedin of Massoud. This is how a UN report[4] describes the factional control of the ministry of defence: 'Massoud became minister of defense, but the "army" he commanded had been formed under the SCN [Supervisory Council of the North] umbrella; there was no real national army'.

In February 1993, the relationship between Wahdat and the Jamiat-Ittehad alliance took a particularly ethnic and sectarian turn when the Rabbani government launched its most coordinated military assault in Kabul on Hezb-e Wahdat headquarters in the predominantly Hazara neighbourhood of Afshar in West Kabul. Hezb-e Wahdat forces were quickly overwhelmed after a number of its military commanders were bribed to switch sides with the Rabbani government, leaving the neighbourhood and its residents exposed to massive destruction, pillage and looting. Once they took control of Afshar, the Ittehad and Jamiat forces engaged in one of the most extensive single episodes of atrocities of the civil war in Kabul. Hundreds of civilian Hazaras including women and children were summarily executed, hundreds and perhaps thousands of others were taken prisoners and the area was reduced to ruins (Afghanistan Justice Project, 2005, pp. 82–8; Human Rights Watch 2005, pp. 70–98). The Afshar Massacre effectively pushed the Wahdat leadership into a new alliance with Dostam's Junbesh, Hezb-i Islami and Jabha-e Nejat Milli of Mojaddedi. The new alliance called 'shuray-e a'ali hamahangi' or 'the supreme council for coordination' became the main alliance of anti-Rabbani forces until 1996, when the Taliban took control of the capital.

Failure of strategy and internal fragmentation

The failure of the *Jabal-seraj* agreement and ethnicisation of the civil war in Kabul had profound consequences for internal politics and future evolution of Hezb-e Wahdat. As an organisation, Wahdat lacked solid internal unity and was consequently exposed to external manipulation. Despite their unification under Wahdat, the member organisations retained separate identities and networks. The grievances and factional identities that had developed during the civil war in Hazarajat undermined the development of a single organisation in Hezb-e Wahdat. After 1992, the internal politics of the party was dominated by two rival approaches and strategies with regard to the future of the party and its external strategy towards other players in the country. At the heart of the internal politics of Wahdat was a disagreement over whether to support Rabbani, as a Tajik bulwark against revival of Pashtun hegemony. Mohammad Akbari, the former leader of Pasdaran-e Jihad-e Islami and chairman of Wahdat's central committee, emerged as leader of the pro-Rabbani faction within the party. Mazari, a former leader of Saazman-e Nasr and secretary general of the party, led the majority with his insistence that Wahdat be conceded a quarter of the political power and direct participation in all decision-making levels of the country. The Rabbani government promoted Akbari as a more amenable ally within the Shi'a community. As the civil war in Kabul intensified, the Rabbani government supported the Akbari faction of Wahdat financially and militarily to consolidate and expand its hold over territories in Hazarajat. Similarly, Harakat-e Islami of Shaikh Asif Mohseni who had refused to join Wahdat, joined the Rabbani government and accused Mazari's faction of unnecessary warmongering and bloodshed. On several occasions, Harakat, which was also predominantly based in the west of Kabul, clashed with Hezb-e Wahdat as they competed for territorial control and political influence (interviews with former Harakat and Wahdat commanders, Kabul April–May 2007).

Another source of tension within Wahdat was the opening of the party by Mazari to former Hazara leftists, including Maoists, PDPA officials and some nationalists. While none of the former leftists was given any formal position of authority within the party leadership, their strengthening relationship with, and perceived influence on,

Mazari angered the more conservative sections of the party. The leftist Hazaras did not seek any official positions within the party ranks as they were mostly concerned with ensuring their personal security against persecution by the mujahedin. Again the most significant opposition in this regard was expressed by Muhammad Akbari, who consistently opposed Wahdat's alliance not only with the leftist Hazaras but also with other non-*jehadi* groups such as General Dostum's Junbesh-i Milli. Akbari was an ethnic Qizilbash and the ideology of his group, Pasdaran, was centred on Shi'a Islamism as compared to the Nasr's dominant tendency towards Hazara nationalism in the 1990s (interviews with former Wahdat officials, Kabul, March 2006 and July 2007).

Over time, the differences between Mazari and Akbari opened the first major split within the party. The growing rivalries and tensions between the two leaders strongly surfaced in preparations for the elections of the party's leadership in the summer of 1994. The venue for the forthcoming elections also proved to be contentious. Akbari was pressing for the elections to be held in Bamyan where he felt stronger. By contrast, Mazari and his supporters pushed for elections in Kabul where he had cultivated a larger support base among the urbanised Hazaras. The party was experiencing its most difficult internal power struggle since it was formed. Eventually, the election was held in Kabul in September 1994, amid a heightened competition between the two contending figures for the leadership of the party. New political fault lines were emerging as the party leaders were trying to define and articulate their political agendas in Kabul. Both sides were determined to win and dominate leadership positions and consequently change the political direction of the party. Akbari hoped that by winning the leadership of the party he could steer it closer to the Rabbani's government (interviews with participants and organisers of the Wahdat elections, Kabul June–July 2006).

With forty-three votes out of eighty-two members of the Central Council, Mazari won the election that was held in an environment of deep distrust and high risks of mass violence between supporters of the two factions. Akbari became his first deputy with thirty-three votes. Similarly, agreements were reached on twenty other key appointments. Akbari's faction won the positions of heads of cultural and military committees of the party, which they had strongly pressed for. He and his supporters believed that by dominating the cultural and military committees they could manipulate the war and propaganda machine of the party in favour of the Rabbani government. Karim Khalili, a Nasri activist from Behsud who would later become the leader of the party, was elected as chief of its political affairs committee.

The voting patterns during the elections offer important insights into the internal politics of the party. Members of Nasr and Pasdaran, the two largest and most powerful factions, numerically and politically, dominated the process as well as the two emergent factions. While Nasr maintained its cohesiveness, most other smaller organisations were divided. All former members of Nasr in the council voted for Mazari, testifying to the lasting cohesiveness of Nasr as a political block within *Wahdat*. By contrast, while most former members of Pasdaran supported Akbari, some of them cast their votes for Mazari. For instance, Ali Jan Zahidi, Ghulam Hussain Shafaq, Hayatullah Balaghi and Abdul Ahmed Fayaz, previously important local leaders of Pasdaran, reportedly threw their support behind Mazari. Similarly, most former members of Harakat and Nahzat followed Pasdaran, while most of Saazman-e Daawat and Mostazafin supported Mazari. Other organisations such as Shuray-e Ittefaq and Jabh-e Motahid were almost evenly divided between the two main factions (interviews with various informants, Kabul, 2006–2007).

While Hezb-e Wahdat stands out among its rivals at that time for opening its leadership to internal democratic contestation in the midst of a bloody civil war, the outcome of the election did not overcome the polarisation of the party between the two factions. Mutual distrust and suspicion continued to undermine the new appointments. The role of external players, and particularly that of Rabbani's government, was crucial. Besides open military warfare, Rabbani's National Directorate of Security (NDS), which was directed by Qasim Fahim at that time, engaged in manipulating and dividing its opposition. It provided covert and over support to smaller factions against the bigger rivals. As the example of the Afshar Massacre shows, the NDS also bribed members of the opposition groups to switch sides, in this case with particularly tragic consequences (interview with a former intelligence official, Kabul March 2007).

On 14 September 1994, just days after the Wahdat's internal party elections, Mazari ordered his troops to attack and expel Akbari and

Harakat supporters from the west of Kabul. The attack was a response to an alleged coup plan by Akbari and sections of Harakat against him. After brief firefights which left several dead, Akbari, his supporters and his allies in Harakat were forced to flee into areas controlled by Massoud in the north of the capital. While the exact details of the alleged plot remain unknown, Mazari later claimed that Qasim Fahim, then Rabbani's head of the intelligence department, was working with Akbari to force him out of leadership. According to the allegations, which repeatedly appeared in my interviews, Massoud was also funding and arming as many as 20,000 troops to allow Akbari to take over Wahdat's leadership in Kabul and establish its control in Hazarajat as well.

The split in Hezb-e Wahdat opened a deep and long standing political division among the Hazaras of Afghanistan. Mazari remained in control of much of west Kabul until he was killed by the Taliban in March 1995. He was succeeded by Karim Khalili, a younger member of Nasr, who has since led a faction of Wahdat in a highly personalised fashion. While Mazari and his successor Karim Khalili commanded the support of most of the Hazaras, Akbari has mostly operated in opposition to them. Khalili reorganised the party, and re-established its control over the Hazarajat region after it lost Kabul in 1995.

Taliban, re-conquest and centralisation

In the midst of the bloodshed and anarchy of the civil war in Kabul, the Taliban emerged on the outskirts of the southern province of Qandahar in October 1994. The Taliban proclaimed their mission was to end the civil war and facilitate the formation of a national government. Their initial agenda of disarming irresponsible armed groups, establishing security, ending the conflict and facilitating the formation of an Islamic government quickly gained them a remarkably high level of popular support. Even though the nature and ultimate objectives of the movement remained a mystery for most of the population, the Taliban gained popular support with their practical and clear agendas and their capacity to deliver results in areas they controlled. About three months after it emerged, the movement had gained control of twelve of the thirty-two provinces of Afghanistan, and were making their presence felt on the outskirts of Kabul to the north and Herat to the west (Rashid,

2000, p. 31). In areas that fell under their control, they established a greater level of stability and security by dismantling the warring armed groups and removing militia check-posts that were notorious for extorting and abusing travellers and traders on highways.

The Taliban, drawn predominantly from the Pashtuns, also galvanised Pashtun nationalism. In the words of Rais (1999, p. 5) 'the Pashtun ethnic factor was very important in generating support for the Taliban'. After two-and-half centuries, the Pashtuns had lost control of the capital to the country's other ethnic groups who were in an equal, if not superior, political and military position in a struggle for power (Rashid, 2000, p. 2). Among Pashtun nationalists, the Taliban's quick victories revived the hope that a new, albeit fundamentalist and reactionary, Pashtun force was on its way to unify the country under Pashtun rule. For the Pashtun nationalists as well as many ordinary people in Afghanistan, the movement was also seen as a temporary force that could facilitate the formation of a Pashtun-dominated state by crushing and disarming other groups. This view was further strengthened by the Taliban's own initial denial of its intentions to form a government. In view of this, the Taliban enjoyed overt or covert support of secular Pashtuns, including former communists and secular intelligentsia in Western countries. The former communists from the Khalq faction of the PDPA ran the Taliban's small air force and military artillery and tanks (Muradi, 2006, p. 156; Sinno 2009, pp. 59–89).

The rapid expansion of the Taliban and their uncompromising attitude took all the major mujahedin organisations by surprise. Deeply engaged in the vicious cycle of bloodletting and factionalism, none of the mujahedin organisations, including Hezb-e Wahdat, was prepared to respond to the fast-growing movement from the south. Most misinterpreted the impact and intentions of the Taliban. The Rabbani government saw the Taliban as a potential Pashtun ally against its long-standing rival, Hezb-e Islami Hikmatyar. In view of this, they provided considerable financial and military support to the movement in its early days. Another predominantly Pashtun party, Ittehad-e Islami, led by Rasul Sayaf, had instructed its commanders in the south to avoid confrontation and negotiate possible agreements with the Taliban (Mozhdah, 2003, pp. 26–7). Similarly, Dostum's Junbesh offered critical technical assistance that gave the Taliban their first air power. In 1995, Dostum sent his technicians to repair the few dormant Russian MiG war planes and helicopters that the Taliban had captured at Qandahar airport. He is also reported to have bombed the positions of Ismail Khan (a Tajik strongman of the region affiliated to Jamiat-e Islami) in Herat in support of the Taliban to advance towards the city (Rashid, 2000, p. 39). Contrarily, Hezb-e Islami saw the movement as an immediate challenge to its political authority, viewing it with a great deal of suspicion and distrust, despite positive signals that were sent by the Taliban (see further below). As the movement began to advance towards Kabul, both Wahdat and Hezb-e Islami deployed armed forces from Kabul to the southern Ghazni province to prevent its further expansion. The Taliban, supported by pro-Rabbani forces in the province, easily defeated the militias and forced them to flee towards Hazarajat and Kabul. Government planes also supported the Taliban assault on Chaharasyab, the main stronghold of Hekmatyar in the southwest of the capital (interviews, Kabul, July 2007; Muradi, 2006, p. 156).

Hezb-e Wahdat and the Taliban in 1994

As the Taliban advanced towards Kabul, Hezb-e Wahdat was in a situation of fatigue and disarray. The Wahdat strategy of building a non-Pashtun alliance had not worked. Contrary to their initial expectations, once in Kabul, the organisation found itself fighting a Tajik-dominated government that—like the Pashtuns—refused to give them a meaningful share of power. The civil war in Kabul had exhausted the military, financial and human resources of Hezb-e Wahdat; the party had suffered its first major split.

The first contact between Hezb-e Wahdat and the Taliban occurred in Ghazni in October 1994. In advance of the Taliban attack on Ghazni, Mawlawi Ehsanullah Ehsan, a senior representative of the movement, held a detailed meeting with the local leaders of Hezb-e Wahdat and Harakat on the outskirts of the city of Ghazni. According to the participants in the talks that I interviewed, Ehsanullah had stressed that the Taliban would not attack the Hazara territories, and that in the future they would support the Wahdat demands for official recognition of Shi'a law, distribution of power based on the population figures of all ethnic communities and some level of autonomy to the Hazarajat.

During the meetings, he had impressed the Hazara delegates, who communicated his message to their senior leaders in Kabul. His messages echoed well across the political spectrum of the Hazaras. As a result, the Taliban faced no notable resistance from the Hazaras in Ghazni. The Hezb-e Wahdat force that was deployed from Kabul to fight the Taliban was rejected and attacked by the local Hazaras, well ahead of the Taliban arrival. It must be noted that the internal division within the Wahdat and an aura of invincibility that the Taliban had gained since their birth in Qandahar also helped. Most Hezb-i Wahdat leaders in Ghazni were convinced that armed resistance would risk a military conflict with the Taliban for which they had little capacity. After the Taliban captured the provincial capital, they removed all Hazara officials from their offices but did not attempt to disarm or persecute them at this stage (interview with Ustad Fekrat, Ghazni January 2007).

Hazara resistance, economic blockade and massacres

This optimistic view of the Taliban by the Rabbani government and many Hazara leaders changed after the Taliban arrived at the outskirts of Kabul in February 1995 and demanded unconditional surrender of all the warring factions in the city. At this point Hezb-e Wahdat still controlled most of the western half of the capital, but was severely weakened as a result of heavy fighting with the Rabbani government. Hezb-e Islami, the main Wahdat ally against the Rabbani government, had lost almost all of its territory to the Taliban, including strongholds in and around Kabul. In February that year, Hezb-e Wahdat positions in Kabul came under intense military attacks by Ahmad Shah Massoud who sought to establish full control over the city before the arrival of the Taliban.

Desperate to readjust to the new political configurations, Abdul Ali Mazari entered into a negotiation process with the Taliban. It seems the friendly gesture shown by the Taliban in Ghazni was an important factor in Mazari's faith in the prospects of a negotiation with the Taliban. On 15 March 1995, during a trip to the district of Chaharasiab, the Taliban base outside Kabul, Mazari and nine other senior figures of Hezb-e Wahdat were captured and then summarily executed by the

Taliban. The Taliban claimed Mazari and his associates were killed in a gun battle aboard an aircraft that was flying them towards Qandahar. While the exact circumstances in which they were killed remain a mystery, most accounts of the examination of the bodies of Mazari and other Wahdat leaders show they were severely tortured before being killed. As for the future, the killing sent shock waves through the entire Hazara community, plainly demonstrating the Taliban's uncompromising attitude. The Taliban handed over the bodies of Mazari and other Wahdat leaders to the Hazaras of Ghazni. The body of Mazari was carried on foot in the cold winter of Hazarajat from Ghazni to Mazar-e Sharif where he was buried after a week-long procession. Besides his leadership in the transformation of Hazara politics, the manner in which Mazari died has gained him an iconic status among the Hazaras, a position he continues to holds more than two decades after his death.

In September 1996, the Taliban movement took control of Kabul, where it also attracted international attention for the draconian measures it sought to impose on the population of the city. It practically pushed the women behind the walls, almost entirely shut down all forms of female secular education, banned music and television and turned the city's main stadium into an execution ground. Domestically, the success of the Taliban and their rapid advances finally threatened all the major mujahedin organisations alike. Threatened by a common enemy, Wahdat, Hezb-e Islami and Junbesh joined their erstwhile enemies in the Rabbani government in a new alliance called Jabhe Muttahed (the United Front), which more popularly became known as the Northern Alliance. Karim Khalili, the younger member of Nasr who succeeded Mazari as leader of Wahdat, focused on reorganising the party in its stronghold of Bamyan. Preparing to fight against the Taliban, Karim Khalili reorganised the party and asserted its control over most of the Hazarajat. In the process, much of the territory controlled by Akbari was taken by Khalili's forces. Reinvigorated popular support that resulted from the circumstances in which Mazari was killed greatly helped Khalili. His forces successfully fought back several Taliban incursions at the southern and eastern fringes of the Hazarajat during 1996–97.

With Herat and Kabul in the hands of the Taliban from late 1996, the centre of gravity of the conflict shifted towards northern Afghanistan. Mazar-e Sharif, which was the second major stronghold of Hezb-e

THE HAZARAS AND THE AFGHAN STATE

Wahdat after Bamyan and of the anti-Taliban alliance generally, became the target of Taliban's military offensives. In May 1997, thousands of Taliban militias swiftly rolled into the city of Mazar after Malik Pahlawan, a major Junbesh figure, defected to the Taliban side. The deal which was orchestrated by the Inter-Service Intelligence (ISI) of Pakistan, the Taliban's main external sponsor, brought the movement its most significant political and military debacle. The Taliban's efforts to impose their version of Islamic law and to disarm Uzbek and Hazaras resulted in an armed uprising which first broke out in Sayed Abad, a Hazara district in the city. Thousands of Taliban fighters were caught in the hostile streets of Mazar-e Sharif. Hundreds were killed while fleeing and hundreds of others were captured by Malik's forces and later suffocated to death inside metal containers. The failure of the Taliban in Mazar-e Sharif was the most significant defeat the movement had experienced since it emerged in 1994. Ironically, because the initial uprising was triggered by Hazaras, the retreat of the Taliban from the city was also interpreted as a victory for the Hazaras. Emboldened by the success of this revolt and the internal bickering within Junbesh, Hezb-e Wahdat took control of most of the city of Mazar-e Sharif and surrounding areas, virtually establishing themselves as the major enemy of the Taliban in the north.

In retaliation, the Taliban imposed economic sanctions on Hazarajat by blocking all the entry routes around it. The siege quickly devastated the fragile local economy which was traditionally dependent on remittances from the cities and foreign countries. Singh estimates that the blockade reduced the number of people who could migrate from the region between three-quarters to four-fifths and the prices of the few goods produced in Hazarajat dramatically dropped, while prices of those that were imported, including much of locally consumed wheat and medicines, skyrocketed. Many starving families started to eat wild vegetables in order to survive. To illustrate the impact, Singh notes that: 'before the blockade one sheep might have been traded for one 100 kg sack of wheat flour (sufficient to feed a family of seven for 1.2 months); by August 1998, however, three sheep were required to buy the same amount' (2001, p. 203).

While the economic blockade was taking its toll in Hazarajat, in August 1998 the Taliban prepared for another attack on Mazar-e Sharif. They swiftly moved towards Mazar-e Sharif, after persuading Uzbek militia commanders to surrender through bribes and securing the cooperation of local Pashtun population. The Hazara forces, numbering 2,000–3,000, who were defending the city suddenly found themselves attacked from all directions. Their resistance was quickly crushed, most of them being killed in battles or captured. The Taliban army was now able to exact full-scale revenge by plainly expressing their hatred of the Hazaras. They waged a campaign of ethnic cleansing against Hazara civilians that was described by Rashid (2000, p. 73) as 'genocidal in its ferocity'. It is estimated that around 5,000–6,000 civilians were massacred in two days after the Taliban took control of the city, and thousands more were taken prisoner. The Taliban clearly aimed to cleanse the north of its Hazara Shi'a population. The killings were partly in response to the Taliban defeat and deaths of hundreds of their soldiers in May 1997 in Mazar, but there was also a strong sectarian component in the Taliban's thinking. Immediately after they captured the city, Mullah Manan Nayazi, the newly installed Taliban governor, declared Shi'as as infidels who should either convert to Sunni Islam or face death and forced removal from the country (Human Rights Watch, 1998; Cooperation Centre for Afghanistan, 1998).

The Taliban's final conquest of the north made it extremely difficult for Hezb-e Wahdat to continue resisting in the Hazarajat. The region was now surrounded by the Taliban from all sides and cut off from ground supply routes. In September 1998, Bamyan, the headquarters of the party, fell into the hands of the Taliban without much resistance. The collapse of Bamyan, which triggered disintegration of the political and military structure of Hezb-e Wahdat across the region, remains a matter of great controversy. In a number of my interviews, some former senior Wahdat political and military officials claimed that the Taliban with the assistance of the Pakistan's ISI had persuaded some high ranking officials of the party to give up resistance in return for an offer of a substantial amount of cash. What has fuelled these speculations is the circumstance in which the city fell without any significant military resistance. Beyond Bamyan, local resistance groups and populations were totally demoralised after enduring the devastating economic embargo for almost two years. As a result, the frontline resistance commanders in Ghazni, Wardak and Parwan negotiated a bloodless surrender to the Taliban.

Resistance or collaboration: 1998–2001

The collapse of Bamyan in September 1998 was a key turning point in the history of Hazara politics. With the fall of the city, Hezb-e Wahdat, the chief Hazara political and military organisation, completely disintegrated and most of its political and military cadres fled into the neighbouring countries. Some of its commanders who surrendered to the Taliban were removed from the region and placed under surveillance in Kabul.

Internationally, the Taliban are often known as a fundamentalist Islamist movement. For the Hazaras in Afghanistan, however, the Taliban was a decidedly Pashtun nationalist force, seeking to restore the historical Pashtun hegemony in the region. For the first time in nearly two decades, after the Taliban took control of Bamyan, almost all provincial and district administrations were staffed by Pashtuns, and the Pashtun nomads also returned to the region in massive numbers. The nomads sought to collect two decades of rents and interests on lands and debts to local Hazaras. This was happening at a time that nearly two years of economic blockade had virtually crippled the local economy.

Concurrent with the state collapse in the region in 1979, the nomads had also lost their privileged status. The local Hazara mujahedin organisations, including Shuray-e Ittefaq, blocked the seasonal Kuchi migration to the region and rejected the nomads' claim of ownership over the region's pasture. Furthermore, high demographic pressure and the scarcity of cultivatable lands also forced the local farmers to turn much pasture land into farming fields. Consequently, throughout the 1980s and most of the 1990s most Kuchis were unable to venture into the region. This meant that, for about twenty years, the exploitative relationship between the local Hazaras and the Pashtun nomads was broken, and the nomads were unable to collect the annual interests on the credits they used to provide to local villagers and the lease of the land they had acquired before 1978. Na'im Kuchi, a Pashtun nomad now allied with the Taliban, organised hundreds of his tribesmen into the Taliban army that invaded Bamyan. In the summer of 1999, months after they took control of the region, Na'im Kuchi and his followers attempted to force Hazaras in Panjab and other districts of Bamyan to pay arrears on debt and land lease for the previous nearly twenty years. Wily aptly describes the Kuchi plan after the takeover:

A dominant Kuchi leader, Naim Koochi, was a senior commander with the Taliban and persuaded the leadership that he should be sent to Panjab to disarm the Hazaras. He arrived in May 1999 with a decree to this effect, and an unspecified number of soldiers (some claimed they numbered 3,000). Valley by valley Naim Koochi proceeded to systematically disarm people (often larger landlords), but he also allegedly collected their live-stock, crops and documents and set about collecting sharecropping debts of the past 12 years. Those who had complained to the earlier council were especially targeted. Their homes, farms and animals were looted. Some were seriously injured in the process. IOUs [documents acknowledging debt] were forcibly extracted, itemising the debts that were still owed over and above the animals taken. More land was signed over to the creditor. (2004, p. 54)

Na'im Kuchi and his militias were ordered to leave the region after the rising discontent threatened the Taliban's already tenuous control. However, it seems the restoration of nomads to their privileged status in Hazarajat was part of a broader policy of the Taliban towards the Hazaras. An internal document, which appears to have been issued by the Taliban intelligence department in Qandahar, reveals some aspects of the Taliban policy towards the Hazaras. The Pashto document which was obtained by interpreters of international journalists who visited Qandahar in the months after the collapse of the Taliban in 2001 was published by Ishaq Muhammadi, a Hazara researcher from Quetta in Pakistan. It is hard to verify the authenticity of the document, but some of the orders included in the document resonate well with many actual Taliban policies towards the Hazaras. For example, it orders 'demoli-tion of Mughals historic cultural heritage and structures; ban on hold-ing Jashn-e-Nauroz (The solar New Year celebration); complete eco-nomic sanction of Hazarajat; strict army measures to disown Hazara tribe from their lands and properties forcibly; and propaganda cam-paign against the Shi'a'. The Mughal historical cultural heritage most likely refers to the ancient Buddha statues of Bamyan which were dynamited by the Taliban in March 2001. The destruction of such invaluable historical artefacts was mostly justified by the Taliban and understood internationally as acts committed on religious grounds: a fundamentalist Islamist movement perpetrating an atrocious act of iconoclasm because idolatry is banned in Islam. However, from the Buddhists of East Asian countries to the international organisations concerned with historical heritage, and to Afghanistan as a country, the statues and their destruction had different meanings and consequences. For the Hazaras, the statutes had particularly significant meaning. In the words of one of my interviewees, they were 'the twin towers' of Hazaras, which symbolised an ancient historical glory and civilisational pride at the heart of the Hazara homeland. Hazara historians have highlighted the fact that, like the Hazaras, the Buddha statues had Central Asian facial features, which they take as evidence of ancient Hazara origin in the country (Chiovenda, 2014; Centlivres, 2008).

Despite the Taliban's strong religious rhetoric, the call for the destruction of Mongolic historical remains, and the stated Taliban intention to forcibly occupy Hazara lands once again demonstrated the importance of understanding how ethnic, political and economic motivations are closely intertwined in Afghanistan. The combination of political and economic motivations and the historical grievances garbed in religious fanaticism was responsible for a series of other less well known massacres of Hazaras. In addition to the August 1998 genocidal killing of Hazaras in Mazar-e Sharif, other significant cases include:

- Kandi Posht: One of the largest and the least known of these was the mass murder of hundreds of Hazaras in an area called Kandi Post, in Shah Joy District of the southern province of Zabul. The victims were civilian Hazaras, including women and children who were taken off their vehicles, killed and dumped on the road side. The remains of bodies of hundreds of people were found in the area after the fall of the Taliban in 2001. It appears most of the victims were killed during 1997–1999, when Hazaras were subjected to routine mistreatment and detention along the highway, and hundreds disappeared between Hazarajat and Qandahar.[5]
- In May 2000, the bodies of thirty-one Hazaras were found in Robatak Pass, between Baghlan and Samangan provinces. The victims who were mostly Ismaili Hazaras from Baghlan had been detained by the Taliban four months earlier (Human Rights Watch, 2001).
- Yakawlang: on 8 January 2001, the Taliban committed a mass execution of Hazaras in the Yakawlang district of Bamyan. The massacre of about 200 civilians, some of whom had raised Taliban flags to welcome the Taliban to the district, was perpetrated after a failed

attempt by Karim Khalili to retake control of the district (Human Rights Watch, 2001).

Despite the evident threat posed by the Taliban to all Hazara political elites, the Hazara strategy towards the Taliban was also greatly shaped by internal rivalries and factional politics, resulting in a lack of coordination and even armed confrontation. Broadly speaking, those who decided to collaborate with the Taliban were the groups that were sidelined by the rise of Hezb-e Wahdat under Mazari and Khalili. These included many members of Pasdaran-e Jihad Islami, Harakat-e Islami, Nahzat-e Islami, former Hazara members of Hezb-e Islami and other smaller groups. The most notable was Mohammad Akbari, the former leader of Pasdaran and the breakaway faction of Hezb-e Wahdat after the split in the party in 1994. Those who resisted the Taliban were mainly from the rival Nasr organisation. Mazari and Khalili, who respectively led the main body of Hezb-e Wahdat, and Mohaqiq, who led the anti-Taliban battles in the north of Afghanistan, were former members of Nasr in the 1980s.

Before the fall of Bamyan to the hands of the Taliban in 1998, the main body of Wahdat under Khalili was close to establishing a monopoly over Hazarajat. In an effort to revitalize the party, Khalili had effectively side-lined Akbari and the other smaller groups. However, less than a month after the fall of Bamyan, Akbari surrendered to the Taliban. To find an appropriate place within the Taliban structure, Akbari travelled to Kabul for meetings with senior officials of the Taliban regime. However, in a highly centralised system of leadership under Mullah Omar, the Taliban authorities in Kabul were unable to negotiate on such important issues. Instead, Akbari and about a dozen other Hazara commanders were flown in to Qandahar to negotiate their demands with Mullah Omar, the Taliban leader. A participant at the meeting told me the delegation was not taken very seriously by the Taliban leadership. The Hazara commanders were in a weak and demoralised negotiating position after the Taliban had already taken control of Hazarajat. Thus, for the Taliban, those forming the delegation were of no immediate political or military significance. The meeting with the Taliban leader lasted only a half an hour. During the meeting, Akbari and other senior Hazara delegates could only outline their demands for the release of hundreds of Hazara who were captured by the Taliban along the highways, and some form of political participation, without getting any meaningful response from Mullah Omar.

The manner in which the negotiation in Qandahar ended without any tangible result showed the Taliban were unwilling to accommodate Akbari and other Hazara leaders or their demands for participation in the overall political structure of the movement. Instead, the Taliban preferred to negotiate deals with local Hazara commanders on an individual basis. These deals turned these individuals into collaborators in the Taliban's repression of their own people without addressing the overall political demands of the Hazaras. These local collaborators lacked any form of significant political credibility. For example, Hussain Sangar Dost, a local commander of a breakaway faction of Harakat led by Sadiq Modabber became a Taliban collaborator in Behsud after he peacefully surrendered to them in 1998. Similarly, Mohammad Ali Sadaqat, in Daikundi and Arif Dawari in Shahristan, former commanders of Pasdaran, were the most significant Taliban allies in the two districts. However, none of these men held any official position in the Taliban military or administrative structure. The only officially appointed Shi'a official of the Taliban was Sayed Gardizi, a Shi'a Sayed from Gardez in the southeastern province of Paktia. He was appointed as the district governor of Yakawlang. The Taliban relied on these local allies to maintain control, collect intelligence on opposition activities and identify weapons caches in the villages. They appointed Pashtun officials in the districts that controlled and supervised the local collaborators with a few dozen Taliban soldiers in each district.

Although many of these local collaborators went to extreme lengths to cooperate with the Taliban, they failed to earn the trust of senior officials of the movement. This meant that, like the past repressive Afghan rulers, the Taliban were seeking local collaborators to impose their authority over the local communities without recognising them as equal participants of the state institutions. This became a major weakness of the movement as it deprived it of the confidence of other communities beyond its birthplace in the south. For instance, after several rounds of negotiation, Akbari was only recognised as a community elder by the Taliban. This was a symbolic recognition with no real authority. He was only allowed to maintain a small group of armed men for his own security and was in return expected to cooperate with the regime in securing control of the province. Even then, he was suspected by the Taliban leadership of pragmatically siding with the Taliban and of working in coordination with the Rabbani government to prevent Hezb-i Wahdat, his rivals, from taking control of Bamyan. According to the Taliban's interpretation, Ahmed Shah Massoud had assigned Akbari to cooperate with the Taliban in order to prevent the Bamyan from becoming a resistance centre for Khalili's Hezb-e Wahdat. The logic was that an independent centre of resistance in Bamyan would also divide foreign assistance that came for the Rabbani government (Mozhdah, 2003, p. 166). Akbari also tried to prove his loyalty to the Taliban. In early 2000, in an unsuccessful bid to gain the ultimate confidence of the Taliban in his loyalty, Akbari mobilised hundreds of militants to fight alongside the Taliban forces against the opposition in Parwan (interviews with former Wahdat officials, Kabul September 2007).

Nonetheless, the local collaborators helped the Taliban in important respects, most notably in conducting a thorough disarmament process, which was implemented by torturing those suspected of holding weapons and through an extensive intelligence system, with countless spies all over the region. The environment of fear and terror that came with the Taliban caused the largest exodus of Hazara refugees around world. It was during this period that a significant number of Hazara refugees reached destinations as far away as Australia.

Cooperation with the Taliban was not without some advantages for the local collaborators. For example, the alliance with the Taliban helped Akbari maintain his influence over Panjab and Waras districts, his traditional strongholds in Bamyan. In the summer of 1999, he successfully lobbied the Taliban officials at the Ministry of Defence in Kabul temporarily to halt the harassment of the populations of the two districts by the nomad militias of Na'im Kuchi. In the repressive environment created by the Taliban, the ability of Akbari to alleviate some of the pressures on the local communities earned him some loyal support, which translated in a high number of votes in the parliamentary elections for him in recent years.

However, Hazara resistance was not totally suppressed in the region. In some areas commanders affiliated to the Hezb-e Wahdat under

Karim Khalili carried on fighting the Taliban, albeit mainly on a small scale. The two most notable areas of Hazara resistance against the Taliban until 2001 were Balkhab and Darra-ye Suf districts in the north of the region. For most of the time until 2001, these two districts were outside Taliban control. The district of Yakawlang continued to be contested after its takeover by the Taliban in September 1998. In 1998, Khalili's forces even managed to repel the Taliban from the district and briefly took control of the provincial capital Bamyan. In January 2001, heavy fighting occurred for the control of Hazarajat between the Taliban and Wahdat. After the Taliban recaptured Yakawlang, they massacred 210 civilians (see above). On 13 February 2001, Wahdat recaptured Bamyan town but quickly lost it in a Taliban counter-offensive. The region was liberated from Taliban control only after the US-led military coalition began bombing the Taliban in retaliation for the Al-Qaeda terrorist attacks on 11 September 2001.

Conclusion

The civil war and anarchy of the 1990s exposed deep fault-lines in Afghanistan's politics. These wars had three mutually reinforcing dimensions. First, there were the external factors, the Western, Arab and the Soviet Union support for the mujahedin and the PDPA respectively during the 1980s. With the end of the Cold War, these super power rivalries receded and Afghanistan became the battlefield of a proxy war between its neighbours. The emergence of the Taliban in 1994, and the resilience of its insurgency in post-2001 years cannot be explained without the destructive strategy of Pakistan, particularly its powerful military establishment, in using extremist forces as instruments of its policy towards Afghanistan. Second, there were deep fault-lines in Afghanistan's national politics, which surfaced in the form of jockeying for power among a number of major ethno-political groups at the national level. Third, there were more localised wars that involved local strongmen and communities that were fought over control of local resources and power at the local level. As the success of Hezb-e Wahdat in overcoming the civil war in Hazarajat and the dramatic speed of the Taliban in gaining control of Pashtun territories in 1994 showed, these localised and intra-ethnic politics in Afghanistan did not have the same level of intractability and ferociousness as inter-ethnic competition for power and resources.

What connected these different wars and actors at these three different levels was a battle over control and the future of the Afghan state and the consequences it had for people's security and their social, economic and political opportunities. The key question to be asked about the domestic dynamics of the civil war is why and how the competition for control of the state took such a zero-sum character? Equally importantly, why did ethnicity become the main driver of political mobilisation for politico-military organisations which purported to seek national goals (liberation of Afghanistan from the Soviet occupation) or more ideological objectives (establishment of an Islamic republic or a socialist country). More specifically, how could an ultra-fundamentalist group such as the Taliban assume such a strong ethnic character and fail to transcend secular divisions along ethnic lines?

This chapter explains some of these dynamics. By accounting for the conflicts and rivalries among the various Hazara groups and between Hezb-e Wahdat and the Rabbani and the Taliban governments, it shows how local and national conflicts were closely interlinked. At the national level, the centralised state was central to the intense political mobilisation among Pashtuns and non-Pashtuns alike. It was closely linked to Pashtun hegemony and as a result created fears among other ethnic groups who either sought to control it (e.g. Jamiat-e Islami) or gained a voice and representation in its institutions (e.g. Hezb-e Wahdat). For the non-Pashtuns, the collapse of the state offered an opportunity for negotiation of the nature of political authority, and for the Pashtuns, in the words of Ahady (1995), it indicated the decline of their power. Central to the ethnicised understanding of the power relations was a historically experienced tendency towards monopolisation of power. As the example of the Rabbani government showed, efforts to resist monopolisation of power replicated the same tendency towards monopolisation and retrenchment of power.

The collapse of the state in 1992 and the Taliban's military campaign to unify the country reveals important insights into historical patterns of political power and the modern state in the country. Significantly, the Taliban's military campaigns can be usefully compared to those of Amir Abdur Rahman Kan in the 1890s. First, like Amir Abdur Rahman

Khan, the Taliban leader Mullah Omar framed his war against its adversaries as a *jehad*, and systematically employed a violent Islamic ideology to mobilise fighters and justify the wars. Thus, like Amir Abdur Rahman, Mullah Omar claimed a divine and religiously sanctioned authority. He claimed the title of Amir-ul-Momenin (commander of the faithful) in a congregation of Sunni clerics in Qandahar, signifying the increase in significance of a particular brand of Islam for legitimation of political power. The interesting point to be made here is that a similar congregation of mujahedin leaders and clerics, the Shuraye- Hal Wa A'aqd, did not confer any comparable level of authority on Burhanuddin Rabbani, who had arguably much higher educational qualifications in matters of religion than Mullah Omar. Second, again like Amir Abdur Rahman, the Taliban owed much of their military superiority to external support, which came from Pakistan and a range of global militant organisations, including Al-Qaeda. Thirdly, the political alignment between the Taliban movement and its main opponents between 1996 and 2001 had strong ethnic dimensions. Despite the presence of significant Pashtun figures in the anti-Taliban alliance or vice versa, the conflict between the Taliban and other groups often took a deadly ethnic and sectarian character. The Taliban's wanton destruction of civilian houses and orchards of the predominantly Tajik Shamali plain in 1999, and the ethnic cleansing campaign against the Hazaras in Mazar-e Sharif in 1998, are only two of several tragic phases of the ethnicisation of the war and politics.

With regard to the Hazaras, the most notable difference in this historical comparison is a change in attitude of the Hazara elites. While the nineteenth-century Hazara *mirs* totally rejected the authority of Kabul, both of the main factions of Wahdat that fought against or negotiated with the Rabbani government and the Taliban sought recognition and political representation in the central government. For those who submitted and explored avenues of working with the state, neither Abdur Rahman, nor the Rabbani or the Taliban governments offered any meaningful role for political participation. This demonstrates one of the major weaknesses of the Afghan state: a historical model of statehood leaves little prospect for accommodation and inclusion of opposition through reconciliation. Historically, Kabul, as a seat of the Afghan state, has shown a consistent tendency towards militarily subjugating its opposition. If experience of durable states around the world offers any lesson for Afghanistan, it is that accommodation and inclusion are integral parts of lasting political orders. Ethnically defined states have been a recipe for disaster.

7

INTERNATIONAL INTERVENTION, STATE-BUILDING AND ETHNIC POLITICS, 2001–2016

This is the conspiracy of the occupation. . . The foreigners are supporting the minority against the majority. Once the Americans leave, a 'balance' will return.

Abdul Salam Zaeef, former Taliban Ambassador to Pakistan
(Interview with *Los Angeles Times*, 16 December 2010)

Introduction

On the afternoon of Saturday 23 July 2016 two suicide bombers targeted a peaceful rally at the Deh Mazang Square of Kabul. The first attacker detonated his vest full of powerful explosives and ball bearings, killing eighty-five and injuring 413 of the protestors. The second attacker died from partial detonation of his own suicide vest (United Nations, 2016a). The attack, which became the 'deadliest single incident recorded by the United Nations in Afghanistan since 2001' (United Nations, 2016a) demonstrated a number of features of Afghanistan's social, security and political dynamics that are critical to understanding Afghanistan and its future, after nearly fifteen years of international intervention and state-building.

First, the rally that came under attack highlighted the growing undercurrents of discontent and frustration among the Hazaras regarding their position in central government and their share of national resources and foreign aid. It was organised by a predominantly Hazara protest movement that became known as Junbesh-e Roshanaye or Enlightenment Movement from its emergence in May 2016. The movement was formed in protest against a government decision to change the route of a major power transmission line, which was previously planned to import electricity from Turkmenistan through the province of Bamyan to Kabul and other provinces in the south and east of the country. Towards the end of April 2016, it was revealed that the government had decided to change the route from Bamyan to the Salang Pass, at the Hindu Kush Mountains, which connected Kabul to an existing power distribution line from the Central Asian Republics. The organisers of the movement saw the decision as another indication of what they called 'systematic discrimination' against the Hazaras (Mitra, 2016; Bengali, 2016).

Second, the attack highlighted the vulnerability of the Hazaras in an increasingly precarious security and political situation (Maley, 2016). The extremist group Islamic State in Iraq and the Levant (ISIL), also known as Daesh and more recently ISIS, claimed responsibility for the attack. Since its emergence in Iraq and Syria in 2014, ISIS had established a presence in the eastern province of Nangarhar where it had recruited former members of the Taliban and other local and Pakistan militant groups. ISIS was influenced by the Wahabi school of Islam and was vehemently anti-Shi'a (Osman, 2016).

Third, the attack also raised serious questions about the future of peaceful politics that were gaining traction after fourteen years of international efforts to promote elections, political pluralism and civil and political rights. The movement was distinctive in mobilising mostly the educated and young generation that grew up after 2001. Among those who died in the attack, seven had masters' degrees, twenty-five had bachelors' degrees and forty were current university students. The educated class that was almost entirely decimated in the course of conflict since 1979 was on the rise again but was finding itself in the middle of mounting insecurity and growing conflict over shrinking jobs and socioeconomic opportunities.

Since the overthrow of the fundamentalist Taliban regime in 2001 by US-led military intervention, Afghanistan has made major strides in a number of areas, ranging from holding three rounds of presidential elections to constructing more than 10,000 kilometre of roads, to the expansion of education and health services across the country. These gains, however, remain extremely tenuous, and the achievements made in numbers are often poor guides to their quality and sustainability. Electoral processes fail to produce credible outcomes, and many of the roads, which were arguably the most potent symbols of post-Taliban Afghanistan, witness regular, illegal check-posts, attacks and road-side bombs by the Taliban. The state institutions are among the most corrupt in the world. Following the withdrawal of the bulk of US and NATO forces at the end of 2014, Afghanistan's hard-won gains are being put to a real test. The Hazaras who were among the most passionate supporters of the post-2001 political process are particularly concerned about the future.

This chapter provides an account of the post-2001 international intervention and state-building enterprise in Afghanistan, with a focus on the political role, aspirations and vulnerabilities of the Hazaras. It critiques the underlying assumptions of the state-building model and the challenges that they posed to the international intervention by highlighting a powerful tension between two competing visions of the Afghan state: state-building as a historical reconstruction that rests on dynamics of selection and exclusion in distribution of state power and resources and thus produces ethnic hierarchies in power relations and the distribution of development assistance; and statebuilding as establishment of a broad-based, multi-ethnic and representative political order. The first section explores the relationship between state-building and ethnic politics between 2001 and 2016. The second contrasts and analyses the divergent responses of different social groups to the state-building process. The third provides an account of how the international donors and the Afghan elites in Kabul used international assistance to reward violence and insurgency at the expense of balanced socioeconomic development across the country.

The ideals and practices of ethnic and political pluralism, 2001–2016

The basic framework of the post-Taliban political order was first laid out in the agreement that was adopted by the conference that was organised under the auspices of the UN in the German city of Bonn in

December 2001. The Bonn Agreement, as it became known, provided a road map for a transition towards the establishment of what its preamble described as 'a broad-based, gender-sensitive, multi-ethnic and fully representative government' in Afghanistan. It established a six-month interim administration, followed by an eighteen-month transitional administration. During the two-year period, a number of major processes were to be undertaken, including disarmament, the demobilisation of armed groups and the drafting of a new constitution.

In practice, the goals of the broad-based and representative government were translated into inclusion of all the major political and military players that attended the conference. The conference was attended by four major Afghan political groups: the Rome Group, a royalist diaspora group which was based in the Italian city of Rome, where the former King, Zaher Shah had lived since he was deposed in 1973; the Cyprus Group, a smaller diaspora group represented by Humayun Jarir, a senior figure of Hezb-e Islami and son-in-law of its leader, Hekmatyar; the Peshawar Group represented by Ishaq Gailani; and the United Front, the main coalition of politico-military organisations that took control of much of the country after the fall of the Taliban. Hamid Karzai, a Popalzai Durrani Pashtun from Mojaddedi's Jabh-e Nejat-e Milli, became the Chairman of the Interim Administration. The five vice-chairmen of the interim administration included two Hazaras, one Tajik, one Uzbek and one Pashtun. The interim cabinet included 11 Pashtuns, 8 Tajiks, 5 Shi'a/ Hazaras, 3 Uzbeks and 2 from other minorities.

Karzai was subsequently elected in the June 2002 Emergency Loya Jirga as Chairman of the Transitional Administration for another eighteen months. Karzai also became the first popularly elected president of Afghanistan in the country's 2004 presidential elections, which completed the transition process set out in the Bonn Agreement. Between 2004 and 2017, Afghanistan held two more rounds of presidential (2009 and 2014) and parliamentary elections (2005 and 2010). In 2014, Karzai became the first democratically elected leader of the country to transfer power peacefully to his successor, Ashraf Ghani. During the same period, dozens of political parties were formed, hundreds of print and electronic media outlets were opened and thousands of national and international civil society and non-governmental organisations participated in the reconstruction of the country, millions of children returned to schools and hundreds of thousands rushed towards the universities of the country.

In 2017, one thing is certain about Afghanistan: despite important achievements, the country remains an extremely fragile state, facing a virulent insurgency and enormous developmental challenges with a tenuous political settlement in the centre. The processes that were completed and the benchmarks that were ticked are poor indicators of the strength of the Afghan state and maturity of the political process in Afghanistan. According to John Sopko (2016), the US Special Inspector General for Afghanistan Reconstruction (SIGAR), as of early 2016, the US alone had appropriated $113 billion in reconstruction assistance for Afghanistan. Despite this massive assistance, Afghanistan struggles with major socioeconomic development challenges, its state institutions are some of the most corrupt in the world, elections are so marred by irregularities and fraud that the 2014 presidential elections pushed the country to the brink of a civil war, and rising violence and insurgency have forced hundreds of thousands to flee the country.

Given its complexity and the number of its national and international actors, the record of the US-led intervention and state-building efforts in Afghanistan since 2001 can be assessed according to a range of factors. Some of the factors highlighted by scholars as the main drivers of continued instability of the Afghan state and the resilience of the Taliban insurgency include the institutional design of the post-Taliban state (Maley, 2013), poor governance and state weakness (Jones, 2008), the role of Pakistan in sponsoring and providing safe haven to the Taliban and other extremist groups (Weinbaum & Harder, 2008), and inherent contradictions of the international actors' simultaneous war-making and peace building and international control over development assistance and local ownership (Suhrke, 2013).

I contend that the state-building and stabilisation efforts were also greatly complicated by contradictory conceptions of the post-2001 state, which were most pronounced over the question of ethnic identities. The ethnic factor was important because it was at the core of the tension and contradictions between the legacy of the Afghan state as a historical entity, and the ideals of pluralism and political representation of the new state that was in the making. A new and inclusive state also required a broader national identity, and a new system of exchange in which the state could offer political representation, rule of law, security and socioeconomic development in return for political loyalty and taxation.

To resolve the tension between the two ideas of the Afghan state, the drafters of the 2004 constitution took an ambiguous approach towards ethnicity. On the one hand, the document listed sixteen major and small ethnic groups as constituting the nation of Afghanistan. The names of these ethnic groups are also mentioned in the new national anthem of the country. Dari and Pashto were recognised as national and official languages of the country. Furthermore, languages spoken by the majority of the population of a province were also given official status in those areas. Thus, regional languages such as Uzbeki, which were historically discriminated against, gained official recognition (Articles 4, 16, 20).[1]

On the other hand, the constitution created a highly centralised political system that concentrates power in the office of the president. Formally, the document makes no reference to ethnicity as a requirement for holding any of the political offices and even explicitly bans formation and functioning of political parties that are based on ethnicity, religion or region (Article 35). However, informally the president is expected to be a Pashtun who shares some of his powers with two vice-presidents from two other major ethnic groups of the country. Thus, the new political order fell short of creating a consociational system by failing to stipulate a formal mechanism for ethnic representation. As a result, it created no defence against perceptions and practices of ethnic discrimination, leaving it to uncertain outcomes of electoral politics and the policies of a formally powerful president.

The outcome of the ambiguous approach is a veneer of national unity that refuses to tackle ethnicity as a problem but allows ethnically-framed grievances and feelings of victimhood to accumulate beneath the surface of elite politics. Amrullah Saleh (2012), who served as Director of the National Directorate of Security (2004–2010), aptly described the situation:

> The ethnic divide is increasing, ethnopolitics is on the rise, and both the literature of hate and demagogic politicians are gaining traction. Politicians, intellectuals and opinion leaders talk of ethnic politics openly when addressing audiences made up of their kin, but resort to vague rhetoric while on the national stage.

In spite of the constitutional ban on ethnic political parties, in practice ethnic parties have been the norm rather than the exception. As described above, the Bonn Conference in 2001 represented four separate coalitions of politico-military factions, but over the following few years the old groups and coalitions fragmented and new ones were established. By 2009, there were 110 political parties registered with the Ministry of Justice in Kabul. However, the proliferation of parties did not result in the institutionalisation of parties or the emergence of broad-based programmatic parties that could appeal across the ethnopolitical lines formed during the preceding two decades of war (Ruttig, 2006; Larson, 2015).

The inclusive design of the post-Taliban government that aimed to ameliorate ethnic and sectarian divisions has inadvertently contributed to a more popular ethnicisation of politics (Wafayezada, 2013, p. 188). Ethnicisation of political parties went in parallel with a process of fragmentation. Popular desire for participation, combined with Karzai's neopatrimonial approach, turned these factions into patronage networks of their individual leaders. Consequently, political factionalism, identity politics and patronage networks greatly overlapped one another. Jamiat-e Islami, which is the one of the oldest of the Islamist parties in the country, became even more closely associated with ethnic Tajik politicians. It maintained a resemblance of unity until the assassination of its leader, Burhanuddin Rabbani by a Taliban suicide bomber in September 2011. However, like most other former mujahedin organisations, Jamiat fragmented into a number of loosely structured networks. These include the Afghanistan Naveen Party established by Yunus Qanuni in 2004, Nahzat-e Milli (National Movement) formed by Ahmad Wali Massoud, a brother of Ahmad Shah Massoud in 2002, and the Eatelaf-e Milli (National Coalition) by Dr Abdullah in 2010 (Tchalakov, 2013). Hezb-e Wahdat experienced greater internal fragmentation. By 2009, it had split into four smaller factions, which almost exclusively appealed to the Hazaras (Ibrahimi, 2009). A similar process has been driving the ethnicisation of Junbesh, which began as a regional multi-ethnic party in 1992 but gradually became a vehicle for the political aspirations of Uzbek and Turkmen elites of the country. Junbesh, however, has been the only major exception in the tendency towards fragmentation among the former armed groups. As of 2015, it had not suffered internal fractures similar to its rival groups (Giustozzi, 2005; Peszkowski, 2012).

The endurance of ethnicity as a political factor was helped by a formula of ethnic hierarchy that followed from the Bonn Agreement. At the top of the arrangement that developed during Hamid Karzai's two terms as President (2004–2009 and 2009–2014) was an informal formula of ethno-factional distribution of power that originated from the Bonn Agreement and became a model for a hierarchy of major ethnic groups' positions (Wafayezada, 2013, p. 184). The first Vice-Presidents, Qasim Fahim (2001–2004 and 2009–2014) and Ahmad Zia Massoud (2004–2009), were Tajiks affiliated to Jamiat whereas Karim Khalili, the leader of Hezb-e Wahdat, served as the second vice-president between 2004 and 2014. Ethnic representation was thus reduced to distribution of offices among the key ethno-political factions, without addressing the underlying sources of ethnic politics.

Furthermore, despite the formal ethnic representation in the offices of the vice-presidents, the actual distribution of power among the main groups in the Afghan government significantly shifted over time. For example, the number of ministers in Karzai's cabinets who had a background in the civil wars of the 1990s and were mainly non-Pashtuns dropped from 45.2 per cent of cabinet positions in 2001 to 28.6 per cent in 2009 when Karzai formed the cabinet for the second term of his presidency. By contrast, during the same period, the share of western-educated technocrats who were mainly Pashtuns, increased from 22.6 to 42.9 per cent of the cabinet posts (Giustozzi & Ibrahimi, 2013, p. 249).[2]

The main point to note is that while the main factions fragmented, this occurred within ethno-political boundaries. This created a situation in which several ethno-political factions competed for the support of the same ethnic group. Often, these factional networks engaged in competitive outbidding, presenting themselves as defenders of the ethnic or regional identities. As a result, ethnicity endured as a powerful force: as a frame for political contention and a dividing line for potential relapse of the country into civil war.

The endurance of ethnic politics became most apparent during the protracted crisis over the outcome of the 2014 presidential elections, which pushed the country to the brink of civil war. The protracted nature of the 2014 election crisis cannot be understood without looking at the composition and dynamics of the political coalitions that supported the leading candidates. The essential building blocks of these coalitions were ethno-political factions and networks. In 2014, Ashraf Ghani, a former World Bank technocrat and an Ahmadzai Pashtun from eastern Afghanistan, chose General Abdur Rashid Dostum and Sarwar Danish, an Uzbek and a Hazara respectively, as the first and second vice-presidents in his ticket. Significantly, his team did not include a Tajik. Abdullah, who is a Pashtun through his paternal descent but has spent much of his political career with the Shuray-e Nazar faction of Jamait-e Islami, had chosen Khan Muhammad Khan, a Pashtun from Ghazni, and Muhammad Muhaqiq, a Hazara, as the first and second vice-presidents respectively. Abdullah received 45 per cent of the vote in the first round on 5 April. He fell short of getting the more than 50 per cent required for victory but was well ahead of his closest rival, Ashraf Ghani, who received 31 per cent. Hence, while Hazara candidates remained in the third rank in both coalitions, for many who framed the outcome of the election in ethnic terms the outcome of the run-off on 14 June became particularly significant. For many Pashtun nationalists, the potential election of Abdullah as president was interpreted as an immediate threat to Pashtun political hegemony.

The second round, which by all credible accounts was deeply tainted by fraud at all levels, placed Ghani ahead of Abdullah. The European Union's Election Assessment Team election observers (2014) estimated that there were more than more than 2 million suspicious votes. Some polling stations were doubted to have opened at all as a result of insecurity. The vast majority of the suspect votes came from the Pashtun provinces of southeast Afghanistan, which were plagued by insurgency and poor central government control. Vote-rigging and electoral mismanagement followed a pattern that began with the industrial-scale fraud and irregularities that brought Karzai to power for a second term in 2009. This time, the allegations of fraud were so serious that after months of political crisis that pushed the country to the brink of civil war, a government of national unity was formed to include both electoral coalitions. According to the agreement brokered by US Secretary of State John Kerry, on 29 September 2014 Ghani was sworn in as the president, and Abdullah as chief executive officer, a new post designed to become a full prime ministerial position through a constitutional Loya Jirga to be convened within another two years. (This did not eventuate.)

Responding to the opportunities of the post-2002 political order

To explore the post-2001 state-building and ethnic politics, I emphasise two main standards against which we can evaluate the dynamics and mutual interaction between processes of state formation and ethnic politics: (a) the social base and ethnic character of the main ethno-political factions that fought one another during the civil wars of the 1990s, and (b) their attitude towards organised violence as a strategy for the attainment and preservation of political power. The former asks whether these ethno-political factions transformed by appealing to broader sections of the society or remained largely limited to the ethnic or other forms of narrow and exclusive constituencies that they developed during the war. The latter asks whether these groups abandoned military wings and organised violence as part of their political strategies. Both of these changes are essential to what Rubin (2006, p. 180) describes as 'warlord democratization', which was essential for the attainment of representative and democratic politics.

Evaluated against these two conditions, the internationally led state-building enterprise shows two significant patterns. The first important pattern that emerges is that all significant ethno-political factions of the 1990s failed to broaden their support base beyond the ethnic, sectarian or regional groups from which they emerged. It is clear that between 2001 and 2016 neither did the former armed factions succeed in becoming multi-ethnic parties nor were any new significant programmatic or multiethnic parties formed. The second puzzle that emerges is that while all significant non-Pashtun groups abandoned organised violence as part of their organisational structure, Hezb-e Islami and the Taliban, the main Pashtun ethno-political factions of the 1990s chose to retain both violent strategies and their Pashtun social bases. In October 2016, the militant faction of Hezb-e Islami, led by Hekmatyar himself, signed a controversial peace deal with President Ghani, according to which the party would disarm and enter the political life of the country in return for protection and complete amnesty by the government for all its members (Rubin, 2016). While the effects of the agreements on the level of violence and politics of the country remain to be seen, I argue that these two responses underscore two different conceptions of state-building in Afghanistan: state-building as a process of historical reconstruction and as building institutions of inclusive and representative politics. I will conclude this section by discussing the first pattern, the resilience of ethnic politics, before discussing the contrast in responses to state-building in the next.

Abandoning organised violence, the case of Hezb-e Wahdat

Hezb-e Wahdat, and the Hazaras more generally, offer the most potent example of a shift from violent conflict towards peaceful and civilian politics and as a result are one of the success stories of the post-2001 Afghanistan. The scale of transformation among Hazaras is often captured by Western newspapers headlines such as 'Afghanistan's success story: The liberated Hazara minority' (Sappenfield, 2007a), 'Afghanistan's Hazaras: Coming up from the bottom' (The Economist, 2007), and the 'Hazaras hustle to head of class in Afghanistan' (Oppel & Wafa, 2010).

In many important respects, for the Hazaras the 2001–2016 period came as a welcome relief, after more than a century of persecution and exclusion. The Hazara political elites have been keenly aware of the significance of this opportunity, which they embraced with enthusiasm. While Hazara political activism failed to transcend ethnic boundaries during this period, organised violence as a strategy for political power and competition completely withered away among them. This was the unmistakable indicator of a different perception among the Hazaras of the opportunities presented by the post-2001 Afghan state. As armed insurgency spread from the south and east of Afghanistan after 2006, the Hazara areas remained the most peaceful and stable regions, indicating a firm determination for the success of the peaceful political process. The districts and villages that separate Hazarajat from the Pashtun areas, stretching from the provinces of Wardak and Ghazni and Uruzgan and Day Kundi, also marked the line of central government control on one side, and Taliban insurgency and violence on the other.

Throughout the course of this research, I encountered many former Hazara political and military leaders who expressed pride in what they often described as their choice of *qalam* over *shamshir*, or pen over gun. Such thinking led to an unprecedented rush to schools and universities among the Hazaras in both cities and remote villages of Hazarajat. Consequently, for the first time in the history of the country, Hazaras constitute a substantial part of the rapidly-expanding educated class in the country, and are at the forefront of civil society and peaceful activism in Kabul and other cities.

At the national level, the Hazaras enthusiastically embraced the ideals of political pluralism and democratic transformation, and Hazara elites were quickly integrated into the political and administrative structure of the government. Karim Khalili served as the second vice-president of Hamid Karzai, first in the transitional administration from 2002 to 2004, followed by two terms of elected presidential terms from 2004 to 2014. In the National Unity Government, which was formed after the controversial 2014 presidential elections, Sarwar Danesh became vice-president and Mohammad Muhaqeq became second deputy of Abdullah Abdullah, in a new office of chief executive officer. During this period, the cabinet also included a few Hazara ministers. At the subnational level, provincial and district administrations across the Hazarajat region were staffed mainly by local Hazaras who were mostly affiliated to one faction or the other of Hezb-e Wahdat.

Hazaras have also been keen participants in popular and electoral politics. In the first post-2001 parliamentary elections in 2005, Hazara won thirty seats, about 12 per cent of the 249 seats of the Lower House of the National Assembly. Other non-Hazara Shi'a candidates won eleven seats that together increased the Shi'a representation to about one-fifth of the parliament (Wilder, 2005, p. 8). In the September 2010 parliamentary elections, Hazaras and other Shi'as won 23 per cent of the seats. The increase largely came from the mixed Pashtun and Hazara province of Ghazni where Taliban threats and insecurity meant that few votes were cast in the Pashtun districts, and as a result Hazara candidates won all eleven seats of the province (Semple, 2011, pp. 5–6).

In response to one of Hazaras' historical demands for reform of sub-national administration, in 2004 Karzai ordered the creation of Day Kundi province, a new, mainly Hazara administrative unit from the former Shahristan and Day Kundi districts of Uruzgan province. The governors of the provinces of Bamyan and Day Kundi were also Hazaras who were appointed from Kabul. Among them was Habiba Sarabi who was appointed as governor of Bamyan in 2005 and became the first woman to occupy such a senior position in the subnational administration of a very conservative country. Beyond these two predominantly Hazara provinces, in ethnically mixed provinces such as Ghazni, Wardak and Balkh, Hazaras have served as deputy governors.

The main point here is that the Hazara aspiration for political participation, which as late as the 1990s was anathema for some of the mujahedin, was accepted with no opposition in the Bonn Conference. Moreover, by recognising the diverse ethnic composition of the nation of Afghanistan, the 2004 constitution became an important step towards the establishment of a harmonious multi-ethnic political system. The constitution (Article 131) also recognised the Shi'a jurisprudence alongside the Hanafi School as a legal source for personal matters of their followers. The article is highly symbolic as it applies only where modern statutory laws does not exist, and both parties to private matters such as family disputes are followers of the same religion. But it carries a highly significant meaning after more than a century of official religious discrimination.

However, the presence of Hazaras as vice-presidents, ministers and governors does not indicate an actual distribution of power in Kabul. The pattern of appointment of Hazara ministers during this period points to a gap between formal and actual distribution of power. Beginning with the December 2001 appointment of Muhammad Muhaqeq to the ministry of planning, Hazara ministers were restricted to powerless or service ministries such as the transport, agriculture, women's affairs and justice. Significantly, during several reshuffles and turnovers in the cabinet during this period, no Hazaras were proposed (interestingly not even by Hazaras themselves) as ministers of interior, defence, finance, foreign affairs or as head of the directorate of national security.

Furthermore, the distribution of power at the level of vice-presidents and cabinets did not broaden the composition of the bureaucratic or security agencies of the state. This is important because despite massive changes caused by the war, bureaucratic institutions are the most potent representation and carriers of the historical legacies and ideas of the Afghan state. The bureaucratic agencies of the Afghan state are also among the most important sources of real and perceived ethnic discrimination, as they are the first points of contacts for ordinary citizens, and the main channel of the provision of highly-demanded resources and services. In a country with little and shrinking employment opportunities for the educated youth after the drawdown of international military and civilian engagement in 2014, the state agencies are becoming the most important employers. Corruption and favouritism that have skyrocketed in recent years might also mean that access to these agencies and the services they offer is affected by the ethnic or political affiliation of their administrators.

In the case of the Hazaras, the legacy of a century of exclusion from the civil service has been one of the most enduring aspects of the historical Afghan state. While formally sanctioned discrimination in the civil service has ceased to exist as a policy, Hazaras remain severely underrepresented in the bureaucratic machinery of the state, particularly in the security, judiciary, finance and diplomatic sectors. In 2006, the Afghan government took a rare initiative to collect data on the background of its senior civil servants along ethnic lines. Because of the highly sensitive nature of the subject, the findings of the survey were not fully published but what was leaked of it showed that Tajiks comprised 53 per cent of civil servants in grade (Bast) 3 and above, followed by 34 per cent Pashtuns, 6 per cecnt Hazaras, 4 per cent Uzbeks and 4 per cent others (Sharan, 2013, p. 8). The Afghan civil service begins at grade 8 and continues to 3 and 1 for the positions of directors and directors general respectively. According to other reports, the imbalance is particularly striking in some important institutions. The court system is a case in point. According to the Centre for Policy and Human Development (Wardak, Saba & Kazem, 2007, p. 72), which was supported by the UN and prepared Afghanistan's first human development reports in 2007, from among 1,442 judges in Afghanistan's courts, only sixteen were Hazaras. Similarly, the report showed Hazaras accounted for only 1.93 per cent of the police force in 2007 (p. 82). In the Afghan National Army, which was created and trained by the international forces with a view to ensuring ethnic representation, the situation was better but the Hazaras still remain highly underrepresented. According to the International Crisis Group (2010), 'Pashtuns represented 42.6 per cent of the army overall, while Tajiks represented 40.98 per cent, Hazaras 7.68 per cent and Uzbeks 4.05 per cent and other minorities 4.68 per cent' (p. 19).

The opening of political space, at least to some Hazara elites, and the internationally funded reconstruction efforts have not meant that perceptions and realities of exclusion and marginalisation have also withered among the Hazaras. To the contrary, most Hazaras feel they are discriminated against in important agencies of the state and are left out of major development projects. Chiovenda (2014) shows how perceptions of exclusion and marginalisation continue to drive socio-political activism in Bamyan. Similarly, Mielke (2015) demonstrates how unplanned Hazara neighbourhoods such as Dasht-e Barchi in Kabul have become the medium through which Hazaras experience 'spatial exclusion and a heightened level of immobility'. Significantly, both studies demonstrate that perceptions and realities of exclusion in both urban and rural contexts are linked to historical and national experiences of exclusion.

Rejection and violence, the case of the Taliban and Hezb-e Islami

In contrast to the shift towards peaceful politics among the Hazaras, the Taliban, Hezb-e Islami and other extremist networks have ensured violence remains the predominant strategy for political survival in the Pashtun majority provinces. The result is an unfortunate parallel between the geographies of armed violence and insurgency and the distribution of Pashtun settlements. As Map VII.1 shows, by 2009 from the plains of Farah and Nimroz in the west of Afghanistan to the mountains and valleys in the east of the country, the Pashtun belt was the epicentre of violence, insurgency and extremism. The spread of terrorist networks and armed violence have followed a similar pattern across the Durand Line, affecting nearly all Pashtun areas of Pakistan. On the surface, it seems that religious fanaticism, extremist politics and violence have established deep roots in Pashtun society and culture.

How can the correlation between presence of Pashtun majority in a region and extremist violence be explained? This is an important question because there is nothing in Pashtun culture and way of life that would predispose them towards violence. An essentialist view of the Pashtun society and culture might locate the root causes of such mass violence in Pashtun tribal system and cultural practices. Pashtuns were leaders of one of the region's best-known non-violence movement. In 1929, Khan Abdul Ghafar Khan, a Pashtun leader from the North West Frontier Province launched the movement Khudai Khedmatgar (servants of God), a non-violent movement that offered peaceful resistance against British colonialism in the Indian Sub-continent. Abdul Ghafar Khan is often celebrated as the Ghandi of Pashtuns.

However, a more nuanced view also reveals profound internal tensions and struggles throughout the Pashtun community, and most importantly the human costs of the war on Pashtun civilians. The brunt of the war and armed conflict between 2001 and 2015 was borne by Pashtun civilians. According to the United Nations Assistance Mission for Afghanistan (United Nations, 2016c), between January 2009, when the organisation began documenting civilian casualties, and the end of 2015, 21, 323 civilians were killed and 37,413 others were injured as a result of the armed conflict. Furthermore, between 1 January and 30 September 2016, the organisation documented another 8,397 civilian casualties, including 2,562 deaths (2016). Given the concentration of intensity of the conflict in Pashtun areas, one can safely deduce that the vast majority of victims were Pashtuns.

Such massive violence and brutality are waged in the name of Islam and for control of the Afghan state. Current explanations focus on a range of factors that are behind the rise of extremist violence in the Pashtun areas. These include the spread of radical Deobandi and Wahhabi militant movements, manipulation and machination of the Pakistani military and religious institutions, and local socioeconomic conditions such as unemployment that drive young men into the arms of the insurgents. A more common explanation blames Pakistan for the spread of insurgency by accusing the country of promoting Islamic extremism to sideline Pashtun nationalist movements on both sides of the border. In his book, *The Pashtun Question* Siddique argues that the 'failure of both Islamabad and Kabul to incorporate the Pashtuns into state structures and the political and economic fabric has compromised the security of both countries' (2014, p. 3). Throughout the book, Siddique also attributes the influence of extremist groups to foreign powers, in particular the support of Pakistan's military and intelligence establishment since the 1980s. He argues that:

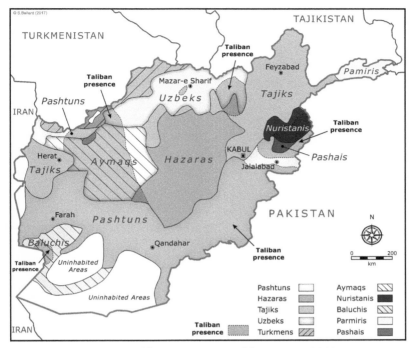

Map 7.1: Taliban activities in Afghanistan in 2009

Source: Dorronsoro, Carnegie Endownment for International Peace 2009.

Pashtuns are no more or less prone to extremism than members of any other ethnicity....Many Pashtun leaders have told me they believe the Pakistani military's myopic view of Pashtuns is the core problem. The war in Afghanistan provided Pakistan with a golden opportunity to act on its longstanding desire to weaken Pashtun nationalism. However, Islamabad's support for pan-Islamism resulted in a new movement that could be described as Pashtun Islamism. This new mindset gained traction during the Taliban's ascent to power in Afghanistan, when pan-Islamist solidarity surpassed the imperatives of tribal relations and ethnic cohesion.

Decades of Pakistani investment transformed Pashtun Islamism into a formidable political force and reduced the Pashtun nationalist threat. But several built-in contradictions in the policy backfired on Islamabad and its goal of enhancing Pakistani security and prestige. Indeed, these contradictions have become so onerous they now threaten Pakistan's survival. (2014, p. 43)

The previous chapters of this book may have made it clear that violence, whether caused by domestic or international factors, was a consistent feature of the history of the Afghan state and religiously justified violence was central to the success of the first Afghan state in extending its control over all parts of the country. While many see radical Islamism as a more recent phenomenon that gained traction only in the 1980s, in his book, *God's Terrorists*, Allen provides a long-term historical account of how radical and revivalist movements such as the Wahhabi Islam combined with Pashtun tribal resistance first against the Sikhs and later in the fight against British colonialism. According to Allen:

> In our times, these two streams [Wahabism and Salafi Islam] re-energised by new political ideologies associated with nationalism, separatism, and pan-Islamism, converged and cross-infected on the Afghanistan-Pakistan fault line. Out of this coming-together emerged two very different bodies, one tight-knit and localised, the other loose-knit ad with global aspirations: the Taliban and Al-Qaeda. (2007, p. 20)

If the policy of promotion of Islamic fundamentalism by Pakistanis backfired in the form of 'Pashtun Islamism' as argued by Siddique, and if Deobandi Islam associated itself with nationalism and separatism as argued by Allen, one must look at the underlying mechanisms and conditions which link various forms of nationalism with radical Islamism. While the role of Pakistan in promoting Islamic radicalism is well established, it can only explain the supply side of the radicalisation process. It does not explain why radical messages and ideologies promoted by Pakistan's religious or military establishment find different receptions in Afghanistan. Moreover, if the geographical proximity of the Pashtun provinces to Pakistan is a factor, the Baluch population similarly straddles both sides of the Pakistan-Afghan border with no marked tendencies towards radical Islamist messages. In recent decades, Baluch nationalism demanding autonomy or outright independence for Pakistan's Baluchistan Province has presented a similar threat to Pakistan's security and territorial integrity. Hence, Pakistan's elite might have a similar incentive to promote radical Islamism among the Baluchs to counteract Baluch nationalism. Moreover, the emphasis on Pakistan does not explain the failure of most secular and even leftist Pashtun elites to stand up and criticise radical and violent groups such as the Taliban.

Without denying the significance of foreign influence and poor governance in inflaming the insurgency, I argue that the dominant form of Pashtun nationalism is a key contributing factor to the success of radical and violent movements among the Pashtuns. In other words, if Pakistani interference explains the supply side of radicalisation, Pashtun nationalism explains the demand side of it. The intersection of religious extremism and nationalist politics is also evident in the manner of Hazara participation in the political process since 2001.

Pashtun nationalism contributes to the violent opposition to the state in two ways. First, the traction and endurance of violence among the Pashtuns benefits from a long history of religiously-justified violence and religiously-framed ethnic identity. As shown in the previous chapters, violence was a consistent feature of the rise to dominance of the Pashtuns over the past two centuries. Consequently, one might argue that a nationalistic history that cherishes *jehad* and mass violence as a path to ethnic or national glory explains the 'demand' side of the radicalisation process. This can be particularly the case if a nationalist ideology that seeks collective glory and pride in violence is not challenged, critiqued and questioned by alterative critical thoughts. The failure to provide alternative political visions and ideologies has often left militant and conservative Islam as the only source of inspiration in many Pashtun provinces.

Second, state-building conceived as a process of historical reconstruction by Pashtun nationalists, including some who participated in the government in Kabul, ensures that there are always some reservoirs of feelings of underrepresentation and discontent among the Pashtuns. The first few years after 2001 saw a powerful line of thinking that argued Pashtuns were alienated from the political process (Crisis Group, 2003). This was despite the fact that state-building as a process of historical reconstruction created the powerful presidential office. In fact, until 2014, it was occupied by Karzai, a Durrani Pashtun and as mentioned above, Pashtun political elites steadily increased their share of the power, particularly in the security, defence and finance sectors, in Kabul.

Lacking the ability to compete with the Taliban for influence and control over the Pashtun areas, the Pashtun elites in Kabul gradually shifted towards Afghan nationalism (a historically controversial and mostly Pashtun-centric ideology) and symbols of independence and resistance against foreign powers to boost their credentials. In competition with other ethno-political groups and bargaining with international actors, they used the Taliban threat as a tool of strategic advantage. Such a strategic approach became more evident after Karzai's relationship with the US and NATO deteriorated following his re-election in the controversial elections of 2009. During his second term, Karzai attempted to restrict and openly criticise Western military tactics against the Taliban whom he famously described as *broderan-e naraz*, disenchanted brothers (King, 2010). In April 2010, in a particularly tense period, Karzai was reported to have addressed a group of sixty Afghan parliamentarians by threatening 'If you and the international community pressure me more, I swear that I am going to join the Taliban' (Rubin, 2010). As will be shown below, the view that the Taliban insurgency was driven by disenchantment and Pashtun alienation with the Afghan state shaped the direction of most of the international aid to the country.

In the course of my own research across Afghanistan I found that throughout the 2001–2016 period perceptions of underrepresentation and marginalisation were present among all major communities. However, perceptions or realties of discontent had different consequences. In many provinces, ethnic, regional and at times linguistic identities and grievances have often offered ready and convenient electoral constituencies to political factions that mostly lack policy programmes and political platforms. In short, while discontent is widespread violence as a medium of its expression is not.

Pashtun nationalism as the dominant ideological framework and historical narrative provides a lens through which political outcomes and changes are interpreted. The effect of such ethnic frames of understanding is evident in the way in which Hazara social, cultural and political transformation is seen in recent years. Among the political elites, there emerged what is described by Amirzada (2011) as Hazaraphobia, a fear and apprehension that results from a combination of historical prejudices towards the Hazaras with recent stereotypical images of them as a motivated, highly-organised and fast-rising group. Over the years, in the course of my own research, I came across numerous politicians, journalists, government officials and even foreign diplomats who pointed to what they viewed as the 'rise of Hazaras' in Afghanistan's politics, civil society and cultural arenas.

Fears of the rise of Hazaras are reflected even more evidently in views of the most ideological groups such as the Taliban and Hezb-e Islami, who also view Afghanistan as a country in which ethnic groups have 'natural' limits and places. Such attitudes are most evident in perceiving the Hazara political participation in recent years. For example, on 7 August 2013 (BBC Persian Service, 2013), Hekmatyar, the leader of Hezb-e Islami, issued a statement in the Shahadat Daily, in which he warned the Hazaras of 'exemplary consequences' for their 'arrogance with the US support and assistance'. In an explicit reference to the Hazaras the statement said:

> The day will come when the oppressed people of Afghanistan will get ready to reclaim their violated rights. At that time, they will not find any refuge for themselves in any corner of the country. Some of them will flee to Iran and Iran will also give them a cruel and savage treatment.

Mullah Abdul Salam Zaeef, the Taliban Ambassador to Pakistan in the late 1990s, in an interview with the Los Angeles Times (Daragahi, 2010) presented a similar opinion about the Hazaras. He described the alleged rise of Hazaras as a 'conspiracy of the [foreign] occupation' that supports 'the minority against the majority', which he predicted will end with the end of foreign occupation. Significantly, in the same interview Zaeef accused the Hazaras of upsetting the ethnic 'balance' by overstepping their place.

Such stereotypical images of Hazaras held by militant groups have gradually translated into armed attacks on Hazara civilians during religious and political events and mass abduction on the highways. On 6 December 2011, a suicide bomber blew himself up among a crowd of Shi'as in Kabul, most of them Hazaras, who had gathered to commemorate Ashura. Another bomb went off on the same day among another Shi'a procession in Mazar-e Sharif. The bomb in Kabul killed at least fifty-five people, with another four killed in the attack in Mazar (Baktash & Rodriguez, 2011).

The attacks on Hazara targets in the urban centres is accompanied by a growing trend of abduction and murder of Hazaras across the highways that connect Hazarajat to Kabul and other major urban centres. In February 2016, the United Nations Assistance Mission in Afghanistan (UNAMA) reported that in 2015 the organisation:

> Observed a sharp increase in the abduction and killing of civilians of Hazara ethnicity by Anti-Government Elements. Between 1 January and 31 December, Anti-Government Elements abducted at least 146 members of the Hazara community in 20 separate incidents. All but one incident took place in areas with mixed Hazara and non-Hazara communities, in Ghazni, Balkh, Sari Pul, Faryab, Uruzgan, Baghlan, Wardak, Jawzjan, and Ghor provinces. (2016b, p. 49)

The year 2016 saw the number of such attacks rise further. Following the attack on the Enlightenment Movement on 23 July 2016, Ashura events were attacked in October 2016 in separate incidents in Kabul and the northern province of Balkh. In Kabul, in the evening of 11 October, an attacker wearing a police uniform engaged in a mass shooting of men, women and children who had gathered at the Karte Sakhi shrine in a predominantly Hazara neighbourhood in the West of Kabul. The attack claimed by ISIS killed eighteen and injured more than thirty others (Reuters, 2016). The following day, an Ashura procession was attacked by a remote controlled bomb in Khoja Gholak area the province of Balkh, killing another fourteen people and injuring many others (Radio Free Europe, 2016). In October 2016, Ghulam Husain Naseri, a Hazara member of parliament speaking at an open session of the assembly, claimed that over the previous fifteen years, 163 Hazaras were beheaded on the highways connecting Hazarajat to the rest of the country (Rasad News Agency, 2016).

Rewarding violence in distribution of development assistance

The ethnic hierarchy that developed in the power relations in Kabul in the 2001–2016 period, and the view held by extremist groups that ethnic groups have natural places and limits to their power in Afghanistan translate into practical consequences for political participation, access to socioeconomic resources and the security of different groups. Two such consequences for the Hazaras are worth exploring here: the distribution of foreign aid at the sub-national level, and organised attacks on, and violence directed against, the Hazaras.

Development aid as instrument of counter-insurgency

In important respects, the success of the US-led state-building effort depended on the extent to which it could bring tangible changes to the lives of ordinary people in the country. However, Afghanistan's post-2001 reconstruction efforts had to address different demands and expectations across the different regions of the country. From the adoption of Afghanistan's first five-year development plan in 1958 many regions such as Hazarajat were left out of the national infrastructural projects. Consequently, the internationally-financed reconstruction that began after 2001 had a very different meaning in Hazarajat. In many parts of Afghanistan, the task was to reconstruct the institutions and infrastructure destroyed by war. By contrast, in Hazarajat, there were no roads, airports, dams, power lines or other significant items of public infrastructure to be reconstructed; the important task in this region was construction, not reconstruction.

At the national level, driven by foreign aid and military spending Afghanistan's economy grew at an impressive average rate of 9 per cent between 2002 and 2012. During this period, the country's total Gross Domestic Product (GDP) increased from $4.1 billion in 2002 to $20.5 billion in 2012, and GDP per capita increased from $192 in 2002 to $690.08 in 2013. In general, the reconstruction efforts that began after 2001 did not prioritise addressing the legacies of the historical discrimination and neglect, or focusing on regions of greatest concerns in terms of poverty and other development indicators. On the contrary, the distribution of foreign aid at the subnational level was influenced by a number of other factors, ranging from political and economic significance of a given region for the international donors, and the ability of the various ethno-political factors to influence the allocation of foreign aid in Kabul, to the military and strategic relevance of the provinces.

One of the country's poorest regions, Hazarajat was particularly excluded from major infrastructural programmes such as construction of roads, dams and distribution of basic services such as electricity. Road construction was one of the main areas of international reconstruction. According to one estimate, by 2014 the US and other donors had spent about US$ 4 billion on roads (Sopko, 2014), most of which went to the ring roads that connect Afghanistan's capital to Mazar-e

Sharif and Qunduz to the north and northeast, Herat to the west, Jalalabad to the east and Qandahar to the south (Amiri, 2013). Hazarajat is excluded from the ring road. Consequently, one of the most important development demands of the Hazaras from the 1960s was construction of the Gardan-e Diwal Highway that connects Kabul through Hazarajat to the western city of Herat. If completed, the 705 km east-west corridor could break the geographic isolation of Hazarajat and reduce the travel distance between Kabul to Herat by 400 kilometres in comparison to the current route that goes through Qandahar in the south. The project was launched in 2007 but as of early 2016 only 180 km of road connecting Kabul to Bamyan, funded by Italy, has been partially completed (Gutsch, 2014).

What is certain is that after the Taliban reorganised and mounted a protracted armed insurgency against the Afghan and international forces in 2006, foreign aid became a central element of a military strategy that aimed to win the hearts and minds of the insurgency-affected provinces. Douglas (2012), who studied the dynamics of provincial allocation of international aid, found that there was 'a significant, positive relationship between the provincial distribution of U.S. aid in Afghanistan and a province's level of combatant violence'. He also found that there were 'some evidence of a negative correlation between the level of poverty by province and the allocation of aid'.

Vast amounts of aid distributed as instruments of counter-insurgency made aid itself a major factor contributing to the instability and vicious cycles of conflict by creating a perverse incentive structure. At the national level, the international donor community appeared to be rewarding violent provinces and districts at the cost of more stable and peaceful regions. According to Zyck (2012), this kind of development spending 'served to create rather than ameliorate grievances... created incentive structures that favour instability...[and] large aid flows in highly insecure areas led to "leakage", which financed insurgent groups' (p. 249).

Consequently, the US and other donors' taxpayers' money was spent in greatest volume where most US soldiers were killed. The subnational development spending by the United States Agency for International Development (USAID), certainly the largest external aid agency in the country, clearly shows these regional disparities. By

2007, only a year into the serious phase of the insurgency, the five mainly Pashtun provinces in the south, which accounted for about 11 per cent of the population of the country, had consumed 35 per cent of the US $1.3 billion the agency had spent since 2002. By contrast, the relatively more peaceful provinces in the north, which account for 29 per cent of the population had received 15 per cent of its spending during that period (Sappenfield, 2007b).

A major factor that determined the level of reconstruction and development assistance each province received was the distribution of the Provincial Reconstruction Teams (PRTs). Launched in 2003 by the International Security Assistance Force (ISAF), the PRTs were military contingents assisted by small numbers of development and diplomatic advisors (Maley & Schmeidl, 2015). Their main objective was to extend the reach of the central government at the provincial level. By 2007, twenty-five PRTs covered Afghanistan's thirty-four provinces. Largely led by a single national contingent, the PRTs became the main channel of distribution of development assistance by their respective nations. The problem was that the level of assistance and amount of funds that were available to a PRT commander sharply varied, depending on the level of commitment, priorities and interests of their respective countries. PRTs led by the major donors were mostly stationed in the southern and eastern provinces. For example, the British led the PRT in Helmand, the Canadians in Qandahar, the Dutch and later Australians in Uruzgan while the US formed the largest number of PRTs in the south and east of the country. By 2008, the varying amount of spending by the PRTs was sharpening the geographical disparity in aid allocation. According to Waldman (2008), if divided per capita, by 2008, at one extreme, Panjsher, which had a US PRT, had received $685 per person in international assistance while the provinces of Day Kundi and Takhar, which had no PRT, and Faryab, which had a Norwegian PRT, had received only $30 per capita. Southern Afghanistan, the birthplace of the Taliban in 1994 and the epicentre of insurgency during this period, attracted the highest amount of foreign military and development spending. In 2008, if considered as a state, Helmand became the fifth largest recipient of funds from USAID. In addition, the province attracted one-fifth of the Afghanistan budget of the British Department for International Development (DFID) (Waldman, 2008; The World Bank, 2012).

According to the World Bank, regions that were historically neglected and geographically isolated but were nonetheless peaceful during this period, lagged behind the main urban centres and the provinces that were most affected by the insurgent violence. The 'lagging regions' included west-central provinces of Ghor, Bamyan, and Daykundi, northeastern provinces of Badakhshan, Takhar, Baghlan, Kunduz and eastern provinces of Nangarhar, Kunar, Laghman, Nooristan. With a poverty headcount rate of more than 50 per cent, (compared to 39 per cent at the national level), these regions were home to more than half of the country's poor population. Despite such sharp regional differences, the average per capita spending of aid in the poor regions was about half of that from the most affluent Central Region which includes Kabul (The World Bank, 2015).

By contrast, regions like Hazarajat, where a 'hearts and mind campaign' was unnecessary, received little attention. In Bamyan, the PRT was formed by New Zealand. In contrast to the resource-rich PRTs in the south and east, the PRT in Bamyan had modest resources and operated in a largely peaceful environment. Despite the highly successful public relations conducted by the New Zealand PRT, the disparity in PRT funding was so sharp that in 2007, Habiba Sarabi, the governor of Bamyan explicitly wished there was an American PRT in her province with more resources (IRIN, 2007).

Another illustrative example is the level of international assistance provided to Day Kundi and Panjsher, the two predominantly Hazara and Tajik areas respectively, which were simultaneously declared as separate provinces by Karzai in 2004. Both provinces were among the most peaceful throughout the 2001–2016 period. Nonetheless, in 2007, Panjsher, which had a well-funded US-led PRT, was connected to Kabul with a reconstructed asphalted road funded by the USAID, which reduced the travel time between the province and Kabul from five hours to two. By contrast, there was no PRT in Day Kundi. As of early 2016, the first ever asphalted road of the province is only 3 kilometre long, which was constructed in the provincial capital, Nili in 2013. Similar patterns can be observed in Hazara districts of multiethnic provinces. The main point here is that Hazara areas were left out of major infrastructural projects, and the regional disparity in reconstruction efforts is central to how Hazaras conceive their relations with the Afghan state in Kabul.

INTERVENTION, STATE-BUILDING AND ETHNIC POLITICS

The Conflict between Pashtun nomads and local Hazaras

In no area can one evaluate the relationship between Hazaras and the Afghan state after the year 2001 as clearly as in the Pashtun nomads' renewed attempt to return to Hazarajat. Beginning with the summer of 2004, the nomads attempted to return to Hazarajat and to reassert their claim on the land and pasture of the region. The main point through which they sought to enter the region was the Behsud region of Wardak province. Fearful of the consequences of the return of the nomads, the Hazaras resisted and Behsud became the main scene of intense conflict in summers of subsequent years. As the conflict broke out every summer, the government of Karzai sent a delegation to the region to investigate the causes and consequences of the conflict, or set up working groups and commissions in Kabul to find a long-term resolution. None of these interventions succeeded in producing a durable solution (Wily, 2013; Foschini, 2013).

In the summer of 2006, the conflict took on wider dimensions as the nomads' effort to enter Hazarajat took the form of armed offensives by hundreds of armed militias. In response, local Hazaras also mounted increasingly organised armed resistance. Nonetheless, they were often overwhelmed by the more heavily armed Pashtun nomads. In the summers of 2007 and 2008, after the local resistance was overwhelmed, the nomad militias engaged in an extensive campaign of looting and destruction, creating an alarming humanitarian emergency.

In the summer of 2008, the conflict nearly escalated to become a fully-fledged ethnic and sectarian war. Hundreds of nomads armed with machine guns and rocket launchers broke the local Hazara resistance and advanced into the districts of Hese Awal-e Behsud, Hese Dowum Behsud and Day Mirdad. In that year alone, the conflict led to twenty-four deaths among the Hazaras. What further complicated the conflict were reports of participation of the Taliban in support of the nomads against the Hazaras. Besides the burning of schools and clinics during their attack in Behsud, which was a distinctive signature of the Taliban insurgency during these years, the militias also left plenty of graffiti on the walls of Hazara houses in Behsud. The graffiti condemned the Hazaras as infidels, significantly associating them with the American invasion of the country (Coghlan, 2008; Linschoten, 2008; IRIN, 2008).

In 2009, the Kuchis did not try to enter Behsud. It was widely reported that President Karzai had distributed about US$ 2–3 million to the main Kuchi militia commanders to persuade them not to enter into the region (IRIN, 2010). This was a critical election year and both Muhaqeq and Khalili supported Karzai's candidacy in the September presidential election. A nomad assault during this year would have deprived Karzai of Hazara votes. In the summer of 2010, a renewed armed attack broke the respite created by the presidential election of 2009. In the summer of 2011, the nomads launched an offensive on the Nawur district of Ghazni province, which was historically both a destination as well as transit route for some of the Kuchi tribes. In 2012, another offensive by some 2,000 Kuchis wreaked havoc in Behsud. After the Hazaras evacuated, Fioriti (2012), one of the rare foreign journalists who visited the region, reported that the looting and destruction in Kajab, an area of Behsud, had turned it into 'a post-apocalyptic wasteland dotted with gutted, fire-blackened mud buildings'.

In its annual report on the situation of human rights in Afghanistan, the Afghanistan Independent Human Rights Commission (AIHRC), provided the following summary of the extent of damage and displacement caused by the conflict:

> From the year 1386 [2007] onwards, annually thousands of inhabitants of districts of Day Mirdad, Behsud and other places in Maidan Wardak Province, and the Nawur district of Ghazni province were forced to flee by armed attacks of armed Kuchis; their farms were destroyed and their houses were set ablaze. Reports from previous years show that in 1386 [2007], around 1900 families were displaced as a result of these conflicts in the districts of Day Mirdad and Behsud in Maidan Wardak. In 1387, these conflicts forced more than 6,000 families to flee from their homes and 84 houses were burnt. In 1389 [2010], as a result of Kuchi attacks 2791 families were forced to leave their homes from the three districts of Behsud I, Behsud II and Day Mirdad, most of them seeking refuge in Kabul. In the year 1390 [2011], as a result of these conflicts in the Nawur district of Ghazni province 36 villages were severely affected, 762 families were forced to flee, and their belongings, properties and household items were plundered. (2013, p. 81)

The reports of Taliban supporting the nomads' offensive against the Hazaras were credible because as the conflict intensified, the Taliban also increased their control over most of the Pashtun districts of

Wardak. The nomads would cross the Taliban-controlled areas before advancing to Hazara villages. A Taliban alliance with the nomads or their support for the attack on the relatively peaceful and pro-government Hazara districts was highly likely and plausible in the context of the broader Taliban objective of destabilizing the country (Foschini, 2013, p. 20). Furthermore, Naim Kuchi, the Kuchi militia commander who led the Taliban attack on Hazarajat in 1998, became the chief organiser of the attack on Behsud. In 2003, he was captured by the US forces in Afghanistan and transferred to Guantanamo Bay where he was detained for his involvement with the Taliban until 2005. In 2007 and 2008, Naim Kuchi and his family were leading the armed offensives in Behsud. He was also believed to have coordinated the attack on Nawur in 2011.

Between 2012 and 2015, the nomads refrained from making any major attempt to enter Hazarajat but the issue was not formally resolved. The complexity and intractability of the conflict serves as an indicator of how the legacies of the historical Afghan state and efforts to reconstruct it shape the present dynamics. In the post-2001 era, the agriculturalist Hazaras believed that western-style democracy would make reconstitution of any form of past exploitative relations an anathema. However, for the nomads, and other Pashtun elites in Kabul, the state-building process was also an exercise of reconstitution of the past. For the Kuchis, the centralisation of power and expansion of state authority also implied the revival of their state-backed claims over pasture of the Hazarajat and the particular social and economic privileges they had acquired in the region after the Hazara War of the 1890s.

Conclusion

Despite its continued fragility, Afghanistan achieved much between 2001 and 2016. The international intervention profoundly transformed the society at all levels. Perhaps, the most significant and long-term effect of the intervention and the relative opening of the political space comes from the exposure of the Afghan society to the forces of globalisation with the potential to shift the underlying social and political dynamics of the country. But could the international intervention have achieved greater success in stabilising Afghanistan and in creating more effective national institutions of pluralist politics and peaceful political transformation? This question will be asked by many Afghan and international scholars who will attempt to make sense of what did not go so well in Afghanistan. Most explanations focus on the shortfalls and inconsistencies of international actors' approach, Afghanistan's neighbours' interference or the institutional design of the post-2001 state institutions. Without discrediting such perspectives or underestimating these factors, in this chapter I attempted to show that the state-building process was also deeply undermined by the tensions and contradictions between Afghanistan's past and the ideals of political pluralism and representative politics in the post-2001 period. I have shown that the underlying assumptions and motivations of reconstructing an imagined Afghan state not only underpinned an ethnic hierarchy in distribution of political power and foreign aid but also fuelled the insurgency and rebellion by providing reservoirs of religious-nationalist ideas and imageries.

In this chapter, I have attempted to explain how these tensions and contradictions influenced the post-2001 state-building process by creating divergent perceptions of the legacy of Afghanistan's past, fuelling ethnic political dynamics among the elites in Kabul, and contributing to the extremist and violent opposition to the state-building enterprise. The intractability of the conflict between the local Hazaras and the Pashtun nomads, and the inability or unwillingness of the state elites to resolve it, are symptomatic of the conundrum of state-building in Afghanistan. Similarly, the militarisation of international development aid show the manner in which the international actors misunderstood and contributed to the contradictions in the state-building process.

The pattern that emerges during this period is that the international intervention and the state-building process that followed it met with different responses across Afghanistan's ethno-cultural landscape. The Hazaras, who were known for their rebelliousness towards the central authority a century earlier, became the most enthusiastic participants in the political process after 2001. The main Tajik, Hazara, and Uzbek ethno-political factions that emerged in the course of armed conflict since the 1980s de-radicalised, largely renouncing organised violence as a strategy for attainment of power. By contrast, their rivals and counterparts among Pashtuns, the Taliban and Hezb-e Islami, retained their ethnic character and organised violence. As a result, opposition against international intervention was largely restricted to the Pashtun majority provinces. By comparison, the Soviet invasion of Afghanistan in December 1979 met with rebellions all over Afghanistan, giving the opposition to the Soviet occupation a national and popular character. How can one understand this puzzle? I argued that besides other external factors such as Pakistan's support for extremist groups and Saudi financing, deep-seated Afghan nationalism contributed to the dynamics of extremist politics by linking national, ethnic and religious historical narratives and imageries. Hence, the intersection between nationalism, power politics and religious extremism is at the core of the insurgency and rebellion against the central state in the period after 2001.

The varying responses to the state-building enterprise also illustrate the processes and dynamics of politicisation of ethnic identities. Ethnicity as a political force retained its resilience through the failure of elites in Kabul to agree on a new social contract in Afghanistan, in which the benefits of the modern state in Afghanistan would be equitably distributed to all groups in the country. This comes down to a simple and disturbing conundrum: the fear that the state may become the instrument of dominance of one group over others. In response to the potential threat of an exclusionary and oppressive state, ethnicity offers itself as a source of security and safety. Hence, the state politicises ethnicity, and war and violence securitise it.

State-building as historical reconstruction rests on a denial that many of Afghanistan's problems are domestic; a denial that violence benefits from a nationalist political imagination and historical narrative that glorifies an imagined past, cherishes *jehad* and mass violence, and creates a hierarchy of power relations among its ethnic groups. The future of Afghanistan hinges on critiquing and exposing this dangerous fusion of nationalism, religious fundamentalism and brutal power politics. I hope this book makes a contribution in opening this debate.

CONCLUSION

Revisiting the main argument of the book

In the first chapter of this book, I made an analytical distinction between two types of scholarship on Afghanistan: the war-centric and the state-centric. The state-centric literature takes a long-term historical approach and locates the primary mechanisms of politicisation of ethnic identities in long-term processes of state formation and emergence of modern Afghanistan. It focuses on uncovering and exposing the long-term structural contradictions and historical legacies of the central state in Afghanistan. Consequently, these scholars challenge, question and deconstruct Afghanistan's official historical narratives, nationalist historiography and myths. By contrast, the war-centric accounts take a comparatively short-term approach by viewing politicised ethnic identities as a product of foreign interference and the failure or weakness of central state institutions since the late 1970s. These scholars and analysts also assume the central Afghan state to be a benign actor, and their accounts often contain an implicit nostalgia for the period before 1978, when Afghanistan was ruled by the Pashtun monarchy. The central point of divergence concerns the institutions and legacies of the centralised Afghan state. Hence, the debate reflects an intense contestation over the legacies and conceptions of the Afghan state as a historical entity, and the strategies for restoring national order and stability to the country.

In the previous chapters, like most state-centric accounts I took a long-term historical perspective to explore specific mechanisms and processes that linked state-building, state fragmentation and war to processes of politicisation of ethnic identities. However, I departed from most state-centric accounts by emphasising historical shifts and evolutions of both the state and the Hazara people as an ethnic group. I conceived the state as a contested set of institutions and field of power relations that experiences periodic crises, and thus rises and falls, consolidates and fragments, expands and contracts. In the course of the contestation over control of the state, ethnicity emerges as a principle of social-boundary making for both the centralising elites, who took control of the state, and the challenging groups, who were excluded from it.

I discussed the relations between Hazaras and the modern state in Afghanistan over three historical periods, with each phase demonstrating the manner in which the state interacted with the Hazaras as an ethnic group. First, state-building and centralisation of power towards the end of the nineteenth century spawned several rebellions, with the Hazaras being one of several such rebellious groups but certainly the most significant and most severely victimised of all. I argued that these rebellions were a response to a process of internalisation of wars of conquests. The centralised Afghan state, which emerged during the reign of Abdur Rahman Khan (1880–1901), was the culmination of a long process of internalisation of an economy of conquest and plunder, which it inherited from its predecessor, the Durrani Empire.

Second, between 1901 and 1978 (with the major exception of the 1929 rebellions) the Afghan state remained mostly stable and hence had the opportunity further to consolidate its power and legitimate its authority by making the state and its resources and service available to its citizenry at large. The central state that the Afghan rulers of this period inherited was based on an exclusive relation of exchange between Pashtun centralisers and a coalition of tribal aristocracy and warriors. The consolidation and legitimation of Afghanistan as a nation state thus depended on broadening the relations of exchange by offering political participation, security, rule of law and socioeconomic development to all inhabitants of the country. I argued that throughout the first three-quarters of the twentieth century, despite periodic experiments of liberalisation, the state continued to engage in the selective distribution of the benefits of control of the state and its resources. The process of selection and exclusion did not benefit all Pashtun tribes and communities. On the contrary, in the process of centralisation of power many Pashtun tribes were also excluded and subjected to violence but at the national level the state control brought sufficient privileges and benefits to sufficient number of Pashtun tribes and elites to transform the state into a vehicle of Pashtun domination. In the case of the Hazaras, this meant that the state demanded that they contribute to the upkeep of the state by committing their political allegiance, paying tax and performing military service without extending to them the benefits of modern state. In addition to more tangible paybacks of integration into a modern state such as political participation and balanced socioeconomic development, the politics of ethnic exclusion also covered more symbolic and non-material components such as exclusive national identity construction, ethno-nationalist historiographies and cultural and linguistic policies.

Third, in response to several decades of selection and exclusion, the Hazara struggle for recognition has sought to broaden the terms of exchange between the central state and various social and political groups of the country. In this system of exchange, the state demands taxation, military services and political loyalty in return for political participation and equitable distribution of public goods such as socioeconomic development, rule of law and general security.

In this broad historical perspective, the sharp increase in consciousness among the Hazaras as an ethnic group emerged as a reaction to the exclusive policies and national identity construction by the state elites. At the core of the group consciousness, which I describe as struggle for recognition, is an effort to broaden the terms of exchange between the Afghan state and all communities of the country. While the Hazara struggle for recognition has emerged as a powerful subaltern narrative that challenges a century of exclusion and persecution, it remains a forward-looking movement for securing and extending the material and symbolic benefits of the Afghan state to all groups of the country.

In a nutshell, the failure of the state to offer such broad terms of exchange to all citizens of the country politicised ethnic identities, and the war and instability of recent decades securitised them.

State-building as historical reconstruction

How can insights of the war-centric or state-centric accounts be used to understand the state-building enterprise that followed the 2001

US-led international intervention in Afghanistan? What are some of the policy proposals and strategic directions that followed from them for reconstituting the state and depoliticising ethnic and other social cleavages? These questions are important because historically the rise and fall of the state in Afghanistan were closely linked to dynamics of ethnic politics. The archetype of the historical Afghan state was created by Abdur Rahman Khan in the nineteenth century, and continues to inspire the imagination of the Pashtun nationalists and centralisers, including the Taliban, up to the present. The sacrosanct element of the model is centralised power held by a Pashtun in Kabul. In its underlying assumption, it equates centralisation with Pashtunisation and any form of decentralisation, distribution or devolution of power with acts of national treason and foreign conspiracies.

There is a well-established historical pattern that links centralisation of power with Pashtun domination in Afghanistan. The most notable centralising rulers of Afghanistan are Amir Abdur Rahman (1880–1901), Nader Khan (1929–1933) and most recently the Taliban's Mullah Omar (1996–2001). Despite important differences in the kinds of governments they formed and the historical context in which they operated, the manner in which they rose to power and the way in which they extended their control over the regions of the country show some stark similarities. First, all three of the centralisers emerged in periods of crises, when the state was either severely weakened or had totally collapsed: Abdur Rahman Khan after the disintegration of state authority in the course of the second Anglo-Afghan War (1878–1880); Nader Khan after the rebellions that forced the modernist king Amanullah Khan into exile and brought Habibullah Kalakani (January–November 1929), a Tajik, to power; and Mullah Omar after the collapse of the PDPA government in Kabul 1992 and the subsequent civil war among the *mujahedin*. Second, in their bid to gain national control each of the three depended on some form of foreign backing, the British in the case of Abdur Rahman and Nader Khan (although to different degrees) and Pakistan in the case of Mullah Omar. Third, all three of them used the selective distribution of state power and resources to form and mobilise coalitions that were largely dominated by Pashtuns against mostly non-Pashtun rebellions or contenders of power. Hence, centralisation of power paralleled Pashtun political hegemony.

CONCLUSION

Thus, the main question facing Afghanistan after 2001 was whether the state could be conceptualised and constructed in a way that it could stand above the ethnic divisions of the country. In other words, could the Afghan state and state-building processes be decoupled from perceptions and policies of ethnic domination? In theory, a liberal and democratic state of the twenty-first century might depoliticise ethnicity by according equal rights and obligations to individuals, rather than large groups like ethnic communities. But depoliticisation of ethnicity in a country disrupted by war, and brutalised by exclusionary regimes, requires much more than the simple provision of equality of individual citizens before the law. For ethnicity to be depoliticised, the state had to be de-ethnicised first, as the privileged influence of any ethnic group over the state brings ethnicity to the heart of struggles for power and competition for resources.

The war-centric account dominated post-2001 thinking and policy-making, by defining state-building as an act of historical reconstruction, pushing the state-centric approach to the margin of political debate as being of no practical relevance. The underlying assumption of the thinking was simple: more than two decades of armed conflict in the country was imposed by foreign interferences and invasion. Consequently, the previous two decades were assumed to be an aberration from the historical trajectory of the Afghan state. Thus, stabilisation required the reconstruction of what had been destroyed by the war. The argument was and may still be intuitively convincing, as state-building as historical reconstruction implies that the contemporary and Western notions of political pluralism, democratic politics, and social and political freedoms should be legitimated through traditional mechanisms and templates. The road to modernity can only go through the territory of Afghan traditions. However, what the proponents of this view ignore is the profound social and political transformation the country experienced during the war.

State-building conceived as a historical reconstruction denied there was a tension between two ideas of the Afghan state: the Afghan state as a historical entity that existed before the April 1978 coup and a state that would meet the demands of a deeply-disrupted and impoverished society in the twenty-first century. The former is informed by a nostalgia for the past, and an out-dated image of the society in Afghanistan, which are constructed and entrenched in the minds of Afghan national-ists. The latter begins with an awareness of the profound contradictions and historical legacies of the past and advocates a radical rethinking of the myths and assumptions of Afghan nationalism.

However, despite the dominance of the conception of state-building as an act of historical reconstruction, the political process began with widespread recognition that the central government in Kabul must be broad-based and representative of the population of Afghanistan. The civil war of the 1990s created a broad recognition, both internally and inter-nationally, that an exclusionary political system based on a single ethnic or political group was no longer tenable. This was important because for the first time in the history of the country, the diverse social fabric of the country and the importance of its reflection in its political dispensation were being recognised. Furthermore, the US-led international interven-tion, at least in theory, also sought to promote liberal democracy that protected the rights of women and minorities. Hence, in theory recon-struction of state institutions was conceived to go in tandem with a democratisation process. The litmus test of a genuine transition from the historically Pashtun-centric conception of the state is whether the elec-tion of a non-Pashtun as head of the state through a democratic process is accepted or allowed to happen. The 2014 presidential elections crisis, which stopped short of unravelling the state and ended through an exter-nally brokered political compromise, showed that there were powerful forces that resisted such transformation.

In 2017, Afghanistan faces an uncertain future. With the departure of most of the US and NATO forces at the end of 2014 and the subse-quent decline in international aid and attention, Afghanistan faces greater challenges with fewer resources. The reduced international presence will increase demands and pressures on the state institutions and may allow the historical dynamism of power relations in Afghanistan to reassert itself. The future of a broad-based and representative politi-cal order will depend on an important, yet simple choice between making the state and its resources accessible to the society at large or reverting to the historical pattern of selective distribution and repre-sentation. The former may not necessarily resolve all of Afghanistan's problems but could certainly increase its resilience and capacity to face the challenges by sharing the costs and benefits through a social con-tract between the state and the society.

NOTES

1. ETHNIC AND TRIBAL POLITICS IN TRANSITION FROM EMPIRE TO STATEHOOD

1. All English translations of quotations from *Sirāj al-Tawārīkh* in this book are from the English translation of the work of Kateb by McChesney and Khorrami (2012).

2. STATE-BUILDING, VIOLENCE AND REBELLIONS: THE PERIOD OF AMIR ABDUR RAHMAN KHAN, 1880–1901

1. The reports of British news writers quoted in this chapter are based on *Diaries of Kandahar*, a collection of such reports gathered from archives by Gulzari (2004).

4. THE RISE AND FALL OF A CLERICAL PROTO-STATE: HAZARA-JAT, 1979–1984

1. It would appear that Ayatollah Beheshti did not have clear ideas about what the *Shura* meant by 'Islamic republic'. When asked in an interview what the Islamic republic would be like, he answered that he would explain that when the time came (Ayatollah Behishti, 1982).
2. Every Shi'a Mujtahed designates Wakil or representatives in each part of the Shi'a world who collect the religious donations and explains religious affairs according to their respective *mujtahed*.
3. There is a significant Hazara community in Quetta, estimated to be close to half a million. Initially formed by the Hazaras who fled the Hazara War in Afghanistan in the 1890s, the community has grown substantially as a result of subsequent labour migration and refugee settlement during the war in Afghanistan.

251

4. Before the formation of the *Shura*, local committees including rebellion leaders were set up in many districts or sub-districts. For example, after collapse of the government administration in Jaghuri district, a committee was set up that included representatives from all major tribes of the district and clerics who were given the role of dealing with disputes according to the Sharia laws (interview with Haji Amanullah Rezayee, Jaghuri, December 2005).

5. AT THE SOURCE OF FACTIONALISM AND CIVIL WAR IN HAZARAJAT, 1981–1989

1. For an anthropological analysis of pre-war religious networks and their implications for the Shi'a religious movements in the region see Canfield (1984).
2. The intelligentsia are here defined as all those who are involved in the production, manipulation and distribution of culture and ideas. In practice, *rawshanfikr*, the Farsi equivalent, is mainly used to refer to graduates of modern schools and universities who engage in diverse professions, including teachers, writers, journalists and authors.
3. The combination of Hazara nationalism and Islamism in Nasr had its roots in the social contexts in which the smaller groups that merged to establish it were formed. During the 1960s and 1970s, the leaders of Nasr were trained in religious madrasahs in Najaf, Iran and Kabul. They had formed separate discussion groups and cultural circles prior to the war in Afghanistan that became the nucleus of Nasr in the 1980s. Those trained in Najaf were more heavily influenced by Khomaini's doctrine of *Welayat e Faqih*, which defined a political role for the *ulema*, while those trained in Kabul were more concerned with the disadvantaged position of the Hazaras under the Afghan state. The Mashhad and Qom circles were more inclined towards the Ali Shariati's political Islam and would send his books to their counterparts in Kabul.
4. In Waras, the head of *Hawzah* was from Pasdaran and his deputy was a Nasr member, in contrast to Laal wa Sarjangal, where Nasr appointed the head and Pasdaran the deputy. In Yakawlang, where Nasr controlled the entire district, the head, military commander, judges and other significant positions were all filled by Nasr. On the other hand, in Panjab there was a mostly equal distribution of power (interviews with former Nasr and Pasdaran leaders, 2006).
5. As a result, Shahristan has one of the highest levels of literacy and school enrolment in the region. Similarly, the district produces one of the finest almonds of Afghanistan, which is an important part of the local economy (interview with Musa Sultani, Director of Regional

Office of the Afghanistan Independent Human Rights Commission, Bamyan July 2006).

6. For instance, control of the Bazaar of Angori by Bashi Habib of Hezb-e Islami provided him access to significant revenues collected as tax on the shopkeepers and tributes paid to him by the Pashtun drivers and smugglers transporting goods, migrants and internally displaced people from Hazarajat to and from Pakistan. He had set up an agency that controlled and coordinated the movement of people and goods through the bazaar.

6. THE SHIFT FROM INTERNAL WARS OF DOMINATION TO NATIONAL STRUGGLES FOR RECOGNITION: HAZARAS AND ETHNICISATION OF POLITICS AND WAR IN 1990S

1. The view that Iranian officials, in particular Husain Ibrahimi, were apprehensive about the formation of *Wahdat* was frequently raised in my interviews and conversations with former senior officials of the party. The overall theme that emerges from these interviews is that the Iranians preferred Shuray-e Eatelaf over a full unification process.

2. Sunnah is the second most important source of Islamic law and guidance after the Holy Quran. It is an Arabic word that is used to refer to the sayings and practices of the Prophet Muhammad. In Shiite Islam it also includes the words and deeds of the Twelve Imams.

3. In his final speech at the ceremony where he handed the power to Rabbani in June 1992, Mojaddedi counted the challenges he faced in stabilising the situation. Among other things, he bitterly complained that he was undermined by Rabbani and Massoud. Significantly, he stated: 'the ministry of defense did not stay neutral in the fighting between Ittehad-e Islami and Hezb-e Wahdat-e Islami and openly sided with Ittehad' (Azimi, 1999, p. 623).

4. The 300-page report, usually called a mapping report, was compiled by the Office of the United Nations High Commissioner for Human Rights and describes the main patterns of human rights violations and war crimes from 1978 to 2001 in Afghanistan. Louise Arbour, the then UN Human Rights Commissioner, presented a copy of the report to President Karzai in 2005. The report has not been officially released but has been widely circulating on several websites since 2010.

5. Like many similar atrocities in the history of the war in Afghanistan, the Kandi Posht massacre has not been investigated by human rights organisations or official agencies. What has made the task of documenting this particular massacre difficult is that it occurred in an area that was strictly under Taliban control in 1997–98 and a resurgence of

Taliban activities in recent years has effectively placed the area off limits to human rights researchers.

7. INTERNATIONAL INTERVENTION, STATE-BUILDING AND ETHNIC POLITICS, 2001–2016

1. A controversial clause in article 16 of the constitution, which provides for preservation of what are called national terminologies, has become the basis of protracted controversies over languages issues and policies. Pashtun nationalists interpret the article to mean that Pashto terms for military, academic and administrative titles and grades can be used in Dari. They are challenged by Dari-speaking politicians and intellectuals who prefer to use the Dari equivalents of the Pashto terms. For example, the use of the Dari word, *Daneshgah*, for university, instead of the Pashto word, *Pohantun*, is the subject of passionate controversies among university teachers, students and politicians.

2. The decline in the number of former mujahedin-affected non-Pashtun was because the Taliban, and senior leaders of Hezb-e Islami, who were mainly Pashtun participants of the civil war in the 1990s, did not participate in the political process. However, a younger faction of Hezb-e Islami, which in May 2005 declared a political party in Kabul with the same name as the militant faction under Hekmatyar, became a highly influential player. Initially led by Khalid Farooqi, a mid-rank commander of the group from the Paktia province, the group steadily increased its influence with many of its members becoming ministers in the cabinet and several other members who served as members of parliament, provincial governors and other senior positions.

BIBLIOGRAPHY

Abu Bakr, M., A.-R. Dihlavi & Azim Khan, M. (1889) *Taqvim Al-Din* (Kabul: Printing Press of the Royal House).

Adamec, L. (ed.). (1977) *Historical and Political Gazetter of Afghanistan: Kandahar and South-Central Afghanista.*(Graz: Akademische Druck—u. Verlagsanstalt (ADEVA)).

Afghanistan Justice Project (2005) *Casting Shadows: War Crimes and Crimes against Humanity* (Kabul: Afghanistan Justice Project).

Ahady, Anwar-ul-Haq (1995) 'The Decline of the Pashtuns in Afghanistan', *Asian Survey* 35 (7): 621–34.

Ali Shah, S. (1899, September 22). *No. 7877* in M. Gulzari (2004) *Diaries of Kandahar.*

Allen, C. (2007) *God's Terrorists: The Wahabi Cult and the Hidden Roots of Modern Jihad* (Boston: Da Capo Press).

Amiri, M. (2013) 'Road Reconstruction in Post-Conflict Afghanistan: A Cure or a Curse?' *International Affairs Review*, XXI (2), 2–16.

Amirzada, H. (2011) 'Khizish hazaraha dar intikhabat-e parlimani wa hazara-phobia' ('Hazara Mobilisation in the Parliamentary Elections and Hazaraphobia'), available at http://www.khorasanzameen.net/php/read.php?id=515 (last accessed March 2016).

Anderson, B. (1991) *Imagined Communities: Reflections on the Origin and Spread of Nationalism* (London and New York: Verso).

Arwin, Ayub (2012) *Salgard-e qatl-e mazari, bahs-e taghir-e nezam bala migirad* (*On Annivarsary of the Death of Mazari, the Discussion of Change of System Intensifies*) BBC Persian Service, available at http://www.bbc.com/persian/afghanistan/2012/03/120312_k02-mazari-fedralism-mohqeq.shtml (last accessed 19 March 2016).

Ayatollah Beheshti, S. (1982) interview with G. Danish, Shura Office in Iran, 11 June.

Azimi, Muhammad Nabi (1999) *Urdu wa siyasat dar she dahey akhir-e Afghanistan*

(*Army and Politics in the Last Three Decades in Afghanistan*) (Peshawar: Maiwand Publications).

Babur, Z. M. (1922) *The Babur-nama in English* (Vol. I), trans. A. S. Beveridge (London: Luzac & Co), available at https://ia801403.us.archive.org/15/items/baburnamainengli01babuuoft/baburnamainengli01babuuoft_bw.pdf (last accessed January 2016).

Baktash, H., & A. Rodriguez (2011) 'Two Afghanistan bombings aimed at Shiites kill at least 59 people', *Los Angeles Times*, available at http://articles.latimes.com/2011/dec/07/world/la-fg-afghanistan-bombings-20111207 (last accessed April 2016).

Barfield, T. (2010) *Afghanistan: A Cultural and Political History* (Princeton: Princeton University Press).

Barth, F. (1969) 'Introduction', in F. Barth (ed.), *Ethnic Groups and Boundaries: The Social Organization of Cultural Differences* (Boston: Little, Brown & Co.) pp. 9–38.

BBC Persian Service (2013). 'Hekmatyar: khariji ha ba hemayat az aqaliatha afghanistan ra tajzia mikunand' ('Hekmatyar: by supporting minorities foreigners are splitting Afghanistan') available at http://www.bbc.com/persian/afghanistan/2013/08/130807_zs_gulbuddin_hekmatyar_eid_message (last accessed April 2016).

Bengali, S. (2016) 'In a first for post-Taliban Afghanistan, a grass-roots protest movement challenges the government', *Los Angeles Times*, available at http://www.latimes.com/world/la-fg-afghanistan-protest-snap-story.html (last accessed 21 October 2016).

Bindemann, R. (1987) *Religion und Politik bei den schi'itischen Hazâra in Afghanistan, Iran und Pakistan* (Berlin: Das Arabische Buch).

Bleuer, C. (2012) 'State-building, migration and economic development on the frontiersof northern Afghanistan and southern Tajikistan', *Journal of Eurasian Studies*, 3, 69–79.

Braithwaite, R. (2011) *Afgantsy: The Russians in Afghanistan 1979–89* (Oxford: Oxford University Press).

Bunyad-e rahbar-e shahid (ed.) (2000) *Manshur-e Baradary (A Manifesto for Brotherhood)* Bunyad-e Rahbar-e Shahid Baba Mazari: n.p.).

Canfield, R. (1972) *Hazara Integration into the Afghan State: Some Changing Relations between Hazaras and Afghan Officials* (New York: The Afghanistan Council).

——— (1984) 'Islamic Coalitions in Bamyan: A Problem in Translating Afghan Political Culture, Revolutions and Rebellions in Afghanistan', in N. Shahrani & R. Canfield (eds), *Revolutions and Rebellions in Afghanistan: Anthropological Perspectives* (Berkeley: Institute of International Studies).

——— (2004) 'New Trends among the Hazaras: From "The Amity of Wolves" to "The Practice of Brotherhood"', *Iranian Studies*, 37 (2), 241–62.

BIBLIOGRAPHY

Cederman, L.-E., A. Wimmer, & B. Min (2010) 'Why Do Ethnic Groups Rebel: New Data and Analysis', *World Politics*, 62(1), 87–119.

Centlivres, Pierre (2008) "The Controversy over the Buddhas of Bamiyan' *South Asia Multidisciplinary Academic Journal*, available at http://samaj. revues.org/992 (last accessed June 2015).

Central Intelligence Agency (1996, 2011 and 2004) 'The World Factbook', Project Gutenberg Issues of the World Factbook, available at http://online-books.library.upenn.edu/webbin/gutbook/serial?name=The%20 World%20Factbook (last accessed 11 November 2016).

———— (2010, 2014 and 2016) The World Factbook, CIA Online Library, available at https://www.cia.gov/library/publications/download (last accessed 12 November 2016).

Chandra, K. (2006) 'What is Ethnic Identity and Does Matter?', *Annual Review of Political Science*, 9, 397–424.

Chiovenda, M. (2014) 'The illumination of marginality: how ethnic Hazaras in Bamyan, Afghanistan, perceive the lack of electricity as discrimination', *Central Asian Survey*, 33 (4), 449–62.

Chiovenda, Melissa Kerr (2014) 'Sacred Blasphemy: Global and Local Views of the Destruction of the Bamyan Buddha Statues in Afghanistan', *Journal of Muslim Minority Affairs* 34 (4): 410–24.

Coghlan, T. (2008) 'Villagers forced out by "Taliban" nomads'. *The Daily Telegraph*, 12 April.

Cooperation Centre for Afghanistan (1998) *Ethnic Cleansing in Mazar: eye witnesses stories*, Department of Human Rights, Cooperation Centre for Afghanistan, available at http://www.afghandata.org:8080/xmlui/bit-stream/handle/azu/3964/azu_acku_pamphlet_hv6322_7_e845_1998_w.pdf?sequence=1&isAllowed=y (lastaccessed February 2016).

Daragahi, B. (2010) 'A Formerly Persecuted Minority Gains Clout in Afghanistan', *Los Angeles Times*, available at http://articles.latimes.com/2010/dec/16/world/la-fg-afghanistan-sects-20101216 (last accessed June 2015).

Dawlatabadi, B. (1992) *Shenasnameh ahzab wa jaryanat-e siyasey-e Afghanistan* (*Introduction to Political Parties and Currents of Afghanistan*) (Qom: Dawlatabadi).

———— et al. (1999) *Shura-ye Eatelaf-e Islami Afghanistan* (*The Council of Islamic Alliance of Afghanistan*) (Tehran: Thaqalain Cultural Organization).

Dawlatabadi, B. A. (2006) *Hazaraha az qatl-e aam ta ehyae-e howiat* (*Hazaras from Massacres to Revival of Identity*) (Qom: Ebterkar-e Danish).

Day Kundi, M. M. (1993) *Shahid Sadeqi Nili setarah-e durukhshan-e inqilaab-e Islami-e Afghanistan* (*Martyr Sadeqi, A Bright Star of Islamic Revolution of Afghanistan* (Iran?: n.p.).

Dorronsoro, Gilles (2005) *Revolution Unending, Afghanistan: 1979 to the Present* (Trans. John King) (London: Hurst & Company).

BIBLIOGRAPHY

———— (2009) *The Taliban's Winning Strategy in Afghanistan* (Washington DC: Carnegie Endowment for International Peace), available at http://carnegieendowment.org/files/taliban_winning_strategy.pdf (last accessed April 2016).

Douglas, J. (2012) 'Military Strategy or Poverty Reduction: Investigating the Provincial Allocation of Aid to Afghanistan', available at http://aiddata.org/blog/military-strategy-or-poverty-reduction-investigating-the-provincial-allocation-of-aid-to-afghanistan (last accessed January 2015).

Dupree, L. (1980) *Afghanistan* (Princeton: Princeton University Press).

Duthie, J. L. (1983) 'Pragmatic Diplomacy or Imperial Encroachment? British Policy towards Afghanistan, 1874–1879', *The International History Review*, 5 (4), 475–95.

Eck, K. (2009) 'From Armed Conflict to War: Ethnic Mobilization and Conflict Intensification', *International Studies Quarterly*, 53(2), 369–388.

Edwards, D. B. (1986) 'The Evolution of Shi'a Political Dissent in Afghanistan', in J. R. Cole & N. R. Keddie (eds), *Shi'ism and Social Protest* (New Haven: Yale University Press).

Elphinstone, M. (1842) *An Account of the Kingdom of Caubul and its Dependencies* (London: Bentley).

Emadi, H. (1995) 'Exporting Iran's Revolution: The Radicalization of the Shiite Movement in Afghanistan', *Middle Eastern Studies*, 31 (1), 1–12.

———— (1997) 'The Hazaras and their role in the process of political transformation of Afghanistan', *Central Asian Survey*, 16 (3), 363–87.

Erfani, Qurban Ali (1993) *Hezb-e Wahdat-e Islami Afghanistan, az kongarah ta kongarah* (Qom: Markaz-e Farhangi-e Nawisendagan-e Afghanistan).

European Union Election Assessment Team (2014) 'Islamic Republic of Afghanistan, Final Report: Presidential Election 5 April and 14 June 2014', 16 December 2014, Election Assessment Team of the European Union (EU EAT). European Union, available at http://www.eueom.eu/files/dmfile/FINAL-REPORT-EUEAT-AFGHANISTAN-2014-c_en.pdf (last accessed 14 June 2014).

Farhang, M. S. (1988) *Afghanistan dar panj qarn-e akhir (Afghanistan in the Last Five Centuries)* (Peshawar: Engineer Ehsanullah Mayar).

Farr, G. (1988) 'The Rise and Fall of an Indigenous Group: The Shura of the Hazarajat', *Afghanistan Studies Journal* (1), 48–61.

Farr, G. & J. Lorentz (n.d) 'Iran and the Afghan Struggle', unpublished paper.

Ferdinand, K. (2006) *Afghan Nomads: Caravans, Conflicts, and Trade in Afghanistan and British India 1800–1980* (Copenhagen: Rhodos).

Fletcher, A. (1966) *Afghanistan: Highway of Conquest* (Ithaca: Cornell University Press).

Fioriti, J. (2012) 'Afghan nomad clashes raise fear of ethnic strife', *AFP*, 8 June 2012.

Foschini, F. (2013) *The Social Wanderings of the Afghan Kuchis* (Kabul: Afghanistan Analysts Network).

Gankovsky, Y. (1981) 'The Durrani Empire: Taxes and Tax System, State Income and Expenditures', in E. Shchepilova (ed.), *Afghanistan: Past and Present* (Moscow: USSR Academy of Sciences).

Gellner, E. (1983) *Nations and Nationalism* (Ithaca: Cornell University Press).

Ghani, A. (1978) 'Islam and State-Building in a Tribal Society Afghanistan: 1880–1901'. *Modern Asian Studies*, 12 (2), 269–84.

————— (1982) *Production and Domination: Afghanistan, 1747–1901*, PhD Thesis. Graduate School of Arts and Sciences, Columbia University.

Gharjistan, M. (1987) *Az Hazarajat ta london (From Hazarajat to London)* (Quetta: Shuray-e Farhangi Islami Afghanistan).

Ghubar, G. (1997) *Afghanistan dar masir-e tarikh (Afghanistan in the Course of History)* (Qom: Sahafi Ehsani).

————— (2008) *Ahmad Shah Baba* (Peshawar: Nashr-e Danesh).

Giustozzi, A. (2005) *The ethnicisation of an Afghan faction: Junbesh-i-Milli from the origins to the presidential elections* (London: Crisis States Research Centre, The London School of Economics and Political Science).

————— (2008) *Afghanistan, Transition without End: An Analytical Narrative on State-making* (London: Crisis States Research Centre, The London School of Economics and Political Science).

Giustozzi, A. & N. Ibrahimi (2013) 'From New Dawn to Quicksand: The Political Economy of Statebuilding in Afghanistan', in M. Berdal & D. Zaum (eds), *Political Economy of Statebuilding: Power after Peace* (London and New York: Routledge).

Glatzer, B. (1998) 'Is Afghanistan on the Brink of Ethnic or Tribal Fragmentation?', in W. Maley (ed.), *Fundamentalism Reborn? Afghanistan and the Taliban* (London: Hurst & Co.), pp. 167–181.

Gopalakrishnan, R. (1981) *The Geography and Politics of Afghanistan* (New Delhi: Naurang Raj).

Government of Afghanistan (1921) *Nezamnah-e taqsimat-e molkiya Afghanistan* (Kabul: n.p.).

————— (1923) *Nezamnah-e naqelin ba samt-e qataghan* (Kabul: Publication Department of the Supreme Council of Ministers).

Gregorian, V. (1967) 'Mahmud Tarzi and Saraj-ol-Akhbar: Ideology of Nationalism and Modernization in Afghanistan', *Middle East Journal*, 21 (3), 345–68.

Grevemeyer, J.-H. (1988) 'Ethnicity and national liberation: the Afghan Hazara between resistance and civil war', in J. P. Digard (ed.) *Le Fait Ethnique en Iran et Afghanistan, Colloque international* (Paris: Centre National de la Recherche scientifique).

Griffin, L. (1888) 'A Page of Afghan History. *The Asiatic Quarterly Review*', VI,

BIBLIOGRAPHY

241–70, available at https://archive.org/details/asiaticquarter-100unkngoog (last accessed 9 November 2016).

Gulzari, M. (comp.) (2004) *Diaries of Kandahar: Hazaras in the Views of British Diaries, 1884–1905*, available at http://www.hazara.net/downloads/docs/Hazaras_In_the_View_of_British_Diaries.pdf (last accessed 7 November 2016).

Gutsch, J.-M. (2014) 'The Road to Bamiyan: A Public Works Debacle that Defines Afghanistan', *Der Spiegel*, available at http://www.spiegel.de/international/world/afghanistan-road-project-tells-story-of-taliban-violence-and-failure-a-994569.html (last accessed February 2015).

Habibi, A. (1967) *Tarikh-e Mokhtasar-e Afghanistan (A Short History of Afghanistan)* (Kabul: Government Press and Historical Society of Afghanistan).

——— (1987) *Jonbesh-e mashrutiat dar Afghanistan (Constitutionalist Movement in Afghanistan* (Kabul: Government Printing Press).

Harlan, J. (1842) *A Memoir of India and Afghanistan: with Observations on the Present Exciting and Critical State and Future Prospects of those Countries* (Philadelphia: J. Dobson).

Harpviken, K. (1995) *Political Mobilization among the Hazaras of Afghanistan*, Dissertation, University of Oslo, Department of Sociology.

——— (1998) 'The Hazaras of Afghanistan: the thorny path towards political unity, 1978–1992', in T. Atabaki & J. O'kane (eds), *Post-Soviet Central Asia* (London: I. B. Tauris).

Herawi, R. M. (1907) *Bahr Al-Fawai'd: Kulliyat-e Riyazi* (Mashhad: Dar al-Tabaat Astan-e Moqaddas).

Hezb-e Wahdat Islami Afghanistan (1990) *Negahi ba aakhirin tahawulat-e siasey-e Afghanistan (A Glance at the Recent Political Developments in Afghanistan)* (n.p: Wahdat Press).

——— (1990) *Tashkil-e Hezb-e Wahdat-e Islami, noqte a'tfi mohem wa ta'in kunenda dar tarikh-e enqelab-e Islami Afghanistan* (Qom: Wahdat Press).

Hopkins, B. (2008) *The Making of Modern Afghanistan* (London: Palgrave Macmillan).

Horowitz, D. L. (1985) *Ethnic Groups in Conflic.*(Berkeley: University of California Press).

Human Rights Watch (2005) *Blood Stained Hands: Past Atrocities in Kabul and Afghanistan's Legacy of Impunity* (New York: Human Rights Watch).

——— (1998) *Afghanistan: The Massacre in Mazar-e Sharif* (New York: Human Rights Watch).

——— (2001) *Massacres of Hazaras of Afghanistan* (New York: Human Rights Watch).

Hyman, A. (2002) 'Nationalism in Afghanistan', *International Journal of Middle East Studies*, 34 (2), 299–315.

BIBLIOGRAPHY

Ibrahimi, N. (2009) *The Dissipation of Political Capital among Afghanistan's Hazaras: 2001–2009* (London: Crisis States Research Centre, The London School of Economics and Political Science).

——— (2012a) *Shift and Drift in Hazara Ethnic Consciousness. The Impact of Conflict and Migration* (Crossroads Asia), available at http://crossroads-asia. de/index.php?eID=tx_nawsecuredl&u=0&g=0&t=1478759527&hash= ef8ba4f405d8f2e5f661627a6863f62cc71161f6&file=fileadmin/user_ upload/webfiles/deliverables/wp05_final.pdf (last accessed 7 November 2016).

——— (2012b) *Ideology without Leadership, The Rise and Decline of Maoism in Afghanistan* (Kabul: Afghanistan Analysts Network), available at http:// www.afghanistan-analysts.org/wp-content/uploads/down-loads/2012/09/NIbr-Maoists-final.pdf (last accessed 7 November 2016).

International Crisis Group (2003) *The Problem of Pashtun Alienation in Afghanistan* (Brussels and Kabul: Crisis Group).

——— (2010) *Force in Fragments: Reconstituting the Afghan National Army* (Brussels and Kabul: Crisis Group).

IRIN (2007) 'PRTs accused of unequal amount on development', available at http://www.irinnews.org/report/71949/afghanistan-prts-accused-spending-unequal-amounts-development (last accessed April 2015).

——— (2008) 'Threat of ethnic clashes over grazing land', available at http://www.irinnews.org/report/77647/afghanistan-threat-ethnic-clashes-over-grazing-land (last accessed May 2015).

IRIN (2010) 'Afghanistan: Kuchi Minority Complain of Marginalization', available at http://www.irinnews.org/report/91172/afghanistan-kuchi-minority-complain-marginalization (last accessed May 2015).

Jamali, G. (2002) *Sahm-e Hazaraha dar hayat-e milli-e Afghanistan* (*The Role of Hazaras in the National life of Afghanistan*) (Kabul: Khalid Press).

Jami, M. A.-H. (2007) *Tarikh-e Ahmad Shahi* (ed. S. Mawlai-e) (Tehran and Kabul: Irfan).

Jones, A. (2006) *Genocide: A Comprehensive Introduction* (London and New York: Routledge).

Jones, S. (2008) 'The Rise of Afghanistan's Insurgency: State Failure and Jihad', *International Security*, 32 (4), 7–40.

Kakar, H. (1971) *Afghanistan: A Study in International Political Developments, 1880–1896* (Lahore: Punjab Educational Press).

——— (1979) *Government and Society in Afghanistan: the reign of Amir Abd al-Rahman Khan* (Austin: University of Texas Press).

——— (2006) *A Political and Diplomatic History of Afghanistan, 1863–1901* (Leiden: Brill).

Kateb, F. (1913) *Siraj-al-Tawarikh* (Vol. I) (Kabul: Hurufi Press).

Katib Hazarah, F. (2012) *The History of Afghanistan Fayż Muḥammad Kātib*

Hazārah's Sirāj al-tawārīkh (trans. R. McChesney & M. Khorrami) (Leiden: Brill).

Kazemi, M. (2004) 'Allama Balkhi wa du tashkilat-e seyasi' (Allamah Balkhi and two Political Organisations), in S. Shujai (ed.), *Setara-e shab-e daijur: Zandagi namah-e allamah shahid sayed Ismail Balkhi (The Star of Moonless Night: Biography of Martyr Allamah Sayed Ismail Balkhi)* (Tehran: Soreh Mehr Press).

Khalili, K. (1990) *Ayari az khurasan, Amir Habibullah khadim-e din-e rasulullah* (Peshawar: Khawar Booksellers).

Khalidi, Noor Ahmad (1991) 'Afghanistan: Demographic Consequences of War, 1978–1987', *Central Asian Survey* 10 (3): 101–26.

Khan, A. (1900) *The Life of Abdur Rahman Khan, The Amir of Afghanistan* (ed. S. Khan) (London: John Murray).

Khomeini, A. (1978) *Welayat e faqih, hokumat-e Islami (Guardianship of the Jurist: Islamic Government)* (Tehran: Entesharat-e Amir Kabir).

King, L. (2010) 'Ethnic divide threatens in Afghanistan', *Los Angeles Times*, available at http://articles.latimes.com/2010/jul/17/world/la-fg-afghan-ethnic-tension-20100717 (last accessed May 2016).

Laali, A. (1993) *Sairey dar Hazarajat (An Overview of Hazarajat)* (Qom: Ehsani).

Lal, M. (1846) *The Life of Amir Dost Mohammed Khan of Kabul* (London: Longman).

Larson, A. (2015) *Political Parties in Afghanistan* (Washington: United States Institute of Peace) available at http://www.usip.org/sites/default/files/SR362-Political-Parties-in-Afghanistan.pdf (last accessed January 2015).

Lee, J. (1996) *The 'Ancient Supremacy': Bukhara, Afghanistan and the Battle for Balkh, 1731–1901* (Leiden: Brill).

Leitner, D. (1894) 'The Amir Abdurrahman and Great Britain (with H.H.'s portrai and a facsmile of his letter on his feelings towards, and his visit to, England)' *The Asiatic Quarterly Review*, VII (13 & 14), 283–95, available at https://ia801409.us.archive.org/17/items/asiaticquarterl01unkngoog/asiaticquarterl01unkngoog.pdf (last accessed 9 November 2016).

Linschoten, A. (2008) 'Behsud: Kuchi atrocities?' available at http://www.frontlineclub.com/behsud_kuchi_atrocities/ (last accessed June 2015).

Maitland, P. (1891) 'Report on Tribes, Namely Sarik Turkomans, Chahar Aimak, and Hazaras', in Afghan Boundary Commission, *Records of Intelligence Party* (Vol. IV) (Simla: Afghan Boundary Commission Government Central Printing Press).

Maley, W. (2006) *Rescuing Afghanistan* (London: C Hurst & Co.).

———— (2013) 'Statebuilding in Afghanistan: Challenges and Pathologies', *Central Asian Survey*, 32 (3), 255–70.

———— (2016) 'Afghanistan on a Knife-edge', *Global Affairs*, 2 (1), 57–68.

Maley, W. & S. Schmeidl (eds) (2015) *Reconstructing Afghanistan: Civil-Military Experiences in Comparative Perspective* (London: Routledge).

BIBLIOGRAPHY

Maqsudi, A. (1989) *Hazarajat sarzamin-e mahruman* (*Hazarajat the Land of Deprived*) (Quetta: n.p.).

Martin, F. (1907) *Under the Absolute Amir* (London and New York: Harper & Brothers).

Masson, C. (1842) *Narratives of Various Journeys in Balochistan, Afghanistan and the Panjab* (London: R. Bentley), Vol. II.

Mielke, K. (2015) 'Not in the Master plan: Dimensions of exclusion in Kabul', in M. Sökefeld & M. Sökefeld (eds) *Spaces of Conflict* (Bielefeld: Transcript Verlag).

Mir Khan, S. (1896, April 4) *D. No. 225 F* in M. Gulzari (2004) *Diaries of Kandahar.*

———— (1896, April 11) *D. No. 242 F* in M. Gulzari (2004) *Diaries of Kandahar.*

Mitra, D. (2016) 'In Search for Power, Afghanistan's Hazaras Vows to Fight On', *The Wire* available at http://thewire.in/63492/search-power-afghanistans-hazara-community-vows-fight/ (last accessed 21 October 2016).

Monsutti, A. (2008) 'The Impact of War on Social, Political and Economic Organisation in Southern Hazarajat', in M. Djalili, A. Monsutti & A. Neubauer (eds), *Le monde turco-iranien en question* (Genève: IHEID).

Montalvo, J., & M. Reynal-Querol (2005) 'Ethnic Diversity and Economic Development', *Journal of Development Economics*, 76, 293–323.

Mousavi, S. (1998) *The Hazaras of Afghanistan: An Historical, Cultural, Economic and Political Study* (Surrey: Curzon Press).

Mozhdah, Wahid (2003) *Afghanistan wa panj sal solte Taliban* (*Afghanistan and Five Years of Taliban Rule*) (Tehran: Nai Publications).

Muradi, Sahebnazar (2006) *Ahmad Shah Massoud wa Tahawolat-e Dahe Hashtad* (*Ahmed Shah Massoud And the Developments of the 80s*) (Kabul: Massoud Foundation).

Nawid, S. (1999) *Religious Response to Social Change in Afghanistan 1919–29: King Aman-Allah and the Afghan Ulama* (Costa Mesa: Mazda Publishers).

Nayel, H. (2000) *Yaddashthai-e dar barh-e sarzamin wa rejal-e hazarajat* (*Notes about the Land and Personalities of Hazarajat*) (Qom: Cultural Centre of Afghanistan's Writers).

Noelle, C. (1997) *State and Tribe in Ninteenth Century Afghanistan: The Reign of Amir Dost Muhammad Khan (1826–1863)* (London: Curzon Press).

Noktadan, S. A. (2004) 'Balkhishinasi' (Recognising Balkhi), in S. Shojai (ed.), *Setara-e shab-e daijur: Zandagi namah-e allamah shahid sayed Ismail Balkhi* (*The Star of Moonless Night: Biography of Martyr Allamah Sayed Ismail Balkhi*) (Tehran: Soreh Mehr Press).

Olesen, A. (1995) *Islam and Politics in Afghanistan* (London and New York: Curzon Press).

Oppel, R. & A. Wafa (2010) 'Hazaras Hustle to Head of Class in Afghanistan',

BIBLIOGRAPHY

New York Times available at http://www.nytimes.com/2010/01/04/world/asia/04hazaras.html?_r=0 (last accessed 7 November 2016).

Orywal, E. (ed.) (1986) *Die ethnischen Gruppen Afghanistans: Fallstudien zu Gruppenidentität und Intergruppenbeziehungen* (Wiesbaden: Dr Ludwig Reichert Verlag).

Osman, B. (2016) 'With an Active Cell in Kabul, ISKP Tries to Bring Sectarianism to the Afghan War', Kabul: Afghanistan Analysts Network, available at https://www.afghanistan-analysts.org/with-an-active-cell-in-kabul-iskp-tries-to-bring-sectarianism-to-the-afghan-war/ (last accessed 21 October 2016).

Peszkowski, R. (2012) *Reforming Jombesh: An Afghan Party on its Winding Path to Internal Democracy* (Kabul: Afghanistan Analysts Network).

Poullada, L. (1973) *Reform and Rebellion in Afghanistan: 1919–1929, King Amanullah's Failure to Modernise a Tribal Soceity* (Ithaca: Cornell University Press).

Radio Free Europe (2016) 'Deadly Attacks Target Shi'a In Afghanistan', available at http://www.rferl.org/a/afghanistan-ashura-shiite-balkh-deadly-bombing/28048205.html (last accessed 21 October 2016).

Rais, R. (1999) 'Conflict in Afghanistan: Ethnicity, Religion and Neighbours', *Ethnic Studies Report* 17 (1): 1–19.

——— (2008) *Recovering the Frontier State: War, Etnicity and State in Afghanistan* (Lanham, MD: Lexington Books).

Rasad News Agency (2016) 'Ghulam Husain Naseri: dar 15 sale gozashta dar masir-e shahrah manateq markazi 163 nafar sarborida shoda and', available at http://www.rasad.af/1395/07/11/highway-taking-hostage-naseri/ (last accessed 21 October 2016).

Rashid, A. (2000) *Taliban: Militant Islam, Oil and Fundamentlaism in Central Asia* (London: I. B. Tauris).

Rawlinson, H. (1875) *England and Russia in the East* (London: John Murray).

——— (1841) 'Report on the Doranees Tribe', in L. Adamec (ed.), *Historical and Political Gazetter of Afghanistan: Kandahar and South-Central Afghanistan* (Vol. V). (Graz: Akademische Druck—u. Verlagsanstalt (ADEVA)).

Reuters (2016) 'Islamic State claims responsibility for deadly mosque attack in Afghan capital', available at http://www.reuters.com/article/us-afghanistan-ashura-idUSKCN12C17E?il=0 (last accessed 21 October 2016).

Rubin, A. (2010) 'Karzai's Words Leave Few Choices for the West', *New York Times* available at http://www.nytimes.com/2010/04/05/world/asia/05karzai.html?_r=0 (last accessed May 2016).

Rubin, B. (2002) *The Fragmentation of Afghanistan: State Formation and Collapse in the International System* (New Haven, CT: Yale University Press), 2nd ed.

——— (2006) 'Peace building and state-building in Afghanistan: Constructing sovereignty for whose security?' *Third World Quarterly*, 27 (1), 175–85.

———— (2013) *Afghanistan from the Cold War through the War on Terror* (Oxford and New York: Oxford University Press).

———— (2016) 'Hard Choices for Peace in Afghanistan', *The New Yorker*, available at http://www.newyorker.com/news/news-desk/hard-choices-for-peace-in-afghanistan (last accessed 21 October 2016).

Ruttig, T. (2006) *Islamists, Leftists—and a Void in the Centre: Afghanistan's Political Parties and Where They Come From, 1902–2006* (Kabul: Konrad Adenaur Stiftung, Afghanistan Office), available at http://www.kas.de/wf/doc/kas_9674–544–2–30.pdf (last accessed 7 November 2016).

Saikal, A. (2006) *Modern Afghanistan, A History of Struggle and Surviva.*(London: I. B. Tauris).

———— (2012) 'Afghanistan: The Status of the Shi'ite Hazara Minority', *Journal of Muslim Minority Affairs*, 32 (1), 80–7.

Saleh, A. (2012) 'The Crisis and Politics of Ethnicity in Afghanistan', *Aljazeera Online*, available at http://www.aljazeera.com/indepth/opinion/2012/06/20126201383044691 3.htm (last accessed January 2015).

Samangani, M. S. (1994) *Salhay-e jihad dar Afghanistan* (*Years of Jehad in Afghanistan*) (Vol. I) (Qom: Samangani).

Sappenfield, M. (2007a) 'Afghanistan's success story: The liberated Hazara minority', *Christian Science Monitor*, available at http://www.csmonitor.com/2007/0806/p06s02-wosc.html (last accessed 7 November 2016).

———— (2007b) 'Bamyan pays the Afghan peace penalty', *Christian Science Monitor*, available at http://www.csmonitor.com/2007/1011/p20s01-wosc.html (last accessed January 2016).

Saramad, M. & A. Pazhman (2013) *wazaiat-e hoquq-e bashar dar afghanistan dar sal-e 1392* (*The Situation of Human Rights in Afghanistan in the 1392*) (Kabul: Afghanistan Independent Human Rights Commission (AIHRC)) available at http://www.aihrc.org.af/home/research_report/3609 (last accessed April 2016).

Schetter, C. (2005) *Ethnicity and Political Reconstruction of Afghanistan* (Bonn: Center for Development Research (ZEF), University of Bonn).

———— (2005) 'Ethnoscapes, National Territorialisation and the Afghan War', *Geopolitics*, 10 (1), 50–75.

Semple, M. (2011) *The rise of the Hazaras and the challenge of pluralism in Afghanistan 1978–2011* "(Cambridge: Harvard Centre for Islamic Studies).

Shahrani, N. (1986) 'State Building and Social Fragmentation in Afghanistan: A Historical Perspective', in A. Banuazizi & M. Weiner (eds), *The State, Religion and Ethnic Politics: Afghanistan, Iran and Pakistan* (Syracuse: Syracuse University Press) pp. 23–74.

———— (2005) 'King Aman-Allah of Afghanistan's failed nation-building project and its aftermath', (review article) *Iranian Studies*, 38 (4), 661–75.

———— (2008) 'Taliban and Talibanism in Historical Perspective', in R. D. Crews & A. Tarzi (eds.), *The Taliban and the Crisis of Modern Afghanistan* (Cambridge: Harvard University Press), pp. 155–82.

Sharan, T. (2013) 'The Dynamics of Informal Political Networks and Statehood in post-2001 Afghanistan: a case study of the 2010–2011 Special Election Court crisis', *Central Asian Survey*, 32 (3), 336–52.

Shojai, S. (ed.) (2004) *Setara-e shab-e daijur: Zandagi namah-e allamah shahid sayed Ismail Balkhi (The Star of Moonless Night: Biography of Martyr Allamah Sayed Ismail Balkhi)* (Tehran: Sureh Mehr Press).

Shura (n.d.) *Ealamiya* (Declaration) Shura Office in Iran (n.d.) Untitled pamphlet.

Siddique, A. (2014) *The Pashtun Question The Unresolved Key to the Future of Pakistan and Afghanistan* (London: Hurst and Co.).

Simosen, S. (2004) 'Ethnicising Afghanistan? inclusion and exclusion in post-Bonn institution building', *Third World Quarterly*, 25(4), 707–29.

Singh, G. (1977) *Ahmad Shah Durrani: Father of Modern Afghanistan* (Bombay: Asia Publishing House).

Singh, I. (2001) 'Exploring issues of violence within the recent context of Hazarajat, Afghanistan', *Central Asian Survey* 20 (2): 195–228.

Sinno, A. (2009) 'Explaining the Taliban's Ability to Mobilize the Pushtuns' in R. D. Crews and A. Tarzi (eds) *The Taliban and the Crisis of Modern Afghanistan* (Cambridge: Harvard University Press).

Smith, A. (1986) *The Ethnic Origins of Nations* (Oxford: Blackwell).

———— (1991) *National Identity* (Harmondsworth: Penguin).

———— (2009) *Ethno-symbolism and Nationalism: A Cultural Approach* (London and New York: Routledge).

Sopko, J. (2014) 'Inquiry Letter: Maintainence of USAID-Funded Roads', available at https://www.sigar.mil/pdf/special%20projects/SIGAR-14–64-SP.pdf (last accessed May 2016).

———— (2016) 'Testimony Before the Subcommittee on Oversight and Ivestigations, Committee on Armed Services U.S. House of Representatives', available at https://www.sigar.mil/pdf/testimony/SIGAR-16-17-TY.pdf (last accessed 20 March 2016).

Suhrke, A. (2008) 'Democratizing a Dependent State: The Case of Afghanistan', *Democratization*, 15(3), 630–48.

———— (2013) 'Statebuilding in Afghanistan: a contradictory engagement', *Central Asian Survey*, 32 (3), 271–6.

Taki Khan, K. M. (1891, July 27). *D.No. 265 F. R.No. 11536 F. No. 5131* in M. Gulzari (2004) *Diaries of Kandahar*.

———— (1892, August 6). *D.No. 341 F. No. 4800* in M. Gulzari (2004) *Diaries of Kandahar*.

———— (1893, January 6). *D.No. 29 F. No. 26 F.C* in M. Gulzari (2004) *Diaries of Kandahar*.

——— (1892, October 14). *D. No. 442 F. No. 6436* in M. Gulzari (2004) *Diaries of Kandahar*.

——— (1893, August 26). *D. No. 390 F. No. 921* in M. Gulzari (2004) *Diaries of Kandahar*.

Tapper, N. (1983) 'Abd Al-Rahman's North-West Frontier: the Pashtun colonisation of Afghan Turkistan' in R. Tapper (ed.), *The conflict of tribe and state in Iran and Afghanistan* (New York: St. Martin's Press).

Tchalakov, M. (2013) *The Northern Alliance Prepares for Afghan Elections in 2014 Afghanistan Report 10, August 2013* (Washington: Institute for the Study of War) available at http://www.understandingwar.org/sites/default/files/NorthernAlliance-2014Elections_1AUG.pdf (last accessed June 2015).

Temirkhanov, L. (1993) *Tarikh-e Milli-e Hazara* (*National History of the Hazaras*) (trans. A. Toghyan) (Qom: Ismailian Printing Press).

The Economist (2007) 'Afghanistan's Hazaras, available at http://www.economist.com/node/8706540 (last accessed 7 November 2016).

The World Bank (2012) 'Afghanistan in Transition: Looking Beyond 2014', Vol. II, The World Bank, available at http://siteresources.worldbank.org/AFGHANISTANEXTN/Images/305983–1334954629964/AFTransition2014Vol2.pdf (last accessed February 2015).

——— (2015) 'Poverty Status Update: An analysis based on National Risk and Vulnerability Assessment (NRVA) 2007/08 and 2011/12', Kabul: The World Bank. available at http://documents.worldbank.org/curated/en/594051468180880731/pdf/100638-v2-WP-P145128-PUBLIC-Box393238B-Poverty-Status-Update-Report.pdf (last accessed 21 October 2016).

United Nations (2016a) 'Attack on a Peaceful Demonstration in Kabul, 23 July 2016', Kabul: United Nations Assistance Mission in Afghanistan, available at http://unama.unmissions.org/sites/default/files/23_july_suicide_attack_against_peaceful_demonstration_-_18_oct_2016.pdf (last accessed 20 October 2016).

——— (2016b) 'UN Chief in Afghanistan Renews Call for Parties to Protect Civilians: UNAMA Press Release, Civilian Casualty Data for Third Quarter of 2016', Kabul: United Nations Assisance Missions in Afghanistan, available at http://unama.unmissions.org/sites/default/files/19_october_2016_-_un_chief_in_afghanistan_renews_call_for_parties_to_protect_civilians_english.pdf (last accessed 21 October 2016).

——— (2016c) *AFGHANISTAN: Annual Report 2015, Protection of Civilians in Armed Conflict* (United Nations Assistance Mission in Afghanistan (UNAMA) and United Nations Office of Higher Commissioner for Human Rights, Kabul) available at https://unama.unmissions.org/sites/default/files/poc_annual_report_2015_final_14_feb_2016.pdf (last accessed April 2016).

Verkoren, W. & B. Kamphuis (2013) 'State Building in a Rentier State: How Development Policies Fail to Promote Democracy in Afghanistan', *Development and Change*, 44(3), 501–26.

Waezi, Hamzah (1999) *Afghansitan wa ta'arozat-e stratezhi haye faramilli (Afghanistan and Conflicts of Transnational Strategies) Seraj*, pp. 27–78. (Qom: Markaz-e Farhangi Nawisendagan-e Afghanistan)

Wafayezada, M. (2013) *Ethnic Politics and Peacebuilding in Afghanistan: The Root Causes of Political Conflicts and the Problems of Democratic Transition* (Saarbrücken: Scholars' Press).

Waldman, M. (2008) *Falling Short: Aid Effectiveness in Afghanistan', Advocacy Series, March 2008* (Kabul: Agency Coordinating Body for Afghan Relief (ACBAR)).

Wardak, A., D. Saba & H. Kazem (2007) *Afghanistan Human Development Report 2007* (Kabul: Centre for Policy and Human Development at Kabul University).

Weinbaum, M. & J. Harder (2008) 'Pakistan's Afghan policies and their consequences', *Contemporary South Asia*, 16 (1), 25–38.

Wilder, A. (2005) *A House Divided: Analysing the 2005 Afghan Elections* (Kabul: Afghanistan Research and Evaluation Unit).

Wily, Liz Alden (2004) *Land Relations in Bamyan Province: Findings from a 15 Village Case Study* (Kabul: Afghanistan Research and Evaluation Unit).

Wily, L. (2013) 'The Battle over Pastures: The Hidden War in Afghanistan,. *Revue des mondes musulmans et de la Méditerranée*, 95–113, available at https://remmm.revues.org/8021?lang=fr (last accessed April 2015).

Wimmer, A. (2002) *Nationalism Exclusion and Ethnic Conflict, Shadows of Modernity* (Cambridge: Cambridge Universtiy Press).

———— (2008) 'The Making and Unmaking of Ethnic Boundaries: A Multilevel Process Theory', *American Journal of Sociology*, 113(4), 970–1022.

———— (2013) *Ethnic Boundary Making: Institutions, Power, Network* (Oxford: Oxford University Press).

Yazdani, H. (2007) *Farzandan-e Kohsaran (The Sons of Mountains)* (Kabul: Said Publishers).

———— (2007) *Farzandan-e kohsaran, negahi gozara ba ba tarikh wa khadamat-e hazara ha dar Afghanistan (The Children of Mountains: a quick glance at the history and services of Hazaras in Afghanistan)* (Kabul: Said Publishers).

———— (2008) *Pazhoheshi dar tarikh-e hazaraha (An Inquiry into History of the Hazaras)* (Tehran and Kabul: Ibrahim Shariati).

Zabriskie, P. (2008) 'Hazaras: Afghanistan's Outsiders', *National Geographic Magazine*, 11 February, available at http://ngm.nationalgeographic.com/2008/02/afghanistan-hazara/phil-zabriskie-text (last accessed 7 November 2016).

BIBLIOGRAPHY

Zyck, S. (2012) 'How to Lose Allies and Finance Your Enemies? The Economisation of Conflict Termination in Afghanistan', *Conflict, Security & Development*, 12 (3), 249–71.

INDEX

271

INDEX

Alizai (tribe): 36; territory inhabited by, 33

Alkozai (tribe): gifting of Hazara families to, 75; territory inhabited by, 33

Allahyar, Haji Nadir: Frontline Commander of Shura, 137

Allen, C.: *God's Terrorists*, 230

Amirzada, H.: concept of 'Hazaraphobia', 232

Arab (ethnic group): 3

Arif, Sayed: Governor of Jaghuri, 132

Armenian Genocide (1915): 79

Aryans: use in ethno-genesis theory of Pashtun identity, 96–7

Australia: Hazara refugee population of, 207

Aymaq: (ethnic group): 3

Azim Beg, Sardaar Muhammad: 73; rebellion led by, 74–5

Babur: 33; founder of Mughal Empire, 31

Badakhshan: 4

Bakhsh, Mir Yazdan: 46–8; execution of, 48–9; reign of, 42

Balaghi, Hayatullah: 194

Balkhi, Ismail: 147; background of, 109, 125; death of (1969), 110; imprisonment of, 110; influence of, 110–11; political parties founded by, 109–10

Balkhi, Sayed Ismail: attempted coup led by (1950), 106

Baluch (ethnic group): 3, 31, 89; displacement/dispossession of, 33, 60; territory inhabited by, 60

Baluchistan: 28, 60; Quetta City, 81

Bank-e Mill-e Afghanistan: founding of (1933), 97

Barakzai (tribe): 26, 34; gifting of Hazara families to, 75; Muhammadzai (clan), 28, 55, 92, 117; rivals of, 28; territory inhabited by, 33

Barfield, T.: 35, 39

Barth, F.: definitions of ethnic group, 8

Beg, Muhammad Ali: Chief of Saighan, 47–8

Beheshti, Ayatollah: 124–6, 129, 138, 151, 184; opposition to, 133; refusal to recognise Ayatollah Ruhollah Khomeini, 138; shortcomings of, 136–7

Behsud (tribe): 82

Beriji, Maqsud Khan: Chief of Shorabak, 36

Bonn Agreement (2001): 215–16, 219–20; holding of national census, 5; provisions of, 216

Brahwui (ethnic group): 3

British Empire: 26, 50, 55; occupation of Punjab (1849), 58; occupation of Sindh (1842), 58; view of Afghanistan, 58

Buddhism: 203–4

Canfield, R.: 100–1

Centre for Policy and Human Development: 226

Charkhi, Ghulam Nabi Khan: 94

China, People's Republic of: 112

Chiovenda, M.: 227

Cold War: end of, 208

colonialism: British, 40, 228, 230; European, 26, 40; Western, 27, 29, 96

communism: 178

Cooperative Mamurin (Cooperative for the Public Servants): 107

Council of Ministers: 99

273

INDEX

Cuba: Guantanamo Bay, 241

Cyprus Group: members of, 216

Danesh, Sarwar: Afghan Vice-President, 224

Dari (language): as official state language, 3, 5, 218

Dawari, Arif: collaboration with Taliban, 206

Dawlatabadi, B.: 111

Deobandism: 228, 230

Dost, Hussain Sangar: collaboration with Taliban, 206

Dostum, General Abdur Rashid: 188, 191; leader of Junbish-e Milli Islami Afghanistan, 187, 193, 196–7

Douglas, J.: 236

Durand Line: 91, 93, 100, 227; establishment of, 60

Durrani (tribal confederation): 26, 231; tribes of, 26

Duranni Empire (1747–1826): 1, 20, 26–7, 35, 40–1, 49–50, 62, 85, 246; founding of (1747), 25, 46; Hazara population of, 27, 41–2; Helmand, 50; Herat, 30, 41, 43–4; Kabul, 30, 38–9, 43–4, 50; military of, 37; Muhammadzai dynasty, 26, 28–9, 40, 42, 44, 50, 55; Pashtun population of, 31–2; Peshawar, 29; Qalat, 36; Qandahar, 30, 32–3, 36, 39–40, 43–4; taxation system of, 34; territory of, 26–8, 39, 43–4; tribal hierarchy of, 29–30, 34, 36–8, 50, 75; use of Turko-Mongolian tribal model in, 35–6

Eatelaf-e Milli (National Coalition): formation of (2010), 219

Edwards, D.B.: 106

Eftekhari, Ali Yawar: 170

Egypt: Al-Azhar University, 113; Cairo, 113

Ehsan, Mawlawi Ehsanullah: presence at Ghazni Hezb-e Wahdat-Taliban meeting (1994), 197

Elphinstone, M.: 35, 40

Emergency Loya Jirga (2002): 216

Emirate of Bukhara: Bukhara, 59

Enlightenment Movement (2016): attacks on, 234

ethnic identities/ethnicity: 2, 6–7, 10–13, 27, 33, 142, 183, 186, 209, 217–18, 220, 243, 245–7, 249; definitions of, 8, 18, 23; ethnicisation of politics, 14–19, 243, 246; mobilisation, 7–9, 19; religious, 231; secular, 130

European Union (EU): Election Assessment Team, 221

Fahim, Qasim: Afghan Vice-President, 220; head of NDS, 194–5

Farsi (language): 5, 7, 31, 97

Fasihi, Shaikh Aman: 131

Fayaz, Abdul Ahmed: 194

Ferdinand, K.: observation of Hazara-Pashtun debt-credit relationship, 104; research in Hazarajat, 101–3

fiqh (jurisprudence): Hanafi, 84, 185; Shi'a, 3, 185, 225

First Anglo-Afghan War (1839–42): 45, 49, 58; political impact of, 49

First World War (1914–18): 91

France: 92–3

Gankovsky, Y.: 30

German Democratic Republic

INDEX

Operation Enduring Freedom (2001–14): 23, 213, 239, 249; casualty figures of, 228; removal of Taliban from power (2001), 203–4, 214–15; state-building efforts during, 217; withdrawal of forces (2014), 215

Ottoman Empire (1299–1923): 27, 95; Damascus, 95

Oxus (river): 59

Padshah, Nayeb: 83

Pahlawan, Malik: 200

Paiman-e Jabal-Seraj: 188, 192; members of, 187–8

pairawan-e khatt-e imam (Followers of the Path of Imam): ideology of, 150

Pakistan: 60, 100, 138–9, 141–2, 173, 208, 217, 229; Baluchistan Province, 230; borders of, 230; government of, 140; Hazara diaspora in, 22; Inter-Service Intelligence (ISI), 200–1; Interim Islamic governments (IIG), 175, 186; Islamabad, 228–9; military of, 156; Pashtun population of, 227; Peshawar, 157, 179, 186–7, 189; Quetta, 22, 130–1, 140, 157, 203; Sindh, 28, 81; Waziristan, 93

Pasdaran-e Jihad-e Islami: 151–3, 167, 171, 180, 183, 194; alliances formed by, 173; ideology of, 193; members of, 152, 163, 165, 168, 205; structure of, 162; supporters of, 160; territory held by, 165

Pashayi (ethnic group): 3

Pashto (language): 101, 203; as official state language, 3, 5, 97–8, 218; poetry, 57

Pashtun (ethnic group): 3, 5, 14, 18, 26, 28–9, 31, 35, 50, 85, 89, 94, 97, 115, 141, 152, 187, 189–92, 201, 227–8, 241–2, 245, 247, 250; Andar, 69; *Badraqa*, 92; conflict with Hazaras, 76–7; cultural traditions of, 19; landholders, 34; military confrontations with, 64; *Naaqilin* (transferees), 3, 98; nomadic behaviour/nomads (*kuchis*), 83, 102–7, 128, 239; political dominance of, 18, 20, 42; population size of, 6; presence in Durrani military, 38–40; presence in Afghan civil service, 226; Shinwari, 56–7; Sunni, 3; tribes, 26–7, 32–3; territory inhabited by, 31, 33–4, 50, 57, 60, 72, 91–2, 98, 173, 208, 224, 227, 230, 237, 240–1

People's Democratic Party of Afghanistan (PDPA): 117–18, 128–9, 139, 143–50, 177–8, 188–9, 192; collapse of government (1992), 178; formation of (1965), 112, 117; ideology of, 150; Khalq faction of, 118, 120, 129, 196; members of, 113, 190; Outlines of the Revolutionary Tasks, 118; Parcham faction, 113, 119; role in Saur Revolution (1978), 95, 117; supporters of, 112–13

Peshawar Accords (1992): provisions of, 189

Peshawar Group: members of, 216

Popalzai (tribe): 216; gifting of Hazara families to, 75; Sadozai (branch), 26, 28, 34–5, 42, 44–5, 55, 62

Progressive Youth Organization